AF412056

Lost Art

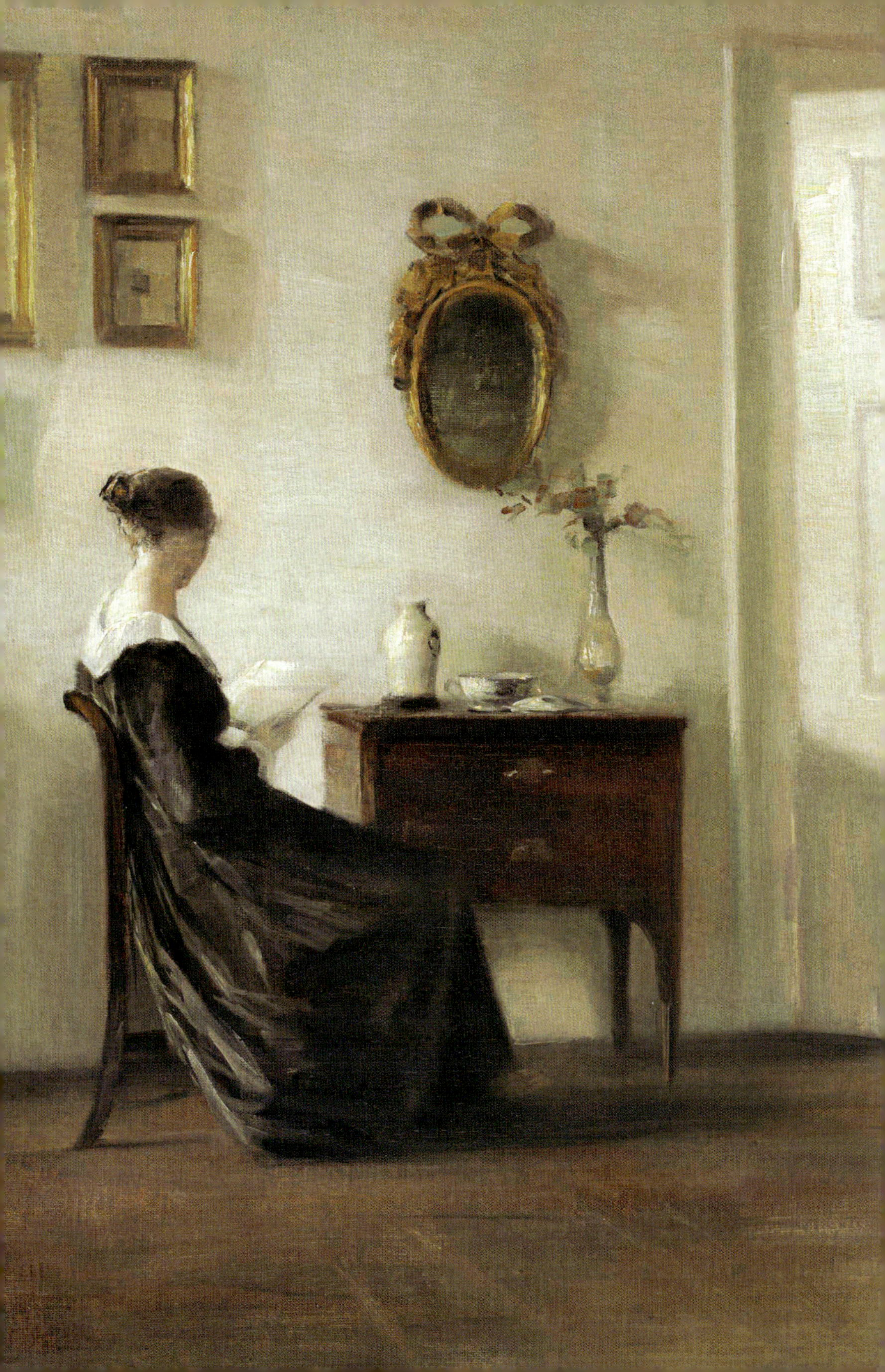

Lost Art

The Art Loss Register Casebook Vol I

Anja Shortland

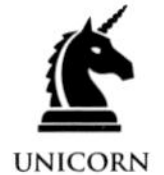

UNICORN

Für meine Eltern
Heide & Klaus Graupe

Published in 2021 by
Unicorn, an imprint of Unicorn Publishing Group LLP
5 Newburgh Street
London W1F 7RG
www.unicornpublishing.org

Thank you to the following sources for providing the images
featured in this book:
The Art Loss Register: 21, 51, 70, 155, 173, 174, 197, 205, 223, 281, 287. © The
Estate of Francis Bacon. All rights reserved, DACS/Artimage 2021. Photo:
Prudence Cuming Associates Ltd: 22. Bridgeman Images/© Christie's
Images: 219. Getty Images/AFP/Joseph Eid: 247, 255; AFP/Gerry Penny: 53.
Metropolitan Police: 268. © Succession Picasso/DACS, London 2021: 177.
Royal Society: 120. Shutterstock editorial/AP/Charles Krupa: 83, 88; EPA/
Hugo Philpott: 135. The Watch Register: 266.

ISBN 978-1-913491-48-2

10 9 8 7 6 5 4 3 2 1

Copy-editor: Linda Schofield
Design: James Alexander at Jade Design
Picture researcher: Katie Greenwood
Indexer: Sue Goodman
Printed in Turkey by FineTone Ltd

1

Introduction

There is a common perception that the art market is a new 'Wild West': a huge international grey market riddled with fakes and forgeries, stolen and looted objects with very limited law enforcement.[1] Yet at the same time, the art market is a highly successful global service industry with a turnover in the region of US$65 billion per annum between 2013 and 2019.[2] Sophisticated investors regularly spend millions, or even tens and hundreds of millions of dollars on rare and fashionable artefacts, suggesting the market is as transparent and liquid as other asset markets. If the art market operates largely beyond state control, how do market participants make and enforce rules that maintain consumer confidence and trust? This book examines a private crime control initiative against art theft: the Art Loss Register (henceforth the ALR), whose database on stolen and looted artefacts provides timely information to buyers, dealers and auction houses on whether an artwork is claimed by a previous owner, and offers a service to resolve such claims before the object is sold. But the ALR is much more than a biddable service provider that keeps its customers out of trouble. The company is controversial because it challenges entrenched business practices in the market: pushing for greater transparency, demanding respect for (largely unenforced) laws and promoting the interests of victims of crime.

Art theft, artnapping, fakes and forgeries, looting of cultural heritage, money laundering and fraudulent investment schemes are recurrent themes in the media. The massive increase in the prices for 'passion assets' since the 1980s has created a multitude of profit opportunities for legal as well as illicit and illegal businesses.[3] As the world's financial elite drive up the cost of fashionable art, antiques, rare cars, watches and antiquities, savvy investors follow suit. Criminals respond to the burgeoning demand for high-status luxury goods by stealing from private and museum art collections, robbing people for jewellery, burgling houses, and looting graves, churches and archaeological sites. Crooks try to pass off brand-new forgeries or old copies and pastiches as authentic works of famous masters. Fraudsters con investors by selling multiple, overlapping financial stakes in desirable artworks. A large service industry stands ready to shelter ill-gotten valuables and counterfeits from law enforcement and (knowingly or unknowingly) sell them on to collectors who do not know how to ask the right questions, or who simply do not care.

The constant threat of art crime raises two fascinating questions. First, how do sellers, dealers and auction houses maintain the trust of buyers in the authenticity and legitimacy of artworks offered for sale? Passionate collectors may have the time, resources and expertise to spot sophisticated scams, verify the authenticity of an artwork and investigate whether there is a former owner somewhere in the world who might try to reclaim the object at some point in the future. Shrewd well-off collectors and investors employ professionals to conduct such investigations. However, most art buyers rely on sellers to exercise due diligence on their behalf. Top prices are only paid when buyers are confident the offered works are genuine and unencumbered. What underpins buyers' trust that artworks are 'as described' and that any problems will be rectified with the minimum of fuss and financial loss?

Second, what has brought about the sea change in art buyers' attitudes over the last thirty years? Until the 1990s, few collectors bothered to make detailed enquiries into an object's recent provenance. Export restrictions designed to protect countries' cultural property were commonly flouted. There was a brisk trade in looted antiquities.[4] Some auction houses were complicit in smuggling art into London and New York, or determinedly turned a blind eye to their consignors' inability to provide a credible history of ownership for their pieces.[5] Theft victims and families who spotted their ancestors' Nazi-looted artworks in private collections, public sales or museums had little hope of recovering them.[6] Fakes and forgeries could circulate freely once they had been accepted as genuine by a single well-known dealer or connoisseur. Nowadays, artworks that have been smuggled, looted or stolen, or whose origin is dubious, are considered suspect and even distasteful. What explains this massive shift in social norms?

It is highly unlikely that improved policing provides the answer to these questions. If anything, states have become less active in policing the art market over the last twenty years. In most countries, police budgets are stretched to breaking point. Police chiefs face tough decisions about how to divide their limited resources between fighting violent, drug and property crime. In times of financial austerity, property crimes can slip silently down the political priority list. To most voters, art crime looks like a luxury problem. As the Director of the UK Police Foundation put it: 'My sense is that [art crime] is not prioritised because of everything else the police have to do that is more pressing.

Acquisitive crime generally is deprioritised with the increased focus on violent and sexual crime, which now make up the overwhelming bulk of investigative work.'[7] Moreover, artworks easily cross international borders into jurisdictions that make it deliberately difficult to seize stolen objects and hold criminals to account. Thus, policing the art market is not only expensive and time-consuming, but also success is far from assured. Major international police operations to track down stolen art or antiquities are therefore the exception rather than the rule.

Some jurisdictions – especially New York – have lowered the barriers for former owners to reclaim their property through the civil courts. However, seeking legal redress brings its own problems. Disputes over art are generally highly complex, making court cases both costly and lengthy. Court cases are also conducted in public and frequently attract significant media coverage. The saying 'nobody looks good in court' could have been coined for the art market. Even if they know they have a good legal case, many people prefer to avoid resolving the problem under the glare of the media spotlights. Does that make the art market effectively lawless?

When we take a close look at 'Wild West' situations and markets, we often find they are surprisingly well-ordered. When states are weak or exercise power only sporadically, individuals, voluntary organisations and private companies step in to fill the gaps. We see private initiatives to protect citizens and their property, gather information, enforce contracts, adjudicate or mediate in disputes, or help the police to enforce the law within their limited budgets. The lack of public law and order therefore does not mean the global art market is anarchic or has been taken over by criminals. It is in the commercial interest of top-end dealers, fair organisers and auction houses to create institutions that maintain the trust of art buyers.

Private solutions

Collectors who display their artworks only to close friends and would never dream of parting with their treasures can choose to ignore gaps in their artworks' provenance. But art investors who frequently flip their assets rely on secure titles. Every public sale is an opportunity for hidden problems to come to light: former owners may spot their possessions being advertised in a catalogue or online and try to reclaim them. Experts attending pre-sale viewings may throw doubt on an artwork's authenticity. Rich and powerful people may acquire art to demonstrate their wealth and good taste. But showing off artworks in glossy magazine spreads, in social media and at glamorous events similarly comes at the price of public scrutiny and potential exposure. Philanthropists who display their collections in private galleries, lend them to public exhibitions or donate important works to museums must expect them to be examined in minute detail by curators, conservators, provenance researchers and academics. When collectors exhibit their treasures, they seek positive publicity and status gain. They do not want the embarrassment of having been tricked or lawsuits brought by former owners. Thus, anyone who wants to serve the world's most attractive client base must be seen to take all reasonable precautions against offering counterfeit, stolen, smuggled or looted artworks. In case something slips through the net, reputable dealers and auctioneers prove their good faith by reimbursing their disappointed (VIP) customers. For example, in 2016 Sotheby's rescinded the 2011 sale of a painting sold as a work by Frans Hals after technical analysis proved it to be a counterfeit and returned the full sale price of £8.5 million to the buyer.[8]

Offering buy-back guarantees is a high-stakes gamble unless one has confidence in the provenance of every object on sale. Yet, not all legitimately owned artworks, antiques or pieces of jewellery have a complete paper trail of consensual sales leading back to the original maker. In fact, relatively few objects have a perfect provenance. Many artefacts just come with some oral history passed down the generations such as 'your great-great-uncle Luke brought this back from Abyssinia in the 1890s'. Tourists on the Grand Tour in the eighteenth century shipped antique statuary home by the cartload. In the past, gifts were rarely formally documented. Even if they existed, import and export licences and receipts are lost over time: through negligent bookkeeping, during moves, house fires, divorces or floods. Bargain hunters can pick up genuine but unprovenanced treasures at flea markets and car boot (or yard) sales for spare change. Can you tell the difference between an object that has become accidentally detached from its provenance from one that was criminally severed from it?

It is not surprising the art market has developed a commercial solution to this thorny question: to facilitate the trade in legitimately owned art and luxury goods, as well as raising the stakes for criminals trying to infiltrate and contaminate this lucrative market. Enter the Art Loss Register.

Serving the art market

The ALR was founded in 1990 as a joint initiative between insurers, reputable art dealers and the world's top auction houses to prevent the circulation of stolen artefacts in the market. It is majority-owned by its founder Julian Radcliffe, with Sotheby's and Christie's as minority shareholders. The ALR has compiled the world's most comprehensive database on lost, stolen and at-risk artworks, antique furniture and antiquities. By July 2020 it had registered more than 700,000 uniquely identifiable objects, gathering data from a wide range of sources. The ALR's team of researchers started off by recording the historic theft data collated by the International Foundation for Art Research (IFAR). This not-for-profit educational and research organisation in New York had collected and publicised detailed reports on art thefts since 1977.[9] The ALR's innovation was to create a searchable database of lost and stolen artefacts, which is constantly updated by adding information on art thefts reported to Interpol, theft reports from various industry associations and insurance records.

In addition, the ALR database offers a direct service to theft victims who can prove ownership and supply a detailed description of the object, high-quality photographs and evidence of the crime (such as a police report number). Families looking for Nazi-looted artefacts can register their art loss on the database. It is also possible to register assets under legal dispute (e.g. in divorce proceedings), works that are mortgaged and cannot be sold without the lender's agreement and well-documented archaeological treasures at extreme risk of looting.[10] The company provides a similar facility for registering stolen luxury watches – The Watch Register – with a total of over 70,000 entries. Although it is theoretically possible for dealers to independently search some of the ALR's source files – taking care to look at foreign police data in addition to the subset of crimes recorded on the Interpol database – this is clearly impracticable and uneconomic. It would also be less reliable, as police and insurers eventually remove objects from their databases and information from private subscribers would be missed. Over a period of thirty years the ALR has thus become the most comprehensive and internationally respected provider of timely information on stolen valuables in the art world.

Anyone who can prove a legitimate interest in an artwork can pay for a search to be carried out. In the first stage, ALR staff conduct a search based on a description of the artwork's key attributes to narrow down the list of potential matches. In the second stage, high-resolution photographs of the object are compared with those submitted by the theft victims. When a search results in an all-clear, the provenance does not raise any red flags and the documents are credible, the item can be sold in good faith. If there is a possible match, the ALR may ask the searching party to examine the artwork physically and send additional photographs (including the reverse of the object). This information is compared to that provided by the registrant to determine or rule out a match. If a match is confirmed, the company or individual commissioning the search and the former owners/lenders/co-owners are alerted. If the holder is suspected of smuggling or fencing stolen goods, the police are informed.

Often, however, many years have passed since the crime was committed, and the holder may be abroad or hiding their identity. In these cases, there is little chance of a successful prosecution. Yet, reputable dealers, art fairs and auction houses will still refuse to sell the object until the title issues raised by the ALR are fully resolved. This puts the artefact in a state of limbo as far as a public sale is concerned. The holders can withdraw the disputed item from sale, sell it privately (probably at a significantly lower price) or seek a settlement. If the last option is chosen, the ALR puts the current holders directly in touch with the former owners or helps to broker a settlement between the rival claimants. Depending on the preferred course of action, the ALR then charges either a location fee or a recovery fee, which are a small percentage of the final benefit for the registrant.

Many dealers and auction houses subscribe to this service and check all valuable objects routinely before a sale. These due diligence procedures reassure customers that they can buy in good faith, and protect buyers, dealers and market makers against scandal and future lawsuits. An increasing number of art and antiques fairs similarly engage the services of the ALR to check the exhibitors' offerings and thereby create a visible barrier against art crime. Private individuals can consult the register to investigate the legitimacy of artworks they wish to purchase. They have to provide their full contact details and the provenance details of the item. Their search history is also recorded. These measures discourage criminals from using the database to try to get an all-clear for an object they know is stolen but may not (yet) have been registered with the ALR.

Helping the victims of crime

The ALR is a last resort for thousands of people who have lost valuable artworks and treasured family heirlooms to thieves, burglars, extortionists and looters. Few theft victims are as outspoken as the British cider magnate Esmond Bulmer, who told reporters that the police officers handling the investigation of £2 million worth of art stolen from his stately home were 'brain dead, incompetent and deplorable'.[11] Many crime victims feel let down by the lack of police effort to protect them and investigate their complaints. In recent years the percentage of crimes leading to prosecutions in the UK has dropped dramatically.[12] Data published by the British Home Office in July 2019 showed that in the previous year only 6 per cent of reported thefts in England and Wales resulted in someone being charged or summonsed, 74 per cent of cases were closed without a suspect being identified and the median time for a theft case to be assigned to an outcome was a mere two days.[13] Many people who report a theft to the police do so mainly because they need a police crime number to be able to claim on their insurance.[14]

Before the ALR started its operations, an insurance payout was the standard remedy after a theft or burglary. Yet for art, antiques, fine silver, porcelain and jewellery theft this is often a partial solution. First, people are emotionally attached to valuables rich in personal and family memories. Financial compensation only ameliorates the sense of bereavement and fury against the perpetrators. Second, given the massive price appreciation of 'passion assets', few people can afford adequate insurance for an Impressionist painting their globetrotting parents brought back from a 1920s summer holiday in Paris, for example. One cannot replace precious antiques from the payout of a standard home insurance cover. The ALR holds out the hope of recovering family assets and reconnecting with cherished memories at some point in the future, while denying criminals the profit from selling stolen valuables in the open market in the meantime.

A partner for insurers

The boom in art prices at the end of the 1980s raised the incentive to commit art crimes and hence the risk exposure of art insurers. As the police proved unable to step up their efforts – and indeed reduced their focus on property crime in subsequent decades – insurers intensified their search for private crime control solutions.

Art insurers have two complementary interests. First, they can reduce art crime by driving down its profitability and raising the risk of detection. Creating a single, trusted and comprehensive register as the point of call for all title searches from buyers, dealers and market makers is an efficient way of hindering the circulation of stolen and looted art in the market. Criminals respond to incentives. By encouraging ever more sellers to search for stolen objects, insurers make it risky for criminals to sell on stolen artefacts and for collectors to buy them. With effective monitoring, prices in the grey market can be decreased to a small fraction of the open market value of artworks. When stolen art is perceived as 'hot' and has to be sold secretly and at rock-bottom prices, criminals move on to other activities offering a better risk–reward profile. This makes art theft insurance commercially feasible and affordable for a wider range of customers. Second, once insurers have paid compensation to theft victims, legal title for the stolen objects passes to them. Over time, art insurers have accumulated a large and valuable portfolio of missing treasures. It makes commercial sense to salvage these objects when they reappear on the market, either by having them seized or by transferring the title back to the original owner on reimbursement of the insured amount, or by negotiation with the current holders.[15]

To further raise the probability of detecting stolen artworks, art insurers also refer suspicious requests from unknown entities to the ALR (especially for transport insurance across international borders). In the event of a match, insurance is refused until the title issue is resolved. This reduces the attractiveness of acquiring unprovenanced artworks, even for otherwise unscrupulous collectors. Buyers who find themselves unable to obtain insurance can either return the disputed object to their dealer or the auction house, or come forward to work out a settlement with the former owners or their insurers.

Commercial resolutions

When a match is made with an object registered on the ALR database, there are three broad scenarios. First, the current holders may have acquired the object in good faith and have enjoyed peaceable possession for a legally specified period of time (known as the statute of limitation). This means that, under most laws, buyers acquire good title after five to ten years after the purchase. If so, they can also transfer good title to subsequent owners. However, the current legal owner may still feel a moral obligation to compensate the former owners once their claim comes to light. When insurers, dealers and auction houses refuse to proceed with a transaction until the problem is resolved, there is a level playing field for negotiating a financial settlement acceptable to both parties.

Second, a match may lead to an innocent holder who has not yet acquired good title to the object. For example, a buyer may have picked up a bargain at an antiques shop or a stall at a flea market. If the item is identified and reclaimed before the statute of limitation has expired, they can only hope for a finder's fee. Similarly, if somebody inherits a stolen object, they do not acquire good title and can – at best – ask for a reward. Setting the reward is up to the legal owner, and it is not something that should be aggressively demanded.

Third, a match may be made when the original criminals or their accomplices try to sell an artwork to a reputable dealer or auction house or seek insurance for shipping. When they find they cannot sell the object, they might decide to enter into a negotiation about its return, but effecting a commercial resolution in these cases is complicated. On the one hand, it is not in the public interest to create a criminal business opportunity in 'artnapping', that is, holding museums or collectors to ransom over stolen artworks. People who broker such deals might well find themselves in court over facilitating criminal transactions or money laundering. On the other hand, it is perhaps naive to assume crooks will just give up their loot when they can also sell it in the shadow economy or to a criminal network. There is therefore a clear conflict of interest between former owners who could get their missing masterpiece back for a fraction of its open market price and protecting the property of potential future victims of theft. This can usually only be resolved on a case-by-case basis. In principle, however, criminals should not benefit directly or indirectly from their illicit activities.

Unfortunately, these three neat categories rarely fit real-world situations. First, it is often difficult to distinguish between crooks and finders. A criminal may pose as an honest finder or pass the loot onto someone else who does. An honest finder may be so adamant in claiming their reward that they seem like an extortionist to the theft victim. Second, the art market is international, but each country has its own laws. Rules for acquiring legal ownership vary across jurisdictions. What constitutes a good faith sale varies greatly between countries as well as over time: due diligence procedures have improved massively in recent years. For example, in the 1960s and 1970s few people considered a sticker from a European Jewish family collection on the back of a painting as a problem. By contrast, nowadays this is regarded as a red flag and a buyer's good faith would be queried if they bought or sold such artworks without a full provenance or (at least) an all-clear from the ALR and other databases recording Holocaust-era art thefts. Statutes of limitation also differ from country to country. A holder may therefore have a fully valid legal title in some countries but not in others. For example, a valid legal title from a buyer-friendly jurisdiction such as Switzerland may be challenged if the artwork is exported to a country that applies rules favouring the claimant, especially the all-important US market and particularly New York.

Court cases tend to be expensive, stressful and immensely time-consuming, and this is especially true for disputes involving choice of law and jurisdiction. Legal action therefore only makes commercial sense for the world's finest and most expensive artworks. Even then, both parties tend to rue the day they decided to bring their argument into a court. In almost every circumstance, an amicable commercial settlement recognised in all jurisdictions is a better option than an acrimonious legal dispute.

A partner for law enforcement

The ALR thus has an interesting position vis-à-vis law enforcement. As a watchman scrutinising the global art market, the ALR is uniquely placed to discover the location of stolen artworks. Dealers and auction houses have created strong norms for protecting their sellers' and consignors' identities to save them the embarrassment of being caught divesting themselves of their collections. However, with a court order the police can demand this information. A single carefully investigated lead can bring down the whole edifice of a smuggling ring, a fencing operation or a money laundering scheme.

The initial match may be a relatively minor artefact for which no police force in the world would actively search. However, people can privately register items of emotional value on the ALR database and subscribing insurers routinely register all uniquely identifiable objects from a theft or burglary. One registration was a child's Austin pedal car valued at £2,000 that had been stolen from a family home near London in 1998. A year later, the ALR researchers found it again, listed in a Christie's sales catalogue, in Melbourne! The match was beyond doubt: the toy's registration plate, its scratches and rust pattern were identical to photographs submitted by the original owner. But what kind of burglar would ship a toy to sell it on the other side of the world? A few pages further on in the catalogue the researchers discovered another clue: a porcelain collection stolen from a house in Oxford around the same time as the pedal car theft. This was enough to spark the interest of the police. The subsequent international investigation led the detectives to a criminal gang in Britain that plundered art and antiques on a huge scale and systematically smuggled containerloads of loot into Australia. Their greed was their downfall: they were caught when they tried to obtain the best price for their booty by selling it through an international auction house. Based on the lead provided by the ALR several arrests were made.[16]

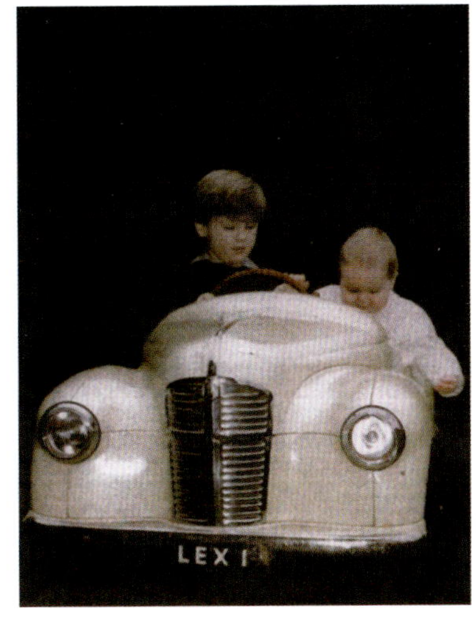

Austin pedal car stolen in 1998: family photo submitted by the theft victim.

Sometimes criminals commission a database search themselves, to check whether they can take the loot to market. The ALR is always on the look-out for 'customers' from outside the art market who may have an ulterior motive for consulting the register. One such suspicious out-of-the-blue search request came from an individual in Spain who sent in photographs of a diptych by Francis Bacon that had been stolen from a friend of the artist in Madrid in 2015. The Spanish police were alerted, and forensic investigators ascertained the model of the camera used. They traced it to a camera rental company that was able to identify the person who had taken the photographs. When the police searched their premises, they recovered three paintings (valued at £19 million) and subsequently made ten arrests.[17] These stories illustrate the immense scope for a public/private partnership in fighting art crime, through which timely information provided by a private company helps the police to detect and apprehend criminals.

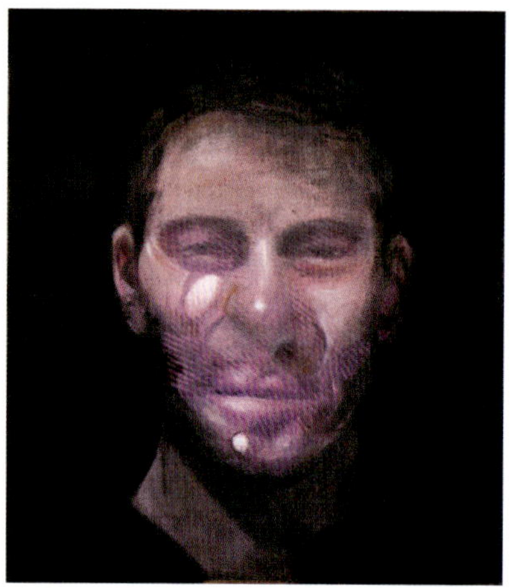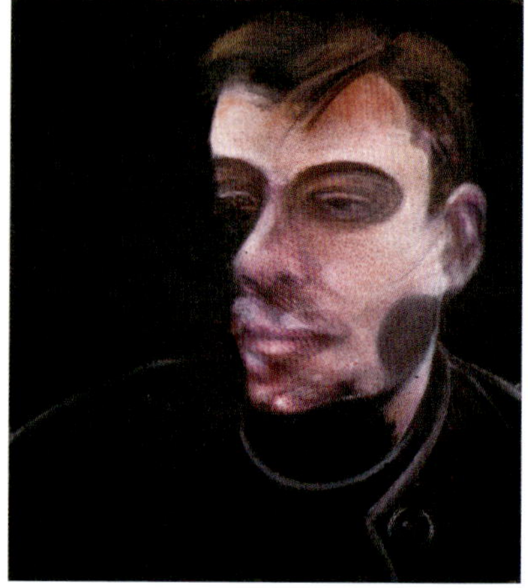

Francis Bacon (1909–1992), *Two Studies for a Portrait* (1990). One of five paintings stolen in Madrid in 2015, three of which were recovered by the Spanish police in 2017.

Unfortunately, many thieves and fences are well aware of this danger. They therefore patiently hide the loot for years before they approach a dealer. It may be decades after the theft when the ALR picks up a first attempt to sell stolen valuables. In this case the police files will have long been closed. But when they are reopened, the thieves' treasure trove may still be largely intact. For example, in 2017 the ALR alerted the Danish police to a match. It had spotted an oil painting in a US auction house that had been registered by the insurer of a Danish family who had paid out for the loss of eight oil paintings in 2000. The shocked seller in America explained they had recently bought the painting at a Danish auction house less than an hour's drive away from the location of the burglary. The Danish police enquired with the auction house who had sold the painting. When they searched the seller's house, they were delighted to find the other seven paintings just where they had been hidden for more than sixteen years. The thieves' calculation that the art world would eventually forget the theft

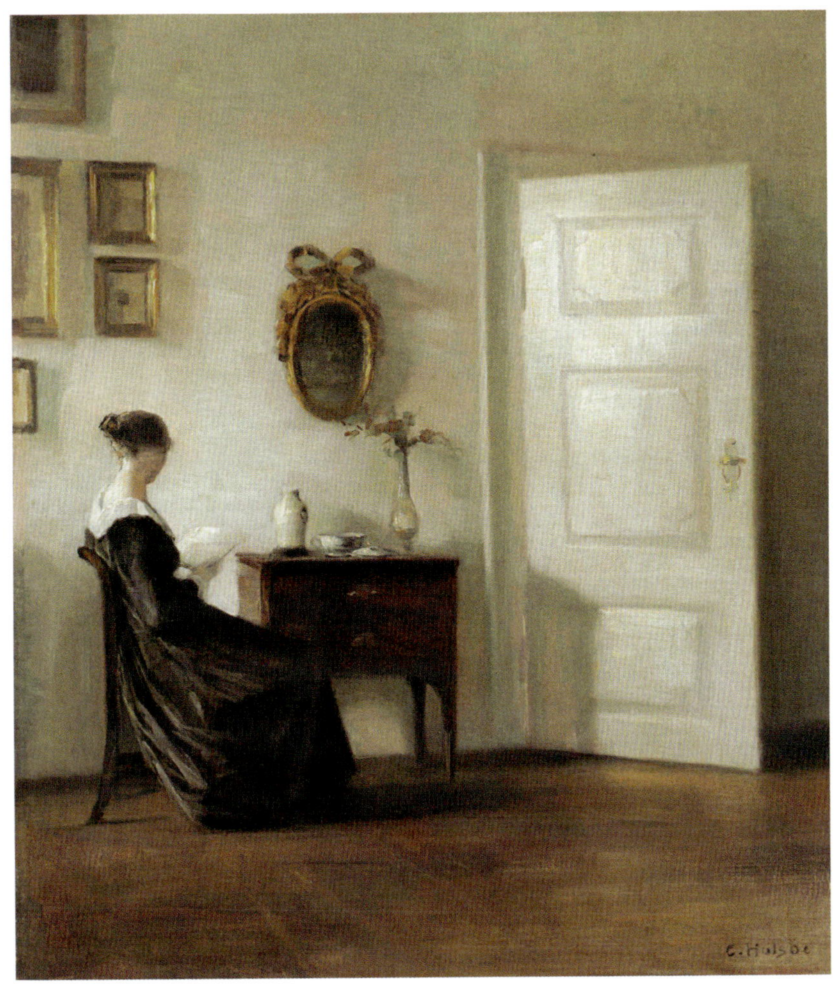

Carl Vilhelm Holsøe (1863–1935), *Lady Reading in an Interior*. Stolen in
Denmark in 2000, found in the USA in 2017.

had misfired: the ALR's record is permanent and its reach is global. Chapter 11 provides a detailed examination of how the private sector can help law enforcement and put criminals behind bars.

Tensions between public law and private interest

Despite these and many other examples of successful public/private cooperation, the commercial interests of the ALR and the objectives of formal law enforcement are not always perfectly aligned. As we will see in Chapter 9, there can be tension between police officers' desire to secure a conviction and the ALR's interest in the timely recovery of stolen objects for their former owners. First, detectives tend to base their legal cases on items for which the evidence is most clear-cut, rather than necessarily investigating a suspicious dealer's entire stock. Second, objects that are needed as evidence in court may be retained for years, pending the trial and any appeals.

The length and cost of legal proceedings is a recurrent theme in this book. We will meet crooks in court for different reasons. Some deliberately exploit the legal system to obstruct justice, to gain time or impose cost on former owners in the hope of wearing them down (Chapters 2, 3, 4 and 9). Cynical criminals wait until the last moment to see what the police can dig up against them before pleading guilty to the specific charges where the evidence is most damning (Chapters 8 and 11). And some rule-breakers appear simply too naive to settle a case they are bound to lose (Chapter 8). In all the cases in this book justice prevails, but often at such a high cost and with such delays that for the original victims their victory may well seem hollow.

Brokering amicable commercial resolutions is central to the ALR's business model. It is heartening to see that many restitutions and settlements are based on generosity and sympathy towards former owners, rather than laws that favour good faith owners. For instance, very few jurisdictions grant ownership to Jewish former owners deprived of their artworks under the Nazi regime, once they have been sold on the open market and held for the statutory period. Yet, people who are told about their property's troublesome past are often willing to share the proceeds of a sale with the former owners' heirs. In Chapter 7, we meet someone who was happy to recognise the moral legitimacy of a Jewish family's claim and pay compensation even though the law would have been on her side. Similarly, people who inadvertently purchase stolen goods in bric-a-brac shops or at flea markets may not insist on their legal rights. For example, a woman who had bought a painting by Thomas Francis Dicksee for £10 at a car boot sale was so shocked to find it had been stolen from the artist's descendants that she immediately volunteered to return it.[18] Human decency can be stronger than the law, but the law cannot command it.

Significant controversy arises when the current holders are suspected criminals. When crooks recognise the ALR's power to interrupt public sales, they may try to negotiate a ransom for the return of a painting instead of selling it to a third party. Extortion is a crime. From a public policy point of view, any individual or company that creates a channel for recovering stolen art from the economic underworld is viewed with extreme suspicion. The issue is analogous to kidnapping: the kidnap for ransom business model would break down if nobody ever paid ransoms. Yet a blanket ban on ransom payments clashes with the understandable interest of the crime victims to retrieve their loved ones, or in this case a prize painting or treasured family heirloom. Under what circumstances is it acceptable to negotiate? Often the issue is ambiguous.

If a strict no-negotiation policy is implemented, stolen artworks can still circulate in the underground economy, so thieves can obtain a payout regardless. Valuable paintings are used as collateral by organised crime groups in drug deals.[19] Preventing the crime of extortion may thus come at the cost of facilitating other – perhaps violent – crimes. If decades pass before stolen artworks resurface it will be near impossible to secure a conviction even if the original thieves are caught. When a person comes forward with information many years after a theft, the informer is unlikely to be the thief or a close accomplice. Often a third party has become aware of the location of a stolen treasure and offers to help the former owner recover it, for a fee. At this point, the ageing former owner or their heirs may be desperate to reconnect once more with an object from their family history. If they agree a deal, the money will be split between an unknown (possibly criminal) current holder and the broker. It is unclear whether the broker is committing a crime. If negotiations are started earlier, it is more likely the original criminals are still in the picture and the police can glean information leading to a conviction.

There are many detectives, lawyers and art recovery businesses that specialise in brokering art retrievals, but all trades involving criminals are a tricky business. In the UK there were two recent high-profile court cases against people who tried to negotiate a finder's reward (or ransom, depending on the point of view) with the representatives of theft victims. In the 2010 case of the Duke of Buccleuch's stolen Leonardo da Vinci painting (the *Madonna of the Yarnwinder*), the police inserted an undercover detective into the negotiation over the return of the (clearly unsaleable) artwork. Just before the transaction was concluded, the police seized the painting and arrested the solicitor who had tried to broker the deal. He had to defend his actions in court.[20] In 2018 an intermediary who helped to broker a deal to return a £2 million art and jewellery hoard to the Bulmer family for £175,000 was also put on trial.[21] The associated media publicity illustrates perfectly the frustration of a theft victim who is told the police cannot do anything to return his property to him, and nobody is allowed to make a limited financial concession to retrieve it privately either. If the intermediaries had been convicted of a crime for trying to broker such deals it would have left just two destinations for stolen masterpieces: organised crime or the bonfire.

Although both court cases ultimately collapsed, they showcase the deep unease in the policymaking and law enforcement communities about deals between legal entities and people with links into the shadow economy. On the other hand, major public museums in the UK have made significantly larger financial outlays to retrieve stolen artworks. The Tate Gallery's bill of £3.5 million to recover two paintings by J.M.W. Turner in 2002 is probably most famous example.[22] Although the word ransom was strenuously avoided in all official communications, it is clear that under certain conditions law enforcement does permit deals to be brokered through which criminals may be among the ultimate beneficiaries.[23]

Playing by the rules with a criminal opposition

As a British company, the ALR must obey the law and is held to account for all its commercial decisions. In this book we will meet a host of shady characters trying to sell stolen artworks, ideally in the open market but, failing that, to their former owners. As a legitimate and accountable company, how do you trade with people who try to hide their identity from you? What if you suspect your counterparty has uncomfortably close links to the original crime, but you cannot prove anything either way? It turns out the police will sometimes sanction the payment of a small 'reward' to recover stolen artworks, but only as a last resort. Obtaining police approval for payments can thus be used as a negotiating position to drive down the criminals' ransom expectations and thereby reduce the incentives for artnapping. Offering minimal compensation certainly works better than trying to talk crooks into giving up valuable artworks for free, while securing (and enforcing) a legal judgment against them can be prohibitively expensive. Chapters 2, 3 and 4 illustrate the complexity of cases when the ALR's clients refused to pay anything to the holders of their stolen property.

Servant of two masters

Even when art recoveries involve only legal entities and above-board transactions, the ALR sometimes has to strike a delicate balance. Much of the ALR's subscription income is from dealers and auction houses, and indeed Christie's and Sotheby's are shareholders in the company. Dealers and market makers are looking for swift and confidential resolutions that protect their customers' commercial interest and maximise commission income. But to be entrusted with recoveries, the ALR must also be perceived to pursue vigorously the interests of former owners and/or their insurers. Thus, the ALR has to negotiate settlements that are acceptable to both sides.

This is clearly a very different business model from the services offered by law firms that are fighting entirely for one side, at a hefty price. However, it turns out that a balance of interests is not necessarily a disadvantage when brokering a deal between opposing parties. Rather than escalating tensions, the ALR effectively takes on the role of mediator, looking for common ground and mutually acceptable solutions. Thus, settlements often can be reached swiftly and at minimal cost for all parties.

Building a business

The business model of retrieving stolen artworks for a reward was already well established when the ALR was founded in 1990. Art detectives have tracked down famous and valuable artworks and negotiated their return for decades. However, these negotiations are only successful if the original owner is the current holder's preferred buyer from a risk–reward point of view. This once again suggests a situation akin to hostage-taking: you are best off selling a kidnapped person back to their family or employer. It is easy to see that some artworks are so famous – for example, iconic masterpieces stolen from major museums – that they are simply unsaleable on the open market. The term 'artnapping' implies exactly this kind of scenario. However, generally it requires a significant effort to make an object sufficiently well known to prevent its sale in a global market. And if this effort is not sustained, thieves may simply lie low until the scandal has died down.

Various national industry associations created processes to alert their members to stolen valuables and hinder their return into the legitimate market. The Stolen Art Alerts published by IFAR from 1977 were the first major international effort to publicise art thefts. As founder of the ALR, Julian Radcliffe's idea was to extend this beyond artworks destined for the very top end of the market. A permanent record of stolen art, internationally recognised as the arbiter of what can and cannot be sold in good faith, would put ordinary families, cash-starved museums and victims of Nazi-era looting in a position to retrieve treasured but not hugely valuable artworks, or demand compensation. Moreover, the knowledge that such a register exists would reduce the attractiveness of committing art theft in the first place, so protecting public and private collections and cultural heritage sites. The ALR would be a private business serving the broader public interest and working hand in hand with (rather than under the radar of) law enforcement.

Yet, to become commercially successful, the ALR had to build demand for its services in the art market. This required a sea change in attitudes towards legitimate ownership and provenance. For decades, dealers and collectors had blithely overlooked that their treasures could have been looted, expropriated or stolen. Many did not want to know and some deliberately ignored obvious clues revealing a potentially awkward history. At the top of the market, dealers and auction houses were effectively looking for someone to have a quiet word in their ear so they could politely turn down problematic commissions. They certainly did not want the information provider to call the police. In the mid-market, the majority of art lovers and service providers just wanted to carry on with business as usual and resisted paying for a service they felt was being forced on them. Radcliffe's – and the insurance industry's – idea about the purpose and reach of the ALR was bound to clash head-on with the prevailing norms of the art market.

Academics who study how social norms change point to the key role of 'norm entrepreneurs'.[24] These are people who are so committed to an idea or an ideal that they are willing to incur significant personal costs to challenge the existing norms. They take controversial actions to reframe the debate on what is appropriate behaviour: for example, suffragettes demonstrating publicly and chaining themselves to railings, political prisoners going on hunger strike, and activists disrupting environmentally harmful economic activities. Challenging social norms is the very definition of 'inappropriate' and 'controversial'. The ALR could not change attitudes in the art market by working entirely with, on behalf of and within the (unwritten) rules of the system. In this book we see the ALR breaking some rules, such as encouraging the consignment of stolen artworks with the intention of having them seized. We observe the ALR stepping on toes, disrupting sales until former owners' claims are recognised and encouraging a client to sue one of its shareholders. In turn, we also see insiders resisting the efforts of the ALR to redefine legitimate ownership to include moral obligations, occasionally taking the ALR close to breaking point. Those who benefit from an unregulated and opaque art market and the holders of stolen, looted and smuggled artworks have used court cases and media campaigns to discredit the ALR. They have also tried to replace Radcliffe in the hope of turning the ALR into a more pliable service that provides confidential alerts rather than working actively to recover stolen and looted art.

The ALR is far from the only institution challenging the prevailing laissez-faire approach to provenance in the art market. For example, archaeologists and governments campaign for greater protection of cultural heritage, while Jewish lobbies champion the restitution of Nazi-looted art. Museum curators, art historians and scientists work tirelessly to protect the integrity of the historical record against fraudsters. Many of the ALR's more controversial actions can only be understood in this broader context of evolving norms in the art market. Norm entrepreneurs are successful if they build institutions to promote their ideals and convince a critical mass of agents to adopt the new norm. A tipping point may be reached where the new norm cascades through the population to replace the old norm. Nowadays, formerly commonplace acts such as the promotion of imperialism, gender discrimination and the hunting of endangered species are considered as unacceptable behaviour. In the art market the process of changing social norms towards greater transparency and fairness is ongoing. But the world's most prestigious museums, auction houses, art fairs and dealers already operate consistently within a new norm that recognises the compensation claims of (at least some categories of) former owners.

Every art recovery story presented here can thus be read as a mini adventure about the pursuit of 'just and fair' solutions in a market slowly and reluctantly adapting to rising moral and ethical standards. Jointly, the stories are about a business being built against the odds with dogged determination, and about investing massive resources into establishing a formidable reputation, so as to convince people it is in their best interest to search assiduously and settle early and gracefully. General acceptance among market participants that a clean provenance is essential for a good faith sale makes the ALR a commercially viable and hence a sustainable business.

We also observe considerable commercial experimentation. In theory, any type of uniquely identifiable valuables could benefit from a dedicated, searchable register. Rare antiques, antiquities, fakes and forgeries, condition reports and any object made unique by a serial number such as guns, machinery and watches are other candidates. Extending the business model into these areas is in the public interest. However, the lower the commercial recovery value of the individual item, the greater the reliance on search income, requiring mass subscription to the service. As we will see, criminals continue to benefit from the art market's traditional culture of secrecy. Traders' adherence to old norms and their resistance to change significantly increase the cost of recoveries. Ultimately, overturning entrenched norms in the mid-market may require a degree of compulsion through industry regulation. To achieve the most from mutually beneficial public/private partnerships, private initiatives such as the ALR need more explicit support from governments.

2

The Moral Maze: Negotiating the Return of a Multimillion-dollar Cézanne

Sotheby's expert for Impressionist paintings was nervous. In the morning his plane from London had flown through a terrifying thunderstorm and now he was in Geneva to assist in a hostage exchange. He had been asked to authenticate and secure an iconic painting by Paul Cézanne that had been missing for over twenty years. Its owner had promised a significant concession if the secretive holders relinquished the original painting, but feared he might be scammed with a copy. It was already several hours after the appointed time. Morning coffee had been served and the painting had not arrived. The fancy celebration lunch had first been postponed, then cancelled. Eventually some sandwiches had been procured instead. The plates had been cleared now, too, and fingers anxiously drummed on chair rests. No more coffee, thank you. Finally, a phone call from the other side's lawyer. There would be a further delay. Was it time to go home? No. Julian Radcliffe, an expert on hostage crisis

> *resolution, was sure the ten-month-long ransom negotiation had run its course. The other side had nothing to gain from extending it further. They would stay and await developments. Coffee, anyone?*

Twenty-one years in the wilderness

There are two general principles guiding companies offering art retrieval. First, one should not pay the original criminal or a near associate to retrieve stolen goods. Second, no money can be paid to organised crime. So, what happens if your counterparty resolutely refuses to reveal their identity? What if you come to suspect that you would have to cross at least one of your red lines to conclude the deal? On the other hand, your ageing client is desperate to retrieve a much-mourned family heirloom. More than twenty years have passed since the heist. The police closed their investigation a long time ago and would give you some wiggle room for paying a small ransom. How would the ALR negotiate its way through this moral maze?

In January 1999 a database search request arrived at the ALR from a Lloyd's syndicate specialising in fine art insurance. A British businessman had enquired about transport insurance for someone who wanted to ship a painting from Russia to Switzerland. The insurer followed its due diligence protocol and checked the ALR for possible issues. Indeed, there was a problem. The details of the picture matched one stolen in 1978 from the house of Michael and Doris Bakwin in Massachusetts, USA. It had been a major theft: seven pictures by famous artists had been stolen from the couple's dining room. The artworks had been gifts from Michael Bakwin's late parents. Looking at the paintings had always brought back lovely memories of the gregarious couple. Both of them had been leading paediatricians, who enjoyed travelling, socialising

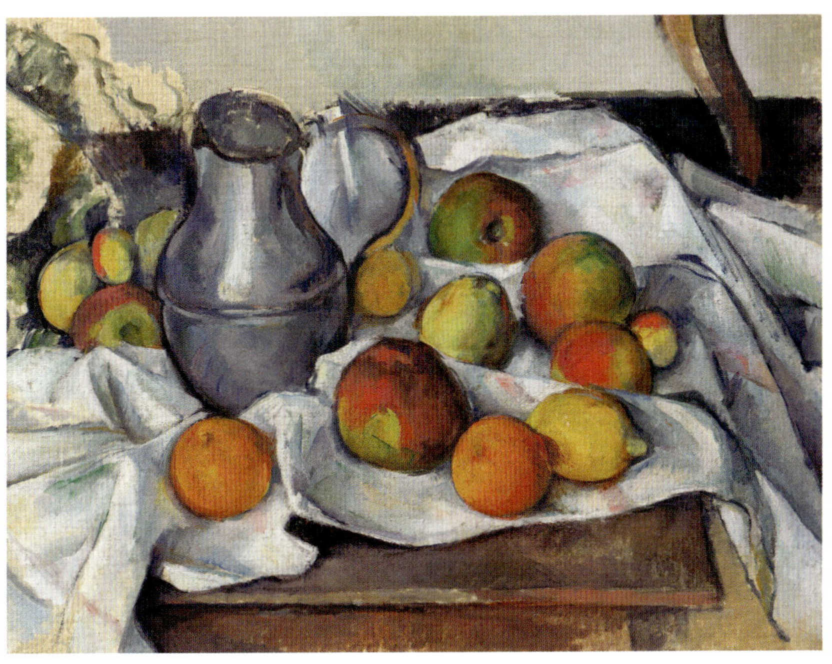

Paul Cézanne (1839–1906), *Bouilloire et Fruits* (1888–90).
Stolen from the Bakwin family in 1978.

and art. In the 1920s and 1930s they had regularly visited Paris and often bought works directly from artists' studios. Some of their collection had become extremely valuable since, especially one classic still life by Cézanne showing fruit and a pitcher, *Bouilloire et Fruits* (1888–90).

The Bakwin family had always felt safe in their neighbourhood and had not been particularly cautious with their treasures. As Doris Bakwin recalled, all their family and friends knew their spare key was under a ceramic frog by the door. Indeed, there was no sign of a break-in when the theft was discovered. Staff and various family members came under suspicion, but the crime was not solved. There was a promising lead once, when the FBI became aware of an illicit firearms dealer in the area. They set up a sting operation. To their amazement their target offered not just guns but a choice of yet to be stolen paintings to the undercover officer. The police decided to focus on the more pressing firearms issue, but before the trap snapped shut, the suspect was killed in an underworld dispute over unpaid poker debts.

The paintings remained at large and the police file on the Bakwin case was eventually closed. The family briefly hired a private detective but terminated his contract when his enquiries led to the same (deceased) suspect the police had identified. From then on, the family's hope of retrieving their paintings rested on someone reacting to the Stolen Art Alert posted by the International Foundation for Art Research (IFAR) at the recommendation of the detective in 1983. They did not even know that from 1991 the ALR was scanning the art and insurance markets for their missing heirlooms based on an IFAR alert posted by their private detective.

A fishy story

Although the Lloyd's syndicate thought Mr W – the person who had made the application for transport insurance – was probably respectable, it declined to provide cover. Instead, it recommended he got in touch with Julian Radcliffe to discuss the matter. Mr W was evasive: his enquiry had been on behalf of someone else. He explained that he was a surveyor and had been approached in his Moscow hotel because he had been introduced mistakenly to the friend of a friend as an art expert. Nonetheless, he had agreed to make the enquiry as he had acquaintances in the art world. Mr W was not at liberty to reveal the identity of his clients, referring to them as a 'Russian institution'. But he really attracted the ALR's attention when in addition to a photograph of the stolen Cézanne he also submitted photos of two paintings by Chaïm Soutine stolen in the same heist. This was extremely suspicious. If there had been a number of good faith sales over the last twenty years, it would be very unlikely that three of the paintings would still be in the same hands. Indeed, Mr W commented that his contact had not seemed particularly surprised by the news that the paintings had been stolen. The 'Russian institution' had received the paintings in settlement of a debt and now wanted to do a deal.

When the Bakwins were told that their missing paintings had finally resurfaced and the holders wanted to engage in a commercial negotiation they were delighted. *Bouilloire et Fruits* had been a particular family favourite and it would be very valuable indeed. Even the 'lesser' paintings were now worth many times more than the amount paid out in insurance twenty years earlier. Although insurance companies automatically acquire legal ownership of stolen valuables on paying compensation, it is customary that they offer to reverse the transaction in return for the insured sum plus interest. Insurers thereby avoid being seen as profiting from crime and denying their customers the joy of reclaiming their lost property. Having received the green light from their insurer, the Bakwins instructed the ALR to pursue the matter on their behalf.

The ALR's recoveries are undertaken on a no-win-no-fee basis. Retrievals can be complex and lengthy operations with uncertain outcomes, meaning the ALR bears a significant financial risk. Although out-of-pocket expenses such as travel costs, lawyers' fees and detectives' bills are paid by the customer, the ALR does not charge for the time it takes to research the case, negotiate the deal and retrieve the object. The customer pays a fixed percentage of whatever financial benefit accrues to them, if and when their treasure is restored to them. It was clear from the outset that this case would be particularly challenging. The mysterious 'Russian institution' that had approached Mr W had raised red flags everywhere. Whenever a holder wishes to remain anonymous, there is a danger the money could go to people involved in the theft, or to someone who would pass on a share to the original criminals. But with an anonymous 'institution' in Russia, there was an additional risk: (part of) the money might go to the mafia or even a terrorist organisation. Unless Mr W's principals were prepared to disclose their identity and come forward with detailed information about how they acquired the paintings to prove their good (or at least tolerable) faith, no deal could be done. The chance of finding oneself drawn into a shady deal with the Russian mafia was simply too high.

Who was Mr W and who were his clients? He persistently gave vague and evasive answers, so eventually the ALR decided to employ private detectives to make confidential enquiries about him and his associates. Mr W turned out to be a British businessman with a string of failed enterprises behind him, but there was no sign of criminal connections. He was a typical middleman and it appeared he was genuinely oblivious of who his clients were. However, over the weeks he gradually revealed that the anonymous holders were not just offering the Cézanne and the two Soutine paintings of a young man and a young woman. They had two more: a landscape painting by Maurice Utrillo and a vase of flowers by Maurice de Vlaminck. Eventually, yet another two photographs arrived. They were quickly confirmed to be two paintings by Jean Jansem, which completed the Bakwins' set of stolen paintings. This made it near certain that the holders were criminals. The seven paintings were very different: not a 'set' that was likely to be acquired by a single good faith buyer. If they were offered together it suggested the thieves or their fence had failed to sell them, or they had been treated as a job lot in some criminal underworld deal.

Over the next months the ALR team became experts on Russian organised crime. Every single contact Mr W mentioned in conjunction with the case was discreetly checked out. The criminals' web included shady businessmen in Russia, Estonia and Monaco, but no promising lead materialised. Radcliffe consulted with the police, the FBI and Scotland Yard, and instructed a London law firm to check out the legal risks of doing a deal with a mystery seller in Russia. Predictably, everyone counselled that no payments could be made to an anonymous Russian institution. Yet, despite this apparent impasse the conversation continued. Often crooks inadvertently give away important information that can ultimately help to resolve a case.

Genuine or fake?

Rather than talking about money, the ALR's ample correspondence with Mr W foregrounded a legitimate concern: the entire deal might be a scam. What if the mysterious sellers were peddling copies of the missing paintings rather than the originals? Until the artworks had been authenticated by an independent expert, there could be no meaningful negotiation about a price. Resolving this problem became the dominant theme of the conversation with Mr W. At its heart is a fascinating question about contract design: how can two parties that do not trust each other agree on a mutually satisfactory authentication process?

The ALR could not hire an international expert on modern and Impressionist art to travel to what was potentially the lair of the Russian mafia. The seller could, of course, send the paintings to a place where it was safe to view them, ideally Christie's or Sotheby's in London. However, this would expose them to the risk of having the paintings seized as stolen goods at customs or upon arrival. The Bakwin family could have given written assurances that they would not mount a civil lawsuit, but could a criminal organisation trust such written assurance, which the family could claim had been signed under duress? Who could predict the actions of law enforcement, even if up to that point neither the US nor the UK police had expressed any interest in the case? Had the conversation reached another dead end?

Fortunately, this kind of tricky contract problem can be solved with the help of impartial third parties. There are countries that are safe for everyone to travel to, where there are respected art experts and where the police are relatively relaxed about the legal status of artworks held, viewed and consensually traded in their territory. Monaco was the first candidate country, but eventually Mr W's clients settled on the idea of authenticating the paintings in Geneva. There was a private bank that would be pleased to make a room available for everyone to meet on neutral ground. The ALR instructed the top art law specialist at a Swiss law firm to explore this option. Would Mr W please put the ALR's Swiss lawyer in touch with the seller's lawyer to negotiate details of the viewing arrangements? Mr W was hesitant, but in the end he grudgingly agreed.

Changing places

The holders' Swiss lawyer introduced himself as Mr F. He had (unbelievably) good news. He knew his clients to be honest and was completely satisfied they were neither involved in the original theft nor in organised crime. His clients had acquired the paintings as an informal payment for services rendered. However, as prominent public figures they would be embarrassed by their names being linked to stolen art. The clients had therefore invented the 'Russian institution' to protect their anonymity. The artworks had been in Switzerland for many years and were owned by a perfectly legitimate offshore trust company. His clients now wanted to retract the cover story about the 'Russian institution' that had apparently become a liability and an obstacle to the resolution process. The lawyer conceded that his clients' wish to protect their identity was less than ideal, but in view of this they were seeking only 10–15 per cent of the paintings' value as their finder's reward.

Having spent tens of thousands of dollars on exploring and mitigating the risks of a potential deal with the Russian mafia, this sudden revelation seemed too good to be true. Could it be trusted? Even with the Russian mafia objection removed, it would be difficult to buy back the paintings on behalf of their lawful owner. As the Cézanne painting alone would fetch between US$10 million and US$30 million, a 'finder's reward' of 10–15 per cent was a substantial sum of money to give to a potential criminal. How to organise the authentication of the pictures had already been worked out in principle, but the plan required significant fine-tuning. And there were five further major areas of concern that would need to be resolved before a trade could go ahead.

Contractual dilemmas

First, despite the Swiss lawyer's assurances, there was every indication that the holders were not acting in good faith. The seven artworks were still together. They had already been worth around a million dollars in the late 1970s and neither the ALR, nor the Bakwins, nor the police could imagine what legitimate professional service could have been rendered by the holders to justify the transfer of possessions on this scale in lieu of payment. Mr W had also let slip information about the circumstances of the theft that indicated the holders had closer knowledge of the crime than had been publicly available. There was no easy way to allay everyone's deep-seated concerns about entering into an unlawful transaction here. The holders could not prove they met the minimum ALR criteria for a negotiation (that is, no link to the theft or organised crime) without revealing their identity. Yet, if they divulged their names, the Bakwins could use that knowledge to threaten them with public embarrassment and thereby drive the purchase price down. What information could possibly be provided to reassure one side without exposing the other?

Second, the holders' demand of a percentage of the paintings' value posed an awkward question: 10–15 per cent of what? The only fair way of determining their value would be by public auction. But in this case the current holders would have to wait until after the auction to receive the money. How could the crooks be guaranteed their payout once the artworks had been handed over? If the money was paid at the handover, the criminals' risk would be lower, but who would provide a truly independent valuation? If either side appointed someone to value the paintings, he or she would be in their employ and thus not independent. Of course, multiple professional opinions could be sought, but each additional valuation would raise the risk of a leak, detection and a possible seizure. In any case, auction houses can get valuations wrong and catalogue estimates are typically conservative. How would the contract protect the holders against an undervaluation and the former owners against overpaying?

Third, the ALR had another worry at the back of its mind. Stolen artworks sometimes serve as securities for deals in the economic underworld, particularly in the drug supply chain. Nobody knew where the paintings had been for the last twenty-one years. How could the Bakwins be sure their property was not encumbered with an underworld debt? Further claimants could come forward when the paintings were publicly auctioned. Proving this negative would be particularly tricky: an anonymous counterparty cannot give a credible guarantee.

Fourth, there was the question of the handover. If the paintings were returned in Switzerland, the lawful owner would want to repatriate them to the USA or perhaps have them sent to auction somewhere else. Unless the import into Switzerland had been completely legal, awkward questions would be asked at customs on export. Yet handing the artworks back in the USA would expose the holders to the risk of border officials seizing the paintings. Who should bear this export risk? And if a disagreement arose after the transaction, which authority would be trusted to adjudicate in this shady deal?

And finally, as Mr F, the holders' lawyer, pointed out in a fax to Mr W: the holders were fully aware they were selling stolen goods. Even if they had not been involved in the original theft, they could now be accused of fencing. The holders knew the only legal way to return the paintings was to give them up. Yet, they wanted to make sure they were adequately recompensed for their honest efforts in bringing about an amicable resolution. All documents relating to the transaction should therefore refer to the holders as the 'finders' and any financial settlement as a 'reward'. However, these particular 'finders' were such tough negotiators that any deal might well look like extortion to an objective observer. Mr F's letter closed with a prescient statement worth quoting in full: 'I should like to point out that while the suggestion I have made is to my belief legal, the whole constellation of returning potentially stolen art remains very delicate and needs careful handling, while at the same time no assurances can be given that matters will work out as expected.' Prophetic words indeed.

The Gordian knot

The next months were taken up with detailed negotiations trying to resolve all of these contractual dilemmas. There are numerous boxes of correspondence, with each subsequent proposal critically evaluated by the ALR, amended as necessary, and then checked over by the Bakwins and their lawyers in Boston, the ALR's own lawyers in London and the Geneva law firm brought in to ensure compliance with Swiss law. The FBI and the Metropolitan Police were regularly kept abreast of events by Radcliffe, while the Geneva lawyers handled communications with Swiss law enforcement.

To unlock a payment, at a minimum the holders had to prove they were not the thieves. It was suggested this might be achieved by revealing the holders' identity to a discreet third party trusted by both sides, who would check the names against a long list of potential suspects provided by the Bakwins and the FBI. A senior partner in a UK law firm was initially selected to take on this role. While the Bakwins compiled their so-called 'no-no' list of wayward family members, staff and their families, friends and acquaintances (to which the police would add the names of known local thieves and gang members), the negotiation moved on to the size of the reward.

Paying a ransom appeared to be the only way of returning the paintings to the Bakwins, so the ALR moved to obtain (informal) police clearance for a payment. Even if the thieves were still in the picture and might get a cut of the ransom, they had waited twenty years to receive their payout. Making a limited financial concession at this stage was therefore unlikely to trigger a spate of new art heists. The FBI, Swiss and UK police forces thus agreed a payment could be made, but the closer the link between the thieves and the holders, the smaller the ransom should be. Did the holders have any evidence to show how they had acquired the property? A sales receipt or agreement, a foreclosure statement, some tax or customs forms, or, in fact, anything at all that would document a legal transaction? Could they prove they had not already sold, promised or mortgaged the paintings to someone else in the meantime? Depending on the quality of the corroborating documents the Bakwins were willing to pay a reward of up to 15 per cent of the value of the paintings.

Unfortunately, there was not a single document that the holders could (or wanted to) provide to prove their good faith. However, they were ready to write an affidavit confirming they had not known or worked for the Bakwins, and they had not participated in or planned the theft. As they had transferred all beneficial rights to an offshore company, they would also swear that nobody in this company had any link to organised crime. This was far from ideal: it raised almost as many questions as it answered. Although Radcliffe described the assurances offered as 'at the de minimis end of inadequate', breaking off the negotiation at this stage was problematic, too. The paintings could still be sold to an unscrupulous collector or shady trader and might be used in illicit deals if they were not returned to the Bakwins. The police and legal advisers counselled the ALR to proceed cautiously. The ALR would work towards a settlement at the bottom end of the reward scale.

After lengthy deliberations, Radcliffe came up with an unusual plan. To obtain police consent for the payment, the holders' Swiss lawyer would formally attest that his clients were not the thieves, putting his own professional reputation at stake. The holders would also sign an affidavit confirming they were not connected to the theft. This document would be sent in a sealed envelope to a senior partner at a London law firm. The lawyers would be paid to hold the envelope in escrow for a period of ten years and destroy it afterwards. The contract between the Bakwins and the holders stated that the envelope would only be released with a court order or with the agreement of both parties.

Predictably, it took many months to thrash out the wording of each and every agreed statement, during which everyone's bills mounted. While the Bakwins took care of the ALR's out-of-pocket expenses (with occasional grumbles over spiralling legal and travel expenses), Mr W was left high and dry. He had been promised a cut of the proceeds by his clients, but now he was on the sidelines while the possibility of a generous settlement was evaporating. The day-to-day work was done by Mr F, who in couching the negotiation in terms of a 'finder's reward' appeared to have overcome his scruples about assisting a potential fence. Who would be responsible for paying the increasingly desperate Mr W? The Russian connection had admittedly been an expensive distraction, but surely the ALR agreed that Mr W had been useful nonetheless? If nothing else, he still had pester power.

As the holders began to accept a lower percentage of the paintings' value as their reward, they became ever more concerned that the ALR might also manipulate the price estimate downwards, thereby hurting them twice. It had been decided that the precondition for the deal was the authentication of the paintings in Geneva by the key Sotheby's expert for modern and Impressionist art. It would be efficient if the expert also provided the price estimates at the same time. The paintings' value crucially depended on their condition and this could be ascertained only by detailed examination. But would the holders receive a fair price estimate from the Sotheby's expert? They began to feel doubtful. Without seeing the pictures, and therefore unable to judge their condition, Sotheby's had given an estimate in the region of US$15 million to US$20 million for *Bouilloire et Fruits*, but only if in tip-top condition. Yet, in May 1999 a similar Cézanne still life had been auctioned at Christie's and broken all previous records. As the *New York Times* reported:

> four bidders fought long and hard to buy Cézanne's 'Still Life with Curtain, Pitcher and Bowl of Fruit' (1893–94), considered a first-rate example of the artist's mature still lifes. After a slow, steady battle that heated up when the price topped $42 million, the painting finally sold to an unidentified buyer … for $60.5 million, far above its $35 million high estimate. The salesroom burst into applause …[25]

The current holders of the Bakwin Cézanne were suspicious. The Sotheby's expert's initial estimate of US$15 million to US$20 million was either very conservative, or was he in cahoots with the ALR? No, came the answer: the Bakwin Cézanne was a bit smaller, not quite as 'first-rate', and the provenance not nearly as attractive as the Whitney family's Cézanne. But Mr F wrote: 'My clients and I are becoming increasingly apprehensive of Sotheby's role in the affair … my clients cannot just accept their estimate as binding.' There would have to be an alternative evaluation arranged by the holders after the painting had been authenticated. So, the Bakwin team would have only a tantalising glimpse of the artworks before they once again disappeared into the underworld.

The next months were spent trying to work around this problem as well as agreeing the wording of the escrow arrangement, the affidavit and the authentication process. How can you give a payment guarantee for something you have yet to authenticate and that is difficult to value if it is genuine? When studying trade in the economic underworld we realise how much we rely on mutual trust in our everyday transactions. Mostly, we select trade partners we trust or who are recommended by friends. Even if we do not personally know a supplier, their high-street presence reassures us they will treat us well to maintain their good reputation. If they do not, we will name and shame them in a damning review or by gossiping about them. And if something goes badly wrong, we trust in state institutions to put things right. But none of this applies in a one-off deal with an anonymous, foreign and quite possibly criminal counterparty. Nobody trusts anybody's assurances on anything, and nothing can be taken for granted.

The so-called 'agreement' that went back and forth between the parties grew ever more convoluted and not a single aspect could be fully settled. The holders felt too exposed to bring their paintings to be authenticated and valued before receiving payment, and the ALR was certainly not going to pay anything to anyone without having seen the goods. A Gordian knot was growing and pulling ever tighter.

An elegant solution?

In October 1999, after many months of fruitless wrangling, Mr F cut through the legal tangle with a bold proposal. Most of the value of the hoard was in *Bouilloire et Fruits*. The six other paintings would probably fetch around half a million dollars at auction and significantly more on a good day. This was less than the holders had expected as their 'reward', but more than the ALR had hitherto offered. The positions had failed to converge, and in any case the parties could not work out a satisfactory scheme for guaranteeing payment to the holders. Under the new proposal, the ALR would be shown only the Cézanne in Geneva. If the experts accepted it as genuine, the Bakwin team would take possession of the Cézanne and formally transfer ownership of the six other paintings to the current holders in return. If the experts judged it a forgery, the deal was off. No money would change hands and the financial risk for both sides would be minimised.

Finally, progress could be made. Mr F staked his own reputation in guaranteeing the holders were not the thieves, linked to organised crime or part of the Bakwins' staff or social circle. The holders' names would appear only on the affidavit that would be held securely by the escrow agent. There was no longer a need to find a neutral territory for the authentication where the crooks could feel secure to show the paintings. The worries about a police seizure evaporated, as the Cézanne was to be handed over anyway. The other paintings would remain with the holders and the Bakwins agreed they would be moved from the 'stolen' to the 'recovered' section of the ALR database. Anyone making an enquiry about these six paintings would be told that they had been stolen in 1978 and recovered in 1999, and that the title had been passed to the current holders in a settlement. Any disputes arising out of the agreement would be settled by a

Swiss arbitrator under Swiss law, about which the holders and their lawyer were absolutely adamant. Having been kept abreast throughout the negotiation, the FBI and Swiss police agreed that the deal met their policy guidelines.[26] With written assurances in place, Swiss customs prepared the paperwork for the legitimate export of the Cézanne.

Within the month, arrangements for the handover were finalised. Mr F suddenly seemed keen to complete the transaction as fast as possible. Although the police had agreed the Bakwins could make the payment, the Swiss public prosecutor was concerned about the shady nature of the deal. The public prosecutor's office informally warned Mr F that he might be facilitating a crime and it seems he became less zealous in pressing for his clients' advantage after this admonition. Would the holders spot that the agreed statement was not exactly the clean bill of health an open market sale would require? They might well get cold feet at the last moment. Whether or not the trade succeeded was very much up in the air.

The return of *Bouilloire et Fruits*

On the morning of 25 October 1999, Radcliffe and two Sotheby's experts met at the ALR lawyer's Geneva offices to wait for the holders' lawyer. Some contracts would have to be signed before the picture was delivered. If the experts accepted it as genuine, the rest of the paperwork would be finalised. However, Mr F did not arrive. Had the deal collapsed at the last minute? A tense three hours passed. Then a phone call reassured the group that it was merely an unforeseen 'complication': the exchange was still on track. Inexplicable hiccups are par for the course in hostage crisis resolutions and you have to learn to wait.

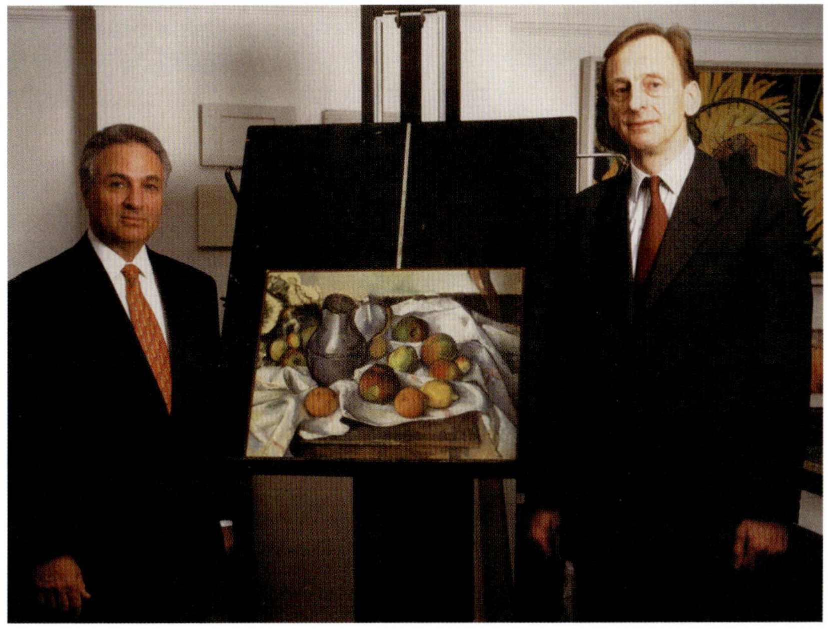

The ALR's Julian Radcliffe and Ron Tauber with the recovered
Bouilloire et Fruits.

At long last the delayed Mr F breezed in without offering an explanation. He unpacked his sheaf of contracts. Both sides' legal representatives and Radcliffe scrutinised each document line by line before appending their signatures. The sealed envelope for the escrow agent was shown and subsequently wrapped in many layers of envelopes and packaging paper, taped up intricately and securely like a mummy. With each layer photographically documented, it would be impossible to take a sneaky peak at the contents without leaving a trace.

Finally, Mr F made a phone call and the whole group proceeded outside. A white car with darkened windows drove past slowly. Mr F followed it around the street corner. Someone passed him a large wrapped package and, tense with anticipation, everyone went back into the office. Sotheby's expert for Impressionist art took charge of unwrapping the parcel. The moment the final layer of paper was peeled back, and the first brushstrokes were revealed, he knew he had a genuine Cézanne in his hands. His local colleague agreed: it was the Bakwins' missing heirloom. Further investigation revealed the picture was in excellent condition. Following this positive verdict, the painting was formally handed over to Radcliffe, and the lawyers resumed their work.

The release agreement was duly signed and was implemented a few days later. Swiss customs expedited the official export of *Bouilloire et Fruits*. After twenty-one years AWOL and nearly ten months of intense negotiations, the Bakwins' beloved Cézanne could finally be returned to its lawful owners. However, the painting had become so valuable that the family decided they could no longer display and enjoy it at their home. On top of paying the significant cost incurred in its recovery, they would have to secure their house and insure it properly. Fine art insurers charge at least 0.1 per cent of the painting's value per annum: a hefty US$30,000 on a US$30 million painting. The Cézanne would be sold at the next suitable auction.

Off to auction

The painting was consigned to Sotheby's London and included in one of its prestigious December evening auctions. The catalogue price estimate was US$15 million to US$20 million: there had not been any deception in the estimate given to its former holders. Sotheby's had provided a genuinely independent valuation. But now the auction house would do the best it could to get a good price for the Bakwins. *Bouilloire et Fruits* was billed as one of the highlights of the Impressionist and modern art sale. The painting was shown in Paris and London prior to the sale and its interesting recent history became one of the features in its advertising.[27] Indeed, the 'Cézanne with the unusual past' was bought by the US media magnate Samuel Irving 'S.I.' Newhouse Jr (of Condé Nast fame) for US$29.5 million.[28]

Finally, everyone on the Bakwin team received their payouts. There were significant lawyers' bills to be settled in London, Boston and Geneva. Even the hapless Mr W, who had been hovering desperately on the fringes of the case for the past six months, was given some money to go away: clearly, his side was not going to pay him. Once all other bills were settled, the ALR received 10 per cent of the final benefit to the Bakwins as its recovery fee. Only the opposition's Swiss lawyer was left out. He would have to extract payment from his own clients. Unless they sold the six paintings, it looked like he would be left high and dry.

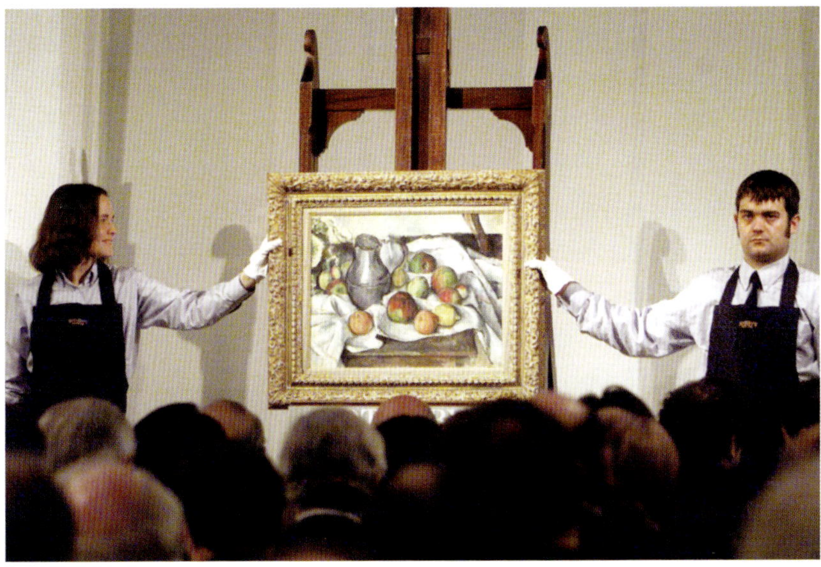

Sotheby's porters present Paul Cézanne's *Bouilloire et Fruits* at auction in December 1999.

One down, six to go

For the ALR the business was not finished, however. There were another six Bakwin paintings out there and Radcliffe would not rest until they too were recovered for the family. It was a point of both honour and principle that unless his mysterious adversaries revealed credible evidence they were not (near-) criminal they should not get a significant financial benefit from the settlement.

A week after the handover of *Bouilloire et Fruits*, Radcliffe was back in touch with Mr F to impart the news that the picture would be sold at auction and to deliver a series of veiled threats. He explained there would be enormous publicity as soon as the recovered Cézanne was exhibited and sold. Journalists would ask awkward questions about the other six paintings. Radcliffe claimed that, although the legal title had formally passed to the anonymous current holders, the transfer was morally questionable. Potential buyers would be concerned by the paintings' tainted provenance, in the same way that collectors avoid Holocaust-era objects with unresolved claims. Radcliffe therefore considered them unsaleable, unless they were sold with the explicit agreement of and ideally in the name of Michael Bakwin. If they were sold in the current holders' names, the police and tax officials might like to investigate the circumstances of their acquisition. Consequently, it would be best for everyone if the current holders came to a confidential, swift and amicable settlement with the Bakwins. There was no response.

Then Michael Bakwin himself made an offer. He would personally buy back the paintings from the current holders, either for a price established by a Sotheby's or Christie's valuation or even at an auction. However, there was one proviso: the money could only be used to cover the holders' legal costs and the balance would go to charity. The promise of payment should at least prompt the Swiss lawyer's interest in a settlement. Eventually, a counter-offer was received. The auction house Phillips had provided the holders with a valuation of US$1.27 million. This was significantly above the previous estimates, but the holders considered it to be a just finder's reward for returning the Cézanne. Would Bakwin be interested in purchasing at this price, with a maximum of US$50,000 going to charity?

We gave you nothing

The fact that a major auction house had valued the paintings without a prior ALR search changed the tone of the subsequent conversations. The holders considered it as evidence the ALR was not as powerful as it had claimed, and that the paintings' poor provenance would not preclude a successful sale after all. The ALR immediately swung into action. Radcliffe confronted Phillips over the valuation and explained the paintings' complex background. The auctioneers apologised and promised greater vigilance in future. But clearly the ALR had to raise public awareness about its quest for the missing artworks. Unless both legal and grey market buyers were put off by the paintings' tainted history, the holders would not come back to the negotiating table.

The ALR therefore decided to brief journalists about the details of the Cézanne recovery. In the final paragraph of an article in the *Boston Globe* Radcliffe defiantly threw down the gauntlet. As the holders had blithely ignored the moral case for a settlement, Radcliffe now threatened them with a legal dispute. He asserted that the transfer agreement for the six paintings was null and void: 'we were coerced to sign over the ownership of those pieces. … As such, those papers are without legal standing. We gave nothing in return for the Cézanne.'[29] This fighting talk was picked up and spread by journalists around the world. Dealers everywhere would now warn potential buyers against acquiring the paintings due to their indeterminate legal status. It was a costly move for the ALR, however. On the upside, putting the paintings in legal limbo shifted the balance of power in the negotiation towards the ALR. But on the downside, most transactions – and particularly underworld transactions – require a degree of trust. Publicly going back on one's word would make subsequent negotiations more complex and could scupper the quest for amicable resolutions: not just in the Bakwin case, but in other art retrievals, too.

3

The Criminal Lawyer: Finder or Fence?

The jury had come back with a guilty verdict and the judge no longer had to hold back his anger and frustration with the defendant. The man in the dock was no ordinary criminal, but an experienced lawyer. Rather than pursuing justice, he had held an innocent crime victim to ransom and had since used every trick in the book to evade punishment. Only a harsh sentence would reflect the profession's revulsion about such 'truly despicable conduct'.[30] The judge banged his gavel. 'The defendant is hereby committed to the Custody of the United States Bureau of Prisons to be imprisoned for a total term of 84 months.'[31] He added: 'The only reason I'm sentencing a 74-year-old man in the early stages of dementia is because you were calculating enough to get away with this for 30 years … You started as a lawyer … As far as I'm concerned, you became a glorified fence'.[32]

The price of justice

The ALR's recovery of the multimillion-dollar *Bouilloire et Fruits* by Cézanne was just the first skirmish in a lengthy campaign on behalf of the Bakwins. There were many unanswered questions. First, where were the remaining six paintings and how could they be flushed out from their hiding place? Second, who was the counterparty of the 1999 agreement and how had they come into possession of the paintings? Third, who was the legitimate owner of the paintings relinquished in return for the Cézanne? Was the 1999 agreement a legally valid contract between sophisticated businesspeople, or was it a concession obtained through extortion? Fourth, were the holders guilty of possessing stolen goods while they believed the agreement to be valid? Fifth, what – if any – compensation should the Bakwins receive? Sixth, who should pay that compensation? The holders clearly had accomplices, but could they be held financially responsible, too? And seventh, could any money judgments be enforced in a global financial system proffering professional asset-hiding services?

These were all fascinating questions. Answering each of them would require a team of private investigators, journalists, lawyers and paralegals, accountants and police officers, and a competent and determined manager to hold it all together and drive the campaign forward. This immediately raised the question of cost. A complex court case can easily rake up a seven-figure bill, but the missing paintings were not that valuable. Even if a judge awarded substantial costs and damages to the winners, the losers could still play an endgame of evasion. Somebody had to foot the bills. Would a coalition of the willing stick together for however long it took? Or would the team fall apart when financial and emotional costs escalated?

Stalemate

The international press had eagerly picked up the thrilling accounts of the ALR's recovery of the Cézanne from a shadowy underworld figure. The art world was on red alert looking for the missing Soutine and Jansem portraits, the Utrillo landscape and the De Vlaminck flowers (see Chapter 2). The ALR therefore wrote to the holders' Swiss lawyer, Mr F, once more. Was it not time to settle the matter by handing back the other six stolen pictures? Unfortunately, Mr F was incensed by the allegation that he had facilitated a coerced transaction. Given the generally amicable nature of the negotiation, the absence of direct threats and the apparently faithful completion of the paperwork after the handover of *Bouilloire et Fruits*, he flatly denied that the agreement could be voided.

Three reputations were at stake here. First, Mr F was worried about his firm being associated with an illicit transaction. The Swiss public prosecutor had already warned him privately, but the ALR's media campaign threatened his public reputation. Mr F had to protest in the strongest possible terms about the ALR's portrayal of the Cézanne deal. Second, if the secretive holders admitted there had been any duress, they would concede they were fences rather than finders. A fence would not only lose the paintings but could end up behind bars. Third, the ALR's reputation was balanced on a knife-edge. Retrieving the Cézanne from a criminal without making a significant concession would be a feat of cunning and a moral victory. But what if the counterparty proved they were honest finders and had been duped and maligned by the ALR? The ALR needs finders to come forward without fear, so this case could backfire on its business, too.

Private resolutions need compromise on both sides. If a dispute is largely about money, then a settlement can usually be found.

But if honour and reputation are at stake, it is much more difficult to reach a compromise. It is certainly impossible to do so in the full media spotlight. Of course, the problem could be resolved in court, with a judge publicly declaring a jubilant winner and utterly shaming the loser. It would be a case with massive stakes: high costs for sure, but perhaps even prison? Everyone decided to lay low for a while. The conversation ended, the media circus moved on and the ALR patiently scanned the world's salerooms for the missing paintings. For five whole years.

For sale at Sotheby's?

Finally, in January 2005, a message came in from Sotheby's. 'An individual' would like to consign four Impressionist paintings for auction. Sotheby's legal department had picked up that there was a small wrinkle with the provenance. The paperwork attesting there was no longer a problem with the pictures seemed a little odd. Would the ALR please confirm that all was in order? Bullseye: the missing paintings were back on the market, except they were still with the seller. If the ALR informed Sotheby's about the contested ownership, the auction house might refuse the consignment and guard the anonymity of the seller. The waiting game for the paintings to pop up somewhere else would begin all over again. To make progress the artworks had to be physically consigned for sale in a jurisdiction where they could be seized by the police. In short, to help the Bakwins retrieve their heirlooms (and collect its recovery fee) the ALR would have to lie to Sotheby's.

This was a moral and commercial dilemma. The Bakwins had waited for more than twenty years to reclaim their Cézanne but they had not been able to keep it. They had endured a further five years of uncertainty over the other paintings since then and really wanted closure. Yet, deceiving the holders into consigning the paintings and then having them seized could inflame an already volatile situation and make an amicable resolution less likely. Moreover, if the subterfuge was made public, a reputation for duplicity might hound the ALR in future art retrievals. The ALR also had a duty of care towards the auction house, which was a loyal long-term customer and a (minority) shareholder. If it encouraged Sotheby's to proceed with a sale agreement and subsequently exposed it with stolen pictures on its hands it would be awkward to say the least. Would the ALR still be trusted by the art market if it occasionally gave false information? Its future reputation depended on being right about this particular consignor being a criminal. Although the holders' actions in the Cézanne deal had been deeply suspicious, it was still possible they had legitimate reasons for disguising their identity.

After a long debate with the Bakwins and their legal advisers, the ALR decided to give a green light to Sotheby's. The Bakwins wrote to the auction house for permission to inspect the paintings well ahead of the June 2005 sale with a view to making a private offer. In the meantime, their lawyers prepared a letter of claim and the ALR informally pressed Sotheby's for more information about the seller. Anti-money-laundering regulation requires auction houses to know their customers. Could the auction house at least tell the ALR whether the pictures were still in the hands of the people who had negotiated the 1999 transfer agreement? However, the auction house would not reveal anything about the consignor's identity without a formal request from law enforcement. When the pictures finally arrived in London in May 2005, Julian Radcliffe confronted Sotheby's with the Bakwins' claim that the transfer agreement was void. In line with the norms of their trade, the auction house moved to protect its client's interest against this unproven allegation. The firm's legal department argued it could not assess whether the 1999 agreement was void or voidable. It would advise its customer of the problem. If they wished to take back their pictures, they would be free to do so.

This was precisely why the ALR had encouraged the pictures' consignment to London. Here the Bakwins could get back-up from law enforcement to resolve the ownership of the paintings. When the lawyers submitted the Bakwins' claim to the High Court in London, Sotheby's immediately withdrew the paintings from the sale and secured them in its strong room. Sotheby's legal team wrote to reassure both sides that the auction house would retain possession of the artworks until it received either joint written instructions from both the consignor and the claimant or a binding court order for their release. At last, there was a level playing field for a commercial negotiation over how much the Bakwins should pay the holders. Yet renewed attempts to resolve the issue amicably were half-hearted and failed. The bargaining positions had hardened. The Bakwins had scented victory and their new cash offer for the paintings was now well below the legal costs incurred by their opposition. The holders, however, were furious about the breach of trust and still considered the release agreement legally binding. The matter would have to be settled in front of a judge.

See you in court

As the consignor had refused to reveal their identity, the Bakwins had to serve a claim against Sotheby's for conversion of stolen property. If Sotheby's responded to this by handing over the stolen paintings to the Bakwins, the consignor would probably sue them. It would cause a scandal and could deter other owners of artworks with gaps in their provenance from consigning their works to Sotheby's in the future. Most auction houses have some experience of managing conflicts between their duty of care towards honest clients and the fallout from unwittingly shielding criminals. When negotiation and informal mediation fail, they do not take sides but elegantly extricate themselves from such disputes. When an innocent third party holds a disputed asset and does not know to whom the asset lawfully belongs, they can file an 'interpleader'. This hands over the controversy to the court and forces the consignor to come forward to fight their own legal action. Thus, in July 2005 the Bakwins finally found out something about their mysterious tormentors: Erie International Trading Company Inc., registered in Panama, was officially entered as the interpleader claimant. In the first stage of the legal proceedings, the High Court in London would have to establish that the dispute was indeed between the Bakwins and Erie International Trading, and Sotheby's an innocent bystander. If so, Erie would be substituted as the defendant in the case. In the second stage, the court would determine ownership of the paintings.

But which court?

As is so often the case in the international art market, the first question that needs to be settled is that of jurisdiction. The paintings were in London, but would the English courts accept responsibility for a dispute arising from an agreement made in Switzerland? The 1999 agreement that handed over ownership of the six paintings in return for the Cézanne stated that any disputes between the parties would be settled by arbitration in Geneva. Erie had insisted on this throughout the negotiation. Confidential arbitration proceedings suited the secretive holder well. Based on Swiss law the International Chamber of Commerce (ICC) in Geneva would likely find in Erie's favour. After signing the agreement, the company had waited for exactly five years before trying to sell the paintings. Under the Swiss civil code, it would have acquired ownership by having been in 'peaceable possession' for this period. So, was there a way for the Bakwins to void the arbitration clause and have the case heard in London? Erie instructed a London law firm to try everything to stay the English proceedings and have the case settled by the ICC. Conversely, the Bakwin team fought for a UK trial arguing this was not just a private commercial dispute. The case involved at least two crimes (fencing and extortion) and should therefore be tried before a UK court.

To win the case in a UK court, Michael Bakwin would have to prove that his title had not been extinguished either in 1999 (when the agreement was signed) or between 1999 and 2005. But which law would the English court apply to settle this question? English law, Massachusetts law (where the theft had taken place) and Swiss law (explicitly specified in the agreement) were all contenders. UK and US law set higher barriers for acquiring good title than the Swiss five-year time limit. By influencing the decision about choice of law, each party could load the dice in their favour. The first stage of the trial was therefore crucial. Once the rules of the game were set, the outcome would become predictable and a fair out-of-court settlement could be reached more easily.

However, manoeuvring the Bakwins into a favourable starting position would take months of work and tens of thousands of dollars in legal fees. The very point of the arbitration clause had been to avoid ruinously costly litigation of the type towards which the Bakwin team was now steering. The Bakwins had no intention of going to trial: they were worried about the cost, stress and time commitment involved. When Erie decided to defend the case, the Bakwins' London lawyer's bill already exceeded the initially agreed threshold 'by a margin'. Yet, although the Bakwins were keen to settle, they felt insulted by the terms suggested by the holder. Thus, their lead lawyer advised them to invest some more money: 'I would like to move quickly on all possible fronts to strengthen our position and weaken the other side, so we can start commercial negotiations as soon as possible.'

The ALR believed that discovering the identity of the people hiding behind Erie would be the key to success. It wanted to apply for a court order for the escrow agent to open the multilayered and taped-up parcel from Geneva. If it contained the names of the holders, one could threaten them with exposure and drive the settlement price down. Time for the Bakwins to open their chequebook again for what Radcliffe described as 'some necessary attritional warfare to shape the battlefield for a commercial settlement.'

Unfortunately, if unsurprisingly, the other side made the same decision. On 4 August 2005 Erie International Trading made an official request to the ICC to arbitrate in the matter of the paintings. Four days later, the British High Court would decide whether to send the case to arbitration. The Bakwins' legal team was genuinely worried: '[T]here is a material risk that the [UK] judge … will … stay the proceedings in favour of arbitration … we cannot say that we are fully confident that we will prevail.' If the case was sent to the ICC, Bakwin would not only lose the paintings but also be asked to pay for Erie's and Sotheby's legal costs in London. Court cases are emotional roller coasters.

Into the long grass

The mysterious holder was perhaps a little too sure of victory in the first round. The junior lawyer pleading their case was hopelessly outgunned by the senior professor brought in by Withers, the Bakwins' London law firm. The judge decided he needed to hear more evidence and set another trial date for November 2005. In the meantime, costs mounted on both sides. The Bakwins' opposition had learnt its lesson: it now instructed a QC, that is one of the highest-ranking barristers in the UK. It also pressed ahead with arbitration in Switzerland, arguing that the British court order for a November hearing did not automatically suspend the arbitration procedure. Even though the arbitrator's orders would probably not be enforceable while UK court proceedings were ongoing, preparing for and engaging in the arbitration process tied up further valuable resources. Just as the UK case generated costs and delays for Erie, running a parallel case in Switzerland escalated the costs for the Bakwin team. Both sides would have to hire both English and Swiss legal experts and prepare two different cases with lines of arguments suited to each jurisdiction. Erie had clearly decided to retaliate in this 'war of attrition' and the lawyers' bills were increasing alarmingly.

The Bakwins were understandably stressed by the spiralling cost of 'shaping the battlefield'. The ALR, too, had gone out on a limb and wanted to settle the case. In early September 2005 the legal advisers thus started to prepare another approach for a negotiated settlement. Several press articles had been drafted and were ready to go. The ALR believed the credible threat of media exposure (and hence police interest) was a more powerful bargaining tool than approaching the opposition after the fact. However, Erie stalled, remaining confident it would win the legal arguments.

Back in court

In November 2005 the UK court needed to resolve whether the arbitration clause in the 1999 agreement was null and void. The Bakwin team argued the Cézanne deal was illegal, immoral and contrary to public policy. It was only entered into under coercion and threat, which made the entire agreement void. Erie therefore had neither title to the stolen paintings nor a right to bring a case for arbitration. Conversely, Erie's lawyers pointed out no threats had been made while the agreement was negotiated and specifically no pressure had been applied when the arbitration clause was agreed. The contract had been signed after the return of *Bouilloire et Fruits*, which would have removed any duress. The agreement had never been formally repudiated either. Thus, five years after the return of the Cézanne the title to the other six paintings had passed to Erie under Swiss law. Moreover, they pointed out that when Sotheby's checked the title to the paintings, the ALR had not indicated there was a problem. This confirmed Erie's ownership.

It was a tense two-week wait for the judgment. On 21 November the judge published an order to stay the Swiss arbitration procedure. He accepted the Bakwins' argument that the entire agreement was made under duress. The threat that the negotiations would be broken off and the remaining six paintings would vanish unless the Bakwins agreed to Erie's terms was unlawful. Importantly, the material threat had not ended with the return of the Cézanne. Erie was still in possession of six stolen pictures and the Bakwins could not formally repudiate the agreement without risking the loss of the remaining pictures. The contract was illegal under Swiss law and therefore the arbitration clause was void. The second battle had been won decisively. Two-nil to the Bakwin team.

Yet, the ownership of the six paintings was a separate issue and would have to be decided by an English court at a subsequent trial. In the meantime, Erie was ordered to pay the Bakwins' full costs related to the interpleader, while both parties would bear equally Sotheby's costs, the innocent third party caught in the crossfire of their dispute. The judge also gave permission to appeal the judgment. In the event that an appeal was received by 6 December all orders would be stayed until after the determination of the appeal.

In early December the Bakwin team drafted yet another offer to settle out of court with Erie. The Bakwins offered to pay their own costs if Erie dropped all lawsuits and released the pictures. Unfortunately, Erie pre-empted the negotiation by appealing the judgment and simultaneously pushing the arbitration process in Geneva forward. The Bakwins were thus forced to invest further money to prepare for the appeal hearing scheduled for 30 January 2006. There would be additional witness statements, more legal advice and the legal team would request a court order to reveal the signatory of the affidavit about the paintings' provenance, still held in escrow. Withers decided that it too needed to engage a QC to present its case. To add insult to injury, the ICC appointed an arbitrator and demanded US$30,000 to cover its administrative costs. The Bakwins reluctantly paid the bill, but Michael Bakwin's emails to his lawyers about his expenses being 'huge' and 'more than expected' reflect his exasperation. Was he throwing good money after bad?

A few days later a letter from the ICC informed both parties that Erie had fallen behind with its payments. Withers' application to Erie's lawyers to pay money to the court as a security to cover the Bakwins' costs to prepare for the appeal was refused, too. Erie's law firm stated that Erie had no liquid assets: it owned the six paintings and nothing else. To obtain reimbursement for its costs, the Bakwin team had to find out who was hiding behind Erie.

The private eyes

Panama's laws are ideal for shielding the owners and assets hidden in its shell companies from detection, tax demands and legal action.[33] Yet, the ALR's private investigators managed to penetrate its elaborate veil of secrecy. They came back with the information that Erie International Trading had been founded in late 1999 by a man called Robert Mardirosian. The timing suggested that it was founded to disguise the identity of the holder just before completing the Cézanne deal. The address for correspondence was that of a private bank in Geneva. It looked like a dead end, except Robert Mardirosian is not a common name. Further investigations revealed that a painter and sculptor called 'Romard' had previously been called Robert Mardirosian and had practised as a criminal lawyer in Massachusetts in the 1970s and 1980s. This put a Robert Mardirosian geographically close to the original crime scene.

When Julian Radcliffe mentioned Robert Mardirosian to Stephen Kurkjian, a *Boston Globe* journalist who had reported on the case before, he immediately recognised him as a fellow Armenian. The Armenians in Massachusetts formed a close-knit community and, indeed, an attorney called Mardirosian had lived in his mother's neighbourhood. Kurkjian offered to make enquiries and soon put Radcliffe in touch with the private detective who had worked for Bakwin in the 1980s. The retired sleuth revealed that he too had come across an attorney named Robert Matirosian: did Radcliffe want to buy his original case notes? It turned out to be a shrewd investment. Matirosian (probably a misspelling) had not only been the lawyer of the suspected thief – the late David Colvin – but had also represented a fence, who had assisted Colvin during his criminal career, and his girlfriend. Attorney Mardirosian's manifold connections with the criminal underworld would explain the surprisingly detailed knowledge of the crime the seller had divulged during the negotiations over the Cézanne painting. Moreover, both the lawyer Mr F and the middleman Mr W had made oblique references to their principal being a lawyer. If the seller had bought the paintings from the thief or his fence, this would also explain the careful wording of the affidavit stating that the holder 'did not participate in these acts nor was even aware of them at the time they were done.' All the pieces of the puzzle fitted together beautifully. If Mardirosian's signature was indeed on the affidavit, he no longer stood a chance of prevailing in a British court.

Radcliffe therefore informed the Bakwins that he was 'near certain' that once the name was known they would win the appeal. Michael Bakwin reluctantly made further funds available so his lawyers could obtain a court order to open the envelope. On 23 January 2006 the court ordered the escrow agent to disclose the holder's declaration to the Bakwin team, on the express condition that the name should not be made public. The many-layered parcel

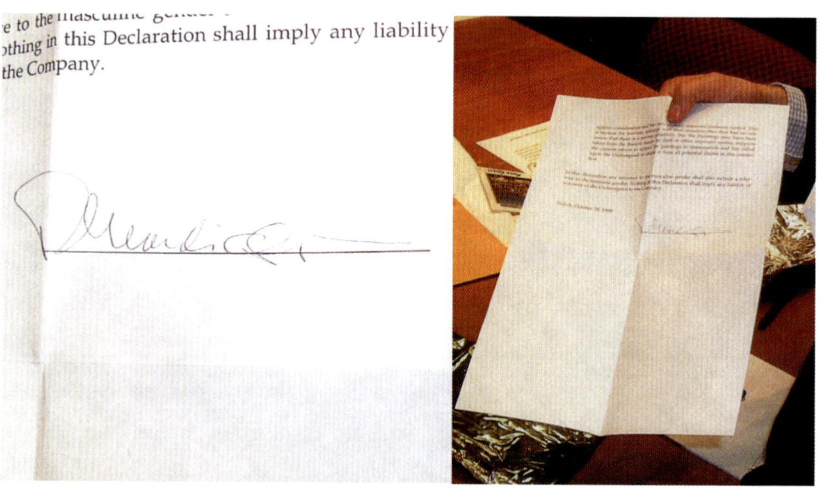

Robert Mardirosian's scrawled signature under his unusual declaration of 'good faith'.

was laboriously unpacked in the lawyer's office to finally reveal the seller's signature. It was undecipherable and there was no name below the illegible signature.

But Radcliffe's team of private detectives was ready for this challenge. They had already obtained copies of several court documents signed by attorney Robert Mardirosian in his capacity as a representative of the suspected thief of the pictures. The signature in some of these court documents was virtually identical to that on the declaration. They had got their man.

With the secretive Mardirosian backed into such a tight corner, everyone thought the fight was over. Rather than pursuing his opponent to the bitter end Bakwin asked his lawyers to make a settlement offer. If Mardirosian returned the paintings and paid them £500,000, the Bakwins would forego the opportunity of reclaiming the cost of retrieving the Cézanne. But there was no response to this proposal. Thus, a watertight fourth witness statement from Radcliffe with sixteen detailed exhibits was forwarded to the court and Erie's lawyers.

An unusual appeal court hearing

On 31 January 2006 the defendant and his lawyers failed to show at the appeal court. Mardirosian had told his legal team to 'give up'. The appeal was dismissed. The judge was most impressed with the ALR's detective work and particularly with the idea of demanding a signed declaration of good faith from the seller. Whose idea had it been? The QC mentioned Radcliffe's insistence that he would not enter into an agreement with someone connected to the theft and requiring this written reassurance before proceeding with the transaction.

Mr Justice Stanley Burton: Is that Mr Radcliffe at the back?

Mr Wardell: It is.

Mr Justice Stanley Burton: He is claiming credit for this, I think.

Mr Wardell: Yes. He has certainly got a big enough smile on his face.[34]

Mardirosian was ordered to join as a party to the interpleader in addition to Erie, so that the Bakwins could recover their costs. A Panamanian shell company could all too easily extract itself from financial responsibility. The size of the award would be determined by the court at a later date. Erie was barred from taking any further steps in pursuing arbitration at the ICC and any assets held by the Mardirosians in England or Wales were frozen.

It is difficult to imagine a more comprehensive victory. Justice had prevailed. But it is also worth considering the financial outlay required to get to this point. According to QC Wardell's testimony in court, the Bakwins had spent £374,121 on court, legal and investigative fees. There was at least one further hearing coming up to settle the issue of ownership of the paintings and it was far from clear whether Mardirosian would actually pay. He had no assets in England and Wales: only a worldwide asset freeze could force him to reimburse the Bakwins. It is therefore not surprising that most people eventually give up on the idea of obtaining justice through the courts and grasp at any opportunity for an early out-of-court settlement. But it takes two to tango: although the Bakwins and the ALR had made several attempts to settle, their opposition never engaged in a meaningful negotiation. Why was the opposition so litigious?

A curious explanation

Mardirosian's next move surprised everyone. Kurkjian had held off publishing his sensational scoop until the court released Mardirosian's name. Immediately after the hearing, he approached the former attorney for an interview. To everyone's utter astonishment, Mardirosian readily admitted he had been in possession of the paintings since 1978. He had a strange story to tell.

Colvin – the suspected thief – had come to his office to seek advice on a gun charge against him. He carried a large bag containing stolen paintings that he was planning to take to Florida for fencing. Mardirosian advised against this: if Colvin was caught with stolen art at this stage he would be in major trouble. As Colvin had nowhere to stay, his attorney offered him a bed for the night. Colvin departed the next morning without mentioning the paintings again. Colvin was shot dead in February of the following year. A year later his lawyer found the paintings in his attic, still stashed in the late thief's bag.

As an upstanding member of society and a practising lawyer, Mardirosian was keen to return the paintings to their lawful owner. But he wanted to see some money: he considered 10 per cent of the paintings' value as his honest finder's due. Unfortunately, *Bouilloire et Fruits* had been insured for a small fraction of its market value and the Bakwins' privately raised reward offer was far below his expectations. So, Mardirosian had decided to take the paintings first to Monaco and then to Switzerland while he figured out how to claim his percentage. When he was finally ready to make a move, the ALR had blocked and crossed him at every juncture. Claiming a finder's reward was not unreasonable. Why had the ALR made it so difficult for him to do so?

Another round on the carousel?

The Bakwin team thought this story sounded like another deceit. It did not think a judge would believe it either. The FBI sent a detective to interview Mardirosian, too, so it looked like the law was definitely on the Bakwins' side. Mardirosian must have come to a similar conclusion: he used his spare passport to flee the USA and hide in his house in the south of France. Bakwin was at the end of his tether and so was Withers. He had not paid his lawyers for several months and their outstanding fees stood at more than £120,000. When the escrow agent put in an eyewatering bill of £4,564.15 – just for opening the mummified envelope at their office – Bakwin nearly lost his patience. Eventually, he grudgingly agreed to transfer US$150,000 to Withers, writing: 'I hope this makes you happy. Now you can make me happy by telling me when you and I can say good-bye. A date please. How much more of this do I have to go through?' The ALR shared his sentiments. When the paintings were recovered, the ALR would receive a fee of 10 per cent of their value, but only after the Bakwins' costs had been taken into account. The paintings were not that valuable, and with spiralling expenses the ALR's prospective return diminished day by day. If the fight continued, it would soon turn into a loss. Feeling weary, the Bakwin team tried to settle once more.

The response from Mardirosian's new lawyer was not promising. His client had little to gain from a making a deal. His reputation had been compromised, the police were after him and the Bakwins wanted most of their costs reimbursed as well as the six pictures. Mardirosian claimed he had no money. He said his only asset was a house owned jointly with his wife Madeline and therefore untouchable. So, unless the Bakwins came up with a serious sweetener, his client would not settle. However, the ALR's private detectives had put together a comprehensive dossier of

Mardirosian's assets in the meantime and estimated he was worth at least US$6 million. Reluctantly, the Bakwins decided to plough on.

The first priority was to obtain a court order to retrieve the paintings from Sotheby's. Then they would sue Mardirosian for the recovery costs. The Bakwins' total costs were close to US$3.5 million if the Cézanne recovery was included. Everyone knew that enforcing a judgment for damages and costs against Mardirosian who owned property in the USA, France and Italy, plus any liquid assets stashed away in shell companies in Panama, Switzerland or Monaco, would require further expense. As Radcliffe explained to Bakwin: 'I am increasingly confident that we will obtain reimbursement of a very major part of all your costs, but it will take patience and persistence!'

Financial restructuring

The court eventually forced Sotheby's to disclose who had consigned the paintings. The seller was a Mr P. He turned out to be the son of a former business associate of Mardirosian and it quickly became clear he had been aware of the paintings' troubled history. If Mr P cooperated with the ALR and the FBI, it would strengthen the case against Mardirosian. If he settled with the Bakwins, it would provide a much-needed cash injection. But Mr P also proved uncooperative. To obtain a settlement the Bakwin team had to put pressure on him, for example by threatening to add his name to the Bakwins' court claim in London. Unfortunately, however, this legal process had stalled. The British court could only proceed to a default judgment after the court papers had been served on the defendants. Mardirosian had been served at his home in Massachusetts, but a Panamanian (shell) company could only be formally served by a Panamanian court. Arranging this would take at least twelve months and require significant financial outlays.

Michael Bakwin was feeling drained, emotionally and financially. He simply could not face any more bills. He went travelling and ignored emails, letters and especially invoices. The clerks at Withers grew exasperated trying to winkle money out of him. There are long email trails in which respectful requests turn into increasingly desperate pleas and finally to threats to end its representation in the Bakwins' case. Moreover, Withers was far from confident that a UK court could force Mr P or Mardirosian to pay its costs. A separate complaint would have to be filed in the USA for the costs of recovering the Cézanne. A US law firm would have to take up the reins stateside. Radcliffe, however, still felt bullish about recovering the Bakwins' costs and hence at least breaking even on the case. He also wanted to see the crooked Mardirosian put behind bars. The media coverage of the court cases had turned the retrieval of the Bakwin pictures into a test case. Demonstrating the ALR's resolve to fight would strengthen its reputation with criminals, the art market and law enforcement. Further publicity would attract new customers to the database, raising both registration and search income.

Radcliffe thus became determined 'to make this the textbook case of all time to show that art crime does not pay.'[35] However, the Bakwins only wanted their pictures back. Radcliffe therefore proposed a different cost allocation model. The ALR and a US law firm – Dwyer & Collora – would assist the Bakwins in the recovery of their costs in return for a (larger) share of the award. In the meantime, the ALR would fund the expenses of the lawsuit. Withers would support the Bakwins to retrieve the paintings from Sotheby's as before, but henceforth any further work on the recovery of costs would be billed to the ALR. After due deliberation, the Bakwins decided to extricate themselves from the financial and emotional stress of their ever-multiplying court cases. They signed the agreement with a huge sigh of relief in November 2006. The ALR was now in charge of taking their case forward. The stress over bills continued for as long as the court actions lasted, but it was now more manageable. The files are still full of long-winded and tiresome arguments over the correct apportioning of costs between the parties, but overall the principal's anxieties about money no longer jeopardised the endeavour to make Mardirosian pay.

In the meantime, Mardirosian persisted with his delaying tactics. Erie's directors refused to accept the service of the English court proceedings in Panama. In October 2006 the judge finally ordered that efforts to serve them had been sufficient and henceforth any further documents could be served on Erie at its London solicitors. The final hearing for delivery of the four paintings at Sotheby's was therefore only delayed to the end of February 2007. But something else was afoot. Anticipating what Radcliffe termed as 'the normal difficulties of finding lawyers' assets', the ALR's team of private detectives kept a close watch on the Mardirosian properties dotted around the world. They noted they were being quietly transferred to Robert's wife and other family members. Mardirosian was preparing to lose his case.

Dark days for Robert Mardirosian

Eventually Mardirosian's spare passport ran out of date and he had to come home. On 13 February 2007 the FBI sent a welcome party to the airport to arrest him on the charges of possession, concealment, storage and attempted sale of stolen art. The district attorney considered it 'disheartening' and 'unconscionable' that as a lawyer Mardirosian had evidently disregarded his duty to uphold the law. If proven guilty, he would face a maximum sentence of ten years in prison followed by a supervised release and a US$250,000 fine on each of the charges. And to further add to Mardirosian's embarrassment, the police officers sent to search his property for evidence found a stash of marijuana worth US$370,000 belonging to his son. On 9 March Mardirosian was formally indicted by a federal grand jury for possessing stolen art, for transporting it across international borders and for trying to sell it.

The ALR and its US lawyers therefore started to prepare civil lawsuits in Massachusetts on behalf of the Bakwins. They sued Robert and Madeline Mardirosian for the fraudulent transfer of their joint property to Madeline in violation of the English court's freezing order. Furthermore, Mardirosian and his accomplices would be sued for the cost of recovering *Bouilloire et Fruits* (conservatively estimated at US$3,400,000), plus interest and any damages a US court might award. Although an out-of-court financial settlement remained a possibility, the ALR team felt it needed to demonstrate it was prepared to follow the court route. Spending significant amounts of money on legal fees to collect evidence signalled its willingness to continue the war of attrition.

The triumphant return of the paintings

On 27 February 2007 the Royal Court of Justice finally awarded the ownership of the four artworks seized at Sotheby's in 2005 and the two missing Jansem pictures to Michael Bakwin. Erie and Mardirosian were ordered to make an interim payment of £75,000 towards damages and another £100,000 towards legal costs to date. On 5 March Sotheby's formally acknowledged the court order and wrote to the ALR to say that the paintings were available for collection. A former employee of a Swiss bank contacted the FBI to make arrangements for handing over the missing Jansem works. The ALR then organised the restoration and reframing of the paintings in London: they had been ripped from their frames and scuffed as they were transferred between their various hiding places. When they were shipshape once more, it was time to have a party. In July 2007, 120 people gathered at Withers to celebrate the formal handover of the four paintings retrieved from Sotheby's to a delighted Michael Bakwin.

Money, money, money

Wringing money out of Robert Mardirosian was a different game, however. He simply failed to comply with the court orders for payment of costs and damages. Thus, the Bakwin team formally registered the orders in France to obtain a charge against the Mardirosians' property on the Côte d'Azur. This time Mardirosian wrong-footed the Bakwins by acting immediately. The house was put on the market, but only for the blink of an eye. When the ALR found out, the house was already under offer and the estate agent took no further viewings. In any case, the agent did not have a key. The house must have been in a terrible condition, because the price was well below any other villa that had sold in the neighbourhood. Mardirosian's 50 per cent share of net proceeds came to just €243,803.50: less than two thirds of the costs awarded. Everyone suspected a dodgy deal, but reluctantly decided to let it go.

In any case, costs and damage awards tend to be more generous in the USA. But tellingly, there is also an entire private 'collection industry' specialising in judgment enforcement. Letters trickling into Bakwin's postbox – and assiduously forwarded to the ALR

– had alerted him to the problem of collecting money awards: 'At this point your unsatisfied money judgment is nothing more than a paper IOU.' But the Bakwins need not worry: 'Locating and seizing any hidden assets from judgment debtors is our speciality!' the professionals claimed. They offered enforcement on a contingency basis: 'you have nothing to lose and a great deal to gain'. Reading this, nobody could be in any doubt that obtaining and enforcing a judgment would be a multistage, long-haul project. Hopefully the cheque from France would encourage Bakwin to stay the course.

The rest of 2007 was spent on the discovery of evidence leading to Mardirosian's US criminal trial. The process was painfully slow. Requests for information were first ignored, then formally objected to and finally had to be compelled. The ALR also investigated Mardirosian's accomplices in storing, transporting, concealing and selling the paintings. Had Mr P, the Swiss lawyer, and Mardirosian's bankers in Geneva known that the paintings had been stolen? Depending on the likelihood of conviction and their ability to pay, their names might be added to the various compensation claims. But further efforts to settle out of court fell on stony ground. Mr P offered a mere US$25,000. There was a similarly paltry offer by Robert and Madeline Mardirosian to advance US$300,000 in exchange for a full and final release 'from any and all claims or demands for costs, expenses, legal fees related to the matter of Bakwin vs Mardirosian et al in the High Court of Justice … from the beginning of time to the present.' With the Bakwins' total recovery costs rapidly rising towards US$4 million, the team reluctantly decided to continue on the court route.

The criminal trial

The judge in the US criminal trial in August 2008 put a very specific question to the jury members. Did Robert Mardirosian possess stolen paintings after 8 March 2002? Mardirosian had already admitted that he knew the paintings had been stolen. His defence relied on the five-year statute of limitation: he could not be convicted for offences committed more than five years ago. It was therefore too late to charge him with possessing, smuggling and selling stolen goods in the 1999 Cézanne deal. He could be held to account only for the 2005 attempt to sell at Sotheby's. For this Mardirosian had a rather sneaky defence. He argued that he had *believed* himself to be the owner of the paintings based on the 1999 contract by which the Bakwins received *Bouilloire et Fruits* in exchange for title to the other six paintings. When he tried to sell the paintings in 2005, he did not know that the 1999 agreement would be voided in 2007. Therefore, he had not committed a crime.

It took six days to hear all the evidence, with Mardirosian's lawyers doing their best to represent the ALR as scheming, duplicitous bullies. They suggested that Radcliffe had cheated poor Mardirosian out of his finder's reward, so that the ALR could charge Bakwin its recovery fee instead. Yet, it took the jury just two and a half hours to reach a unanimous guilty verdict. Although the formal charge had been for possession of stolen property only, the jurors had instinctively understood this was really a case of extortion. Common sense and a desire to see justice done had prevailed over narrow legal definitions and clever dodges. The fact that it was a former attorney who had extorted, and on top of this had given false testimony at a pre-trial hearing, aggravated the judge's outrage. He was determined the punishment should 'send a firm deterrent message to those who believe that their status might enable them to get away with serious crimes.'[36] Mardirosian faced up to ten years in jail, a substantial fine and liability for the Bakwins' costs.

Round we go again

Within minutes of the guilty verdict the Mardirosian team raised objections and declared its intention to appeal. The defendant's twenty-two-page-long sentencing memorandum raised countless legal issues and counterclaims. Moreover, Mardirosian claimed he was unable to afford a fine or the costs the Bakwins had submitted to the court. Perhaps the judge became concerned that a harsh punishment might backfire. Although he imposed a tough seven-year prison sentence on Mardirosian, no monetary sanctions were applied. The Bakwins would have to obtain all their costs through a separate civil process.

Robert Mardirosian was factually accurate when he stated he was a poor man. He had made sure of that. His bank accounts had been swept clean. However, Madeline Mardirosian was now the owner of large investment portfolios and annuities guaranteeing a generous monthly income. The family trust was awash with funds. Madeline Mardirosian, their son and their son-in-law were property and restaurant owners. On his release from prison Robert Mardirosian would be their tenant and dependant.

Efforts to ensure his wealthy accomplices contributed to the costs fell flat, too. Although the ALR put together damning evidence that Mr P and Mardirosian's Swiss banker had known the paintings were stolen, they simply brushed away the threats of legal action against them. They speculated that although the Bakwin team had a good legal case, it probably would not commit the resources to pursue them in court. This was true, but there was one more chance. Litigation insurance and litigation funding can help financially disadvantaged parties to fight for their rights, as long as they share the proceeds afterwards. Yet, the companies approached with the Bakwin case files were unanimous: despite the legal merits of the cases against the accomplices, it would not be profitable for them to join in. The Bakwin team took the hint and refocused its attention on the still elusive main target.

Mardirosian had appealed against the verdict of the criminal trial, which allowed him to stave off the day of reckoning by more than a year. His appeal was heard in October 2009 and the verdict was announced in April 2010. The judge found no merit whatsoever in the arguments brought forward by the appellant and affirmed both the judgment and the sentence. Even if justice

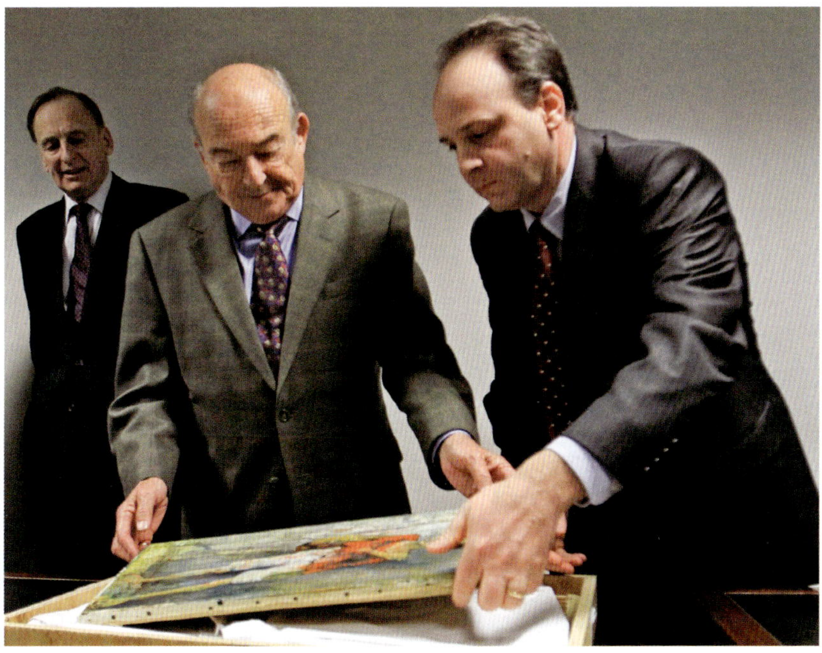

The painting *Boy* by Jean Jansem (1920–2013) is returned to Michael Bakwin at the US attorney's office in Boston in November 2010 (Julian Radcliffe in the background).

is sure, it is definitely not swift. Moreover, putting an old man behind bars was not the kind of justice the Bakwins were looking for: what they really wanted was an apology and their money back. It took until November 2010 for the Bakwins to be reunited with their last two stolen paintings – the Jansem pictures that had stayed in the Swiss bank vault when the others were taken to Sotheby's. The FBI could only release them after the conclusion of the appeal proceedings.

The civil trials

The ALR and Dwyer & Collora had made a massive investment of time and money already. They could either walk away from this loss or fight a further (civil) lawsuit to try to recoup the millions of dollars the Bakwins had spent in their efforts to recover their stolen paintings. As Mardirosian had transferred most of his assets to various family members, they would have to take on the entire Mardirosian clan. Tracing all the relevant transactions – with characteristically minimal cooperation from the family – and proving them to be fraudulent was a complex undertaking. However, it was rather telling that Robert Mardirosian's generosity towards his wife and children began exactly a week after his identity had been revealed in the UK court case in 2006.

Indeed, in August 2011 the Superior Court jury found Robert Mardirosian responsible for the US$3 million in costs incurred by the Bakwins to recover the Cézanne and the other six pictures.[37] He was also convicted of seven fraudulent transactions and judgment was entered for a sum totalling US$4.3 million in damages, interests and costs. Another victory, but with the Mardirosians' refusing to cooperate, the judgment proved impossible to enforce. Massachusetts law protects innocent non-debtor spouses. Half of the value of any real estate, savings and investments in joint ownership belonged to Madeline Mardirosian and her primary residence could not be touched. The couple's son had squandered most of his father's gifts in the meantime and gone bankrupt. The judge had immediately given up on any money ever being recovered from him. Unless specific money judgments were made against each of the claimants, the Bakwins, the ALR and Dywer & Collora would not see anything close to the sum awarded. They had to go to court once more to clarify who exactly could be held responsible for paying the damages.

A further court hearing finally resolved the matter in April 2014, largely in the Mardirosians' favour. The family was not responsible for covering Robert Mardirosian's debt. Madeline Mardirosian's marital home could not be sold to liquidate her husband's 50 per cent share and would be hers alone if he predeceased her. Although Madeline Mardirosian admitted her husband had earned all their money and made all the financial decisions, the court decided to protect her 50 per cent share in the couple's joint deposit, saving and investment accounts. The Bakwins could only claim the money that was fraudulently transferred in 2006, or rather what was left of it. Where assets had appreciated in the meantime, the gains would accrue to Madeline Mardirosian. Where investments had depreciated, the Bakwins could lay claim to only half of the remainder. Any money that Robert Mardirosian had withdrawn in cash and that did not immediately turn up in other family members' accounts was also lost. The bankrupt son's debt to the Bakwins was reinstated, but clearly he would never pay them anything.[38]

Finally, the Mardirosians were prepared to settle, but for less than a quarter of the US$4.3 million awarded by the court. The money was split according to the terms of the tripartite agreement. The Bakwins were reimbursed for their legal costs and a small fraction of their Cézanne recovery bill. Dwyer & Collora made a small profit on its hard-fought seven-year campaign in the US courts, but the ALR could not quite cover the massive cost of the US trials from its share. To people familiar with US law, the outcome looks like a substantial victory: the Bakwins got their paintings back, Mardirosian went to prison and those who footed the bills (largely) managed to recover their costs. But to outsiders, it may seem like too little too late, especially if they took the massive cost award at face value. It is sobering to find out that the huge damages awarded to the victims were effectively grandstanding and empty promises.

A flawed system

The Bakwin case gives a fascinating insight into how the legal system works if one party is prepared to go down every possible alley to delay the day of reckoning and the other side is determined to pursue them. The English High Court's judgment in 2007, the jury verdicts in the 2008 US criminal trial and the 2011 civil trials demonstrated that the legal profession and twenty-four randomly chosen citizens' instincts agreed with Radcliffe's initial assessment of the matter: Mardirosian was a crook. He had seriously wronged Bakwin and should compensate him. Yet, the court verdicts were largely 'moral' victories: the implementation of justice was slow and partial.

As a former attorney, Mardirosian knew how to play the system. He skilfully exploited the weaknesses of different jurisdictions to draw out the process and wear down the Bakwins. First, the international dimensions of this case provided ample opportunities to complicate the process. Who had jurisdiction and what law should be applied had to be settled not just initially, but was re-examined at every stage. Fighting multiple, overlapping court and arbitration cases escalated the cost, complexity and risks for the Bakwins. By contrast, someone inside the legal profession with a network of accomplices working for free, on 'mates' rates' or on commission could keep their costs to a minimum.

Second, Mardirosian used jurisdictions specialised in protecting their customers' anonymity and hiding their physical and financial assets. Monaco, Panama and Switzerland have comprehensive service industries to facilitate all manner of secretive business. As long as the Bakwins' paintings were stored in one of 'the most impenetrable places in the Western world: the vault of a Swiss Bank',[39] and Mardirosian's identity was hidden behind a Panamanian shell company, they were untouchable. Formal law enforcement cannot operate effectively within a limited taxpayer-funded budget if such subterfuges are employed. Law enforcement was also hindered by the norms of the art market that were specifically created to guarantee the anonymity of clients. Even though in the Bakwin case these hurdles were overcome through private efforts, they bought Mardirosian and his accomplices valuable time, while inflicting costs and stress on the Bakwins and their team.

The third highly successful delaying tactic was pure and simple: non-compliance. The legal system is built on two implicit assumptions: civil obedience and residency. If someone fails to comply with an order, it is extremely cumbersome and costly to obtain a remedy. And if the person is not a resident of the country in which the legal remedy was issued, enforcing it is unlikely to be cost-effective.

Finally, the British and US legal systems have a great number of safeguards to prevent miscarriages of justice. The saga of the Bakwin paintings shows that these safeguards can be abused to put off the delivery and implementation of a just verdict almost indefinitely. All requests and orders come with a generous deadline for compliance or objection. If there is an objection, there is a lengthy process of deciding whether to compel. If compliance is partial, the process may have to be repeated. If a judgment leaves open the possibility of an appeal, that gives the losing party many months of reprieve, and then the process starts all over again. When the opportunities generated by international complications, obfuscation and non-compliance are added into the mix, this means years of misery for the wronged party.

Given the complexity and cost of obtaining and enforcing legal judgments, it is not surprising we see so many out-of-court settlements. We also observe a large number of private businesses offering (costly) remedies to those let down by the legal system, as well as expert services to avoid detection and punishment. In fact, many private service providers seem entirely indifferent about serving crooks and criminals, as long as they get paid. All efforts to make Mardirosian's accomplices contribute to a financial settlement and compensation for the unnecessary costs they inflicted on the Bakwins fell apart. Ultimately, this case was not about culpability and justice, but about money and determination – and everybody knew it.

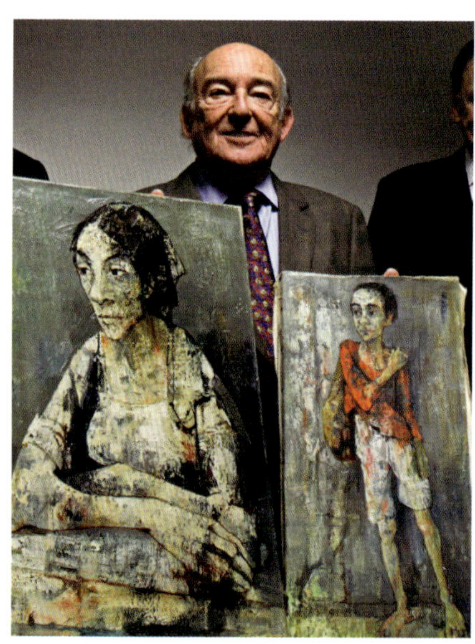

Michael Bakwin holds up the two recovered Jean Jansem paintings – *Woman Seated* and *Boy* – at the US attorney's office in Boston in November 2010.

Conclusion

The Bakwins' odyssey through the courts was an emotional roller coaster, made acute by the massive financial outlays required to obtain justice. The legal profession thrives on charging several hundred dollars per hour for gathering and reading information, drafting and amending documents, having long discussions either in person or on the phone, and arguing its cases in court, year after year, unless or until the parties are willing to settle. Throughout the Bakwins' lengthy campaign, various protagonists made references to a 'war of attrition'. In attritional conflicts, each side's strategy is to wear down its opponents to the point of collapse. Wars of attrition are usually won by the party with the greater resources. However, they can also be won by guerrillas hiding in impenetrable jungle and mounting inexpensive raids that impose high (psychological or economic) costs on their opposition.

A war of attrition is a very apt framework for analysing the Bakwin case. Mardirosian and his accomplices were experts at hiding and inflicting losses on their opposition at a low cost to themselves. Understandably, the ageing Bakwins were the first to be dragged down by the relentless barrage of bills and the apparent futility of winning their court cases. Withers was next to fold: it correctly predicted it could win the legal battles and yet lose the war over extracting compensation. Litigation insurers took a good look at the odds and they too declined to participate. Dwyer & Collora was a risk-taker and made a different calculation. It became a vital ally for the ALR, bringing in expertise and fresh resources for the US court actions with minimal upfront cost. The ALR had done well out of the Cézanne recovery, and Radcliffe felt obliged to retrieve the other paintings for the Bakwins, too. Moreover, the ALR's relentless pursuit of Mardirosian for costs was not only about recovering its investment, but also about sending a signal to shady dealers and law enforcement. Publicising its determination to bring criminals to justice if at all possible and its willingness and ability to fight costly legal battles to the bitter end greatly enhanced its reputation in the art world.

As a law-abiding citizen, one assumes (or fervently hopes) that law and justice are but different sides of the same coin. But the Bakwin case shows the law can be abused to shield a criminal from justice. Mardirosian exploited every single loophole and weakness of the legal system to delay punishment. Obtaining justice through the courts thus became a battle of financial resources, knowledge, resolve, risk tolerance and emotional resilience. The problem of insiders subverting the system was explicitly recognised by Judge Wolf in the criminal trial in 2011, when he described Mardirosian's conduct as 'truly despicable'.[40] His stiff seven-year prison sentence for an ailing elderly man was a clear message to insiders not to use their knowledge of the legal system to impede justice. However, the lesson would have been much stronger if swift and punitive fines had been imposed not just on Robert Mardirosian but also on his crooked accomplices.

4

The Santamarina Impressionists: A 'Very Political' Recovery

The raid on the Museo Nacional de Bellas Artes in Buenos Aires, Argentina, in December 1980 had always seemed a little odd. The thieves were clearly familiar with the museum. It was more of a walk-in than a break-in. The burglars apparently gained access through a gap in the roof opened during the reconstruction of the museum's second-floor galleries. Ladders for access had been left lying around by workers painting the museum's exterior. Surprisingly, the thieves left the most valuable artworks on the walls and instead targeted lesser paintings and drawings from the Santamarina family's collection of Impressionist art, as well as taking early Chinese porcelain and jade figures and vases. The burglars had not been in a rush: they had carefully removed the sixteen paintings from their frames and opened the glass display cases with blowtorches. There were rumours an army truck had waited near the museum that night and the Junta had been involved. However, the

State Security Forces (Secretaría de Inteligencia del Estado) arrested the two hapless guards who had been on duty and roughed them up. To no avail: nobody was ever charged with the 'robbery'.

The theft of the artworks was a significant loss for a country down on its fortunes. The wealthy rancher and politician Antonio Santamarina had assembled an important collection of Impressionist works in Paris between 1895 and 1930. The Argentine government had put considerable pressure on him to donate his entire collection to the country, but the family auctioned off the most famous works at Sotheby's in London in 1974. After Santamarina's death, the remaining objects were reluctantly committed to the Bellas Artes Museum in Buenos Aires by his widow, including sketches and drawings by Paul Cézanne, Edgar Degas, Paul Gauguin, Henri Matisse and Pierre-Auguste Renoir. Now these were gone, too. Buenos Aires art lovers were in uproar. The distraught director of the museum pleaded with the thieves to keep the objects safe, 'even if you hide them away for 20 years'.[41] His bereft staff notified Interpol and sent out photos and descriptions of the missing works to the International Foundation for Art Research to prevent them from being sold abroad. But nobody ever responded to IFAR's Stolen Art Alert.

Almost exactly twenty years later, in May 2001, a search request came to the ALR from Sotheby's. Its experts had carried out a valuation of sixteen Impressionist paintings for a customer in Taipei. Although the customer did not want to consign the artworks, they had asked Sotheby's to carry out a due diligence title search. Could the ALR please confirm that all was in order? Unfortunately, it could not. The pictures from the Bellas Artes Museum haul in 1980 had finally reappeared and, suspiciously, all of them together. The ALR researchers checked their current status with the museum: if the paintings were still reported stolen, they would ask for the museum's authorisation to retrieve them. As no sale was intended it was also possible that a fraud was afoot, so the ALR immediately alerted Scotland Yard. Noting the potentially political nature of the 1980 'theft' in Buenos Aires, the ALR also notified the UK's Foreign and Commonwealth Office (FCO).

The director of the Bellas Artes Museum was delighted with the news and confirmed his museum was indeed the legal owner of the paintings. He would very much like them to be returned. However, his museum had no money at all. This was not a promising start for a recovery mission. But then Sotheby's wrote to say their customer was happy for Julian Radcliffe to contact her on a Spanish mobile number, and indeed she would be delighted to meet him in person. Could there be a quick and easy resolution here? Intrigued, Radcliffe boarded a plane to Málaga to resolve the puzzle, but the ALR would soon find itself entangled in a global web of double-dealing and deceit.

All for charity

The vivacious lady with the huge blonde wig who collected Radcliffe from the airport with her recently acquired husband in tow was a surprise. Dripping with gold and diamond jewellery, Mrs W had a chequered career of businesses and marriages behind her, but of late she had found God and was poised to do good works. Having demonstrated her sincerity by clutching Radcliffe's hands to say grace at the hotel table, she was bursting to talk about the pictures. Her company Humana Way International – a not-for-profit organisation incorporated in Texas – was on the cusp of a major breakthrough. The munificent De Lavor Trust in Suriname had recently had its collection of sixteen fine Impressionist paintings valued at US$350 million. Embarrassed by these riches, the trustees had decided to use the paintings to raise funds for the poor. The chairman of the trust, Mr LL, had sent the pictures to his brother Mr L in Taipei, who would have them insured and offer them as collateral for a loan. The money would be invested in a high-yield private placement programme. Mrs W had been enlisted to help the De Lavor Trust to implement this scheme. In return, some of the profit would be invested through Humana Way International to relieve poverty in Suriname.

Of course, it was all above board. Mrs W was an experienced businesswoman and had checked everything carefully. The artworks had been expertly valued by the Fine Arts Institute of Suriname and its director, a Mr Venoaks, had signed off the valuation himself. She had also received a letter from the office of an 'Ambassador Rupert L. Christopher' in Suriname attesting the pictures had been in the possession of Senator de Lavor's family in Brazil for more than five decades. Her husband had even consulted the Interpol database of stolen art and the search had come up clear. She had therefore travelled all over the world and met lots of lovely, generous people. They had wined and dined together and had written sincere resolutions and letters of intent. They had appointed each other as board members of their respective charitable trusts, and their contracts were embellished with elaborate stamps and elegant signatures.

Admittedly, things had unravelled a little of late. Mrs W had approached an insurance company, but it had insisted on an independent valuation of the artworks by a major auction house as well as a full provenance check. Therefore, she had arranged the appraisal by Sotheby's in Taipei. It had been a fiasco. She was 'totally gobsmacked' when the pictures arrived. The supposedly famous artworks were mostly sketches, and the paintings were off their stretchers: 'You could have rolled them up in a tin!'[42] This lowered their value, of course, but she had still been completely taken aback when the experts gave an estimate that was US$348 million below her expectations. What kind of good works was she supposed to do with a share of the proceeds from investing a mere US$2 million? And then came the shock of the art being stolen.

When the ALR later checked out the papers the upset Mrs W had eagerly shared, the scheme descended further into farce. There was no Fine Arts Institute in Suriname, nor an art expert by the name Venoaks. The whole 'valuation' document was a (not terribly sophisticated) forgery. The letter attesting the ownership of the paintings was a complete fiction. Although there was a British ambassador called Robin (not Rupert L.) Christopher, he was in Brazil and not in Suriname. The true purpose of Humana Way International was also nebulous. It had not carried out any humanitarian projects up to this point, nor could its board members name a single living beneficiary apart from its president: Mrs W.[43] She was paid a six-figure salary, plus expenses. When Mrs W was told that her great fundraising scheme was a scam, though, she was indignant and categorically stated she would have nothing more to do with these crooks. Henceforth, Mr L in Taiwan and Mr LL in Suriname were on their own as far as she was concerned.

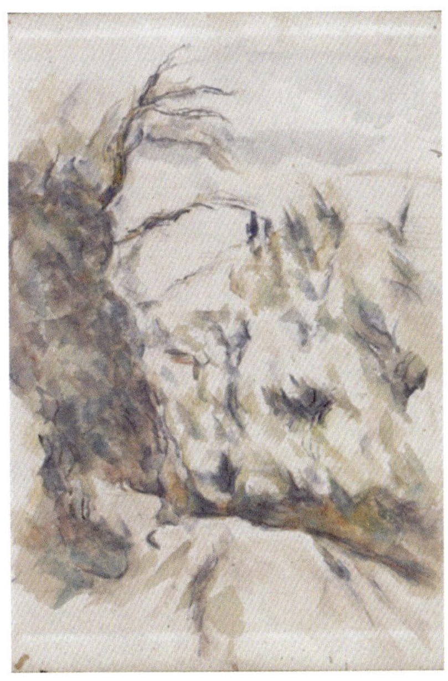

Paul Cézanne (1839–1906), *The Road* (1902–6), Museo Nacional de Bellas Artes, Buenos Aires.

'A difficult case at both ends'

When Radcliffe phoned Mr LL in Suriname he seemed keen to help return the paintings to the Bellas Artes Museum. He faxed a very encouraging reply in mid-June 2001: 'I am pleased to know the truth from you and also more happy to give assistance to return those art works to original owner. We shall meet to discuss this case and supply all information I had for further investigation at earliest convenience.' Mr LL said the pictures were still with his brother in Taipei who would gladly assist the ALR with their retrieval. Such eager compliance is somewhat unusual. Financial compensation might be mentioned at a later time, and there was also the possibility of a further fraud scheme. Thus, as well as booking Radcliffe's flight to Taiwan, the ALR team wrote to Sotheby's. Radcliffe would need an expert on hand to authenticate the paintings. If genuine, the artworks would be packaged professionally, insured and shipped back to Argentina with proper customs documents. Even a smooth recovery would therefore entail significant costs. Radcliffe had to go back to the Bellas Artes Museum to negotiate the ALR's fees and to request the formal authorisation to retrieve the paintings.

The museum's director could not help. He wrote to the ALR that he had 'no authority' to deal with the recovery: it was a 'very political problem'. If the rumours swirling around the involvement of the military Junta in the theft were true, reclaiming the missing artworks might upset those who instigated the 'theft'. The Junta had come to power in a military coup in March 1976, overthrowing President Isabel Perón. They proceeded to wage a 'dirty war' against dissidents in which tens of thousands of citizens were killed or 'disappeared' by the security forces. When the paintings were stolen in late 1980, the Junta was facing significant civil opposition and an economic slump. To distract the increasingly restive population from these problems, the leadership had decided to challenge Great Britain over possession of the Falkland Islands. However, the initial groundswell of patriotism accompanying the Argentine invasion of the islands in April 1982 gave way to disillusionment when British naval forces drove the Argentinian soldiers off the islands in June 1982. The military government was so discredited by this failure that civilian rule and democracy were restored in Argentina in 1983.

In the interest of a peaceful transition, most of the political and moral issues of the dictatorship were suppressed rather than the 'Generals' being held to account. Some were still rich and influential, and the politically astute museum director knew better than to cross them. He would not take personal responsibility for authorising any action that might well embarrass a former official. The ALR would have to seek direct approval from the Argentinian government. Radcliffe therefore consulted with FCO and British Council officials. Ultimately, they thought the return of the stolen pictures would be received positively by the current administration. The FCO could not take on the case itself, but it would meet with Radcliffe in Buenos Aires and make the necessary introductions at the Ministry of Culture. As the communications received from Suriname and Taipei looked extremely promising, Radcliffe made the trip to Buenos Aires.

It became immediately obvious that money rather than politics would be the major sticking point in this restitution case. In the summer of 2001 Argentina was in the throes of a financial crisis. Public officials had not been paid for months and had just agreed to a significant salary cut to stave off a debt default. The country's unemployment rate stood at 25 per cent. The ALR predicted that it would need at least £50,000 to cover the costs of this intercontinental recovery, plus whatever compensation the current holders expected. But even raising the money for Radcliffe's airfares was an insurmountable problem with public budgets squeezed and monitored by the International Monetary Fund. The junior officials meeting Radcliffe in Buenos Aires suggested the ALR should seek a sponsor among the country's financial elite instead. One of the 'Friends of the Museum' might be willing to make a donation to retrieve the Santamarina collection.

The ALR faced a difficult decision: could it balance the commercial imperative to be paid with the political necessity to offer a free service to the Argentine government to obtain swift authorisation to act? Clearly, the ALR could not spend tens of thousands of pounds on a *pro bono* case, even if Radcliffe decided to donate his time. But the team reasoned that if the worst came to the worst, there were sixteen pictures worth at least US$2 million. Even if one or two artworks had to be sold to cover the costs of returning the others, it would still be a positive outcome for the Bellas Artes Museum. The ALR therefore decided to proceed.

Bureaucratic time runs on a different clock to the world of commerce, a matter not improved by a major financial crisis. The meeting in Taipei had to be postponed when the Culture Secretary in Buenos Aires failed to produce the authorisation letter. August, September and October 2001 passed without significant developments. The Taipei meeting had been scheduled for December, so in November Radcliffe was back in Buenos Aires to try to expedite matters and meet potential sponsors. But Argentina's economic situation was far worse than before. The government was close to defaulting on its bonds and focusing on matters of national importance only. The slimmed-down organigram of the state apparatus no longer even featured a Culture Secretariat. The chance of finding a rich sponsor to recover the artworks was negligible in the volatile economic and political climate. And there was a whole host of legal barriers preventing the sale of some of the pictures to pay for their recovery. For the moment, the only viable option would be to put the surrendered paintings into a trust until things could be worked out to everyone's satisfaction. Although the ALR thought a successful recovery would boost the company's profile and credibility, it was at risk, too. Without proper authority to act, its operation would be in an economic and political grey zone.

Mr LL in Suriname wanted to settle the issue swiftly, but his brother in Taiwan seemed more reticent. Eventually, Radcliffe managed to set up an appointment for mid-January

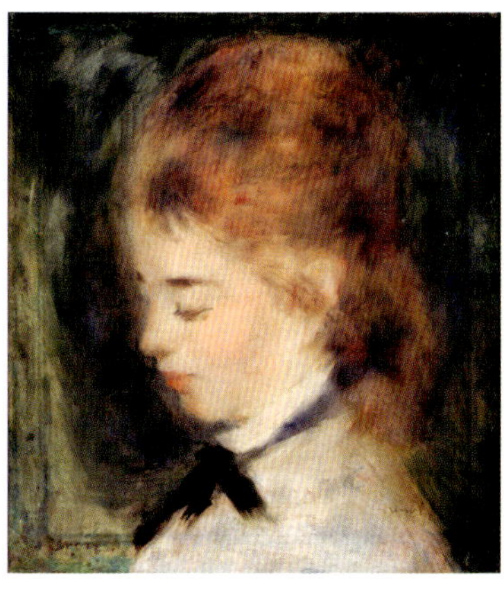

Pierre-Auguste Renoir (1841–1919), *Portrait of a Woman* (nineteenth century), Museo Nacional de Bellas Artes, Buenos Aires.

2002 in Taipei. The local Sotheby's expert who had valued the paintings the previous year joined him at the hotel to be on hand to authenticate the pictures. Hopes for a speedy resolution were dashed, however, when Mr L turned up without the artworks. He explained he had bought them from the De Lavor Trust in good faith having first checked them against the Interpol database. He planned to sell the paintings, not to give them away. When Radcliffe asked him why he had put him through all the expense of flying out to Taiwan the inscrutable Mr L shrugged: 'I guess I had nothing to lose.' He did not believe the ALR could block the sale of the paintings. Radcliffe's veiled threat that the stolen pictures might be seized from him had no effect either. Mr L said he had excellent relations with the Taiwanese government. He was an arms dealer.

Eight months into the case, the ALR was back where it had started, except now a reason for the 'very political' nature of the issue suggested itself: was the theft from the museum linked to weapons purchases from Taiwan for the Falklands War?

On the market

After the interview with Mr L, Radcliffe predicted the paintings would appear on the art market in the near future. When the director of the Bellas Artes Museum finally expressed an interest in revisiting the matter in late January 2002, the ALR decided to use this window of opportunity to obtain the authorisation to recover the artworks. It engaged a law firm in Buenos Aires to drive the matter forward, on a no-win-no-fee basis. The local lawyers were therefore highly motivated to persuade the museum director or the Culture Secretary to commit to paying their costs and fees. The ALR's costs were also mounting as Radcliffe flew out to Buenos Aires for a third time. The meeting in March 2002 was constructive. The museum director indicated he could probably work with the new government. Everyone agreed in principle that in the event of a successful retrieval two of the paintings would be held back and, if necessary, sold to cover the costs of repatriating the other fourteen. Yet once again, week after week went by without a formal letter confirming this arrangement. Another attempt was made through the newly appointed Culture Secretary, but still there was no movement.

In May 2002 a search request came in from a gallery in Paris for three of the missing paintings: a Cézanne, a Renoir and a Gauguin. Another urgent reminder was sent to Argentina stating that the ALR was powerless to prevent their sale without official authorisation. Finally, the following letter arrived from the Bellas Artes Museum:

Dear Radcliffe

I want to authorise you to follow dealing for the possible recovery of the paintings and drawings that have been stolen from this Museum of Fine Arts in December 1980.

Sincerely Yours

[Illegible]

That was it. There was no mention of fees or costs. It was just about sufficient to enable the ALR to ask the gallery to hold the paintings temporarily and enquire how it had obtained them. The dealer explained that a Taiwanese consignor – a Mr Y – had brought the artworks to Paris on behalf of his uncle, Mr L. Radcliffe wrote to Mr L again: was he prepared to surrender the paintings now the ALR had demonstrated its power to stop the sale of the pictures? If so, there was some scope for negotiating his 'expenses'. Mr L did not respond but sent his nephew to the gallery to demand the release of the paintings. The gallerist was mortified by the *grande scène* on his premises and was on the brink of giving the pictures back. He was scared: could the ALR please get the angry consignor off his back? The ALR engaged the services of a lawyer in Paris, but she would only proceed after receiving proper authorisation from Buenos Aires.

A more formal letter was produced in record time, but this still did not refer to the ALR's fees or costs. The ALR's Paris lawyer managed to obtain an *ordonnance* from the commercial court that the paintings should be held by the gallery for ten days. Unless things were resolved within this period, the ALR would have to start court proceedings for restitution on behalf of the museum. At this stage the ALR had invested thirty-five days of work and £25,000 in out-of-pocket expenses. With only three paintings on hand, there would be a problem with the informal agreement that had been reached in Buenos Aires in January, that is, to retain two of the lesser pictures to pay for the recovery costs of the rest. The artworks in Paris were the most valuable three of the sixteen and the Argentinian government might well object to one of them being sold off to return the other two, especially if the remaining thirteen paintings disappeared into the illicit market. To prevent this, Radcliffe tried once again to negotiate an amicable settlement with the consignor.

Radcliffe's first meeting in Paris with Mr Y at the end of May 2002 to negotiate the return of the paintings was not promising. Mr Y repeated that Mr L had bought the pictures in good faith after checking the Interpol records. Unless the ALR made a 'decent proposal' to buy them, they would not meet again. A check with a Taiwanese law firm explained Mr L's defiant stance. To force a surrender of the artworks under Taiwanese law, the ALR would have to prove that Mr L had purchased the paintings in bad faith. Even if it could, the museum's claim against an illegal holder would have lapsed after fifteen years under the Republic of China's law. As regards the crime of receiving stolen goods, Mr L was protected by the ten-year statute of limitations unless his acquisition was recent. By contrast, under French law the Argentinian government's title had not been extinguished: for this, Mr L would have to prove that he had acquired the pictures in good faith. The ALR therefore asked the French police to seize the artworks, while keeping the communication channel open.

Reluctantly, Mr Y agreed to a further meeting, at which Radcliffe reiterated that the pictures were unsaleable. Argentina could only pay a reward if there was evidence of a good faith purchase, and the paperwork presented so far was clearly a fiction. Even in the best-case scenario, Argentina's government was effectively bankrupt. Radcliffe's most optimistic estimate of what could be raised was 1 per cent of the Sotheby's valuation of US$2.5 million, that is, $25,000. Mr Y was petulant and angry: he was looking for US$3 million. He argued that, after all, his price was less than 1 per cent of 'Mr Venoaks's' valuation of US$350 million. In addition to this massive gap in expectations a further unforeseen financial complication arose. When the French police had been asked to seize the paintings, they noted that their import had not been declared at customs. Their owner (whoever that might be) now faced a five-figure bill to cover the import duties and a late payment fine if they wanted them back.

Back in Buenos Aires the ALR's Argentinian law team tried to convince the museum director to finally commit to paying their own and the ALR's costs when the pictures were returned. Nobody could be expected to take on such a complex recovery and foot the bill for expert and attorneys' fees, insurance, transport and duties without eventual compensation. Given the value of the paintings at stake, all costs could be covered by selling just one of them. In principle, this was fully understood, but none of the ministers was prepared to put such a commitment in writing. For the signatory, the potential political damage from selling national patrimony was considered greater than the benefit of retrieving the other paintings. Giving up at this stage, however, would leave the ALR with nothing but unpaid bills, so it decided to press on and call Mr Y's bluff.

When Mr Y was served with a court order, his lawyer wrote to the ALR's lawyer to say that they would not contest the case. They

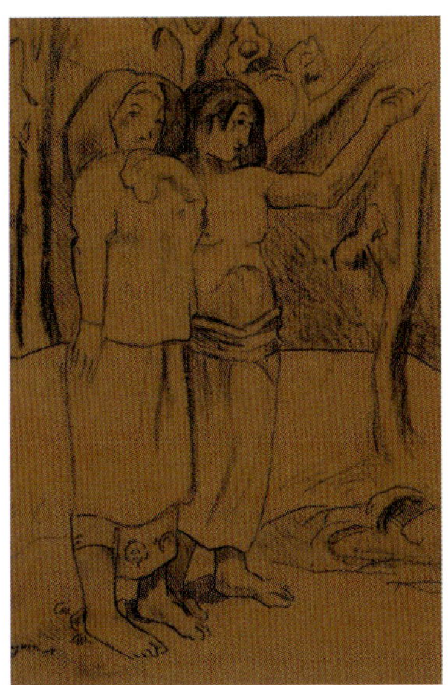

Paul Gauguin (1848–1903), *The Call* (*c.* 1902) Museo Nacional de Bellas Artes, Buenos Aires.

were ready to surrender the three paintings in Paris if the ALR assumed responsibility for the customs duties. However, Mr L wanted to negotiate a payment for the other thirteen artworks. He was now thinking of US$10 million, but without a definitive commitment on recovering the ALR's costs from Argentina, Radcliffe had to stick with the rock-bottom US$25,000 offer. If the ALR spent money irresponsibly by paying potential criminals, it would completely undermine its negotiating position for recovering its costs afterwards.

The threat of court action and the outstanding fine were essential to keep the negotiation going, but in the background the case was falling apart. The Argentinian government was prevaricating about whether the theft of the paintings was 'a criminal matter'. The military Junta had already been tried and the statute of limitation prevented any further prosecutions. If there was no crime, there was no reason for the French police to be involved at all, except for the illegal import of the pictures into France. However, this was a relatively minor transgression unlikely to deter a wily businessman from driving a hard bargain. Indeed, unbeknown to Mr L, French customs had already informally agreed to drop the charge and waive the fine if the pictures went back to Argentina. A different problem arose when the Argentinian government's lawyers asked for an expert valuation of the paintings to decide which of them – if any – could be sold to pay for the recovery cost. If the consignors found out that an internationally renowned Impressionist expert had turned up at the gallery to value the pictures it would completely undermine the ALR's negotiating position that there was no money at all. To keep up the pretence, Radcliffe travelled to Paris to accompany the specialist on his gallery visit to make sure he would talk about a 'condition report' throughout. The last thing the ALR needed at this stage was any sort of publicity on the case.

Betrayed

In September 2002 three major Argentinian newspapers broke a sensational story. The Bellas Artes Museum and the Culture Secretariat were said to be involved in secret negotiations with a shady British company dealing in stolen art.[44] This dubious enterprise had located the artworks from the 1980 heist and demanded one of them as payment for its services. Some journalists realised that international art recovery is not cheap and thought that some compensation might be in order. Others, however, surmised that the Argentinian government was being blackmailed. National patrimony was being held hostage. Was this not a matter for Interpol? As the journalists clearly had extensive access to the ALR's correspondence with the Bellas Artes Museum, the ALR's horrified Buenos Aires lawyers suspected the museum director himself had briefed the journalists. Was he testing public opinion before committing himself to a specific course of action?

The ALR went into damage limitation mode, explaining its business to countless journalists. However, after years of inaction the Argentinian police finally decided to take an interest in the missing paintings and requested assistance from Interpol: to investigate the ALR. Unless Radcliffe could satisfactorily explain the ALR's operations and its mandate in this affair, he faced the threat of being interviewed under caution by the Metropolitan Police. Similarly, a French Interpol officer was despatched to interview the ALR's legal adviser in Paris. Both the French and UK police quickly concluded that no crime had been committed and sent their evaluation and the information they had collected on to Buenos Aires. But no deal could be done in this febrile atmosphere, either in Taiwan or in Buenos Aires. The three seized pictures were left in Paris until the waters calmed. There would be elections in Argentina in 2003 and there was the hope of a fresh start with a new government.

As the French court proceedings were delayed from quarter to quarter, the Argentine police mulled over the information sent to them by Interpol. They soon realised the Argentinian government could start its own proceedings to reclaim the paintings in a French criminal court. A criminal trial would take priority over the ALR's claim in the civil courts. If successful, the Argentine police could take credit for the retrieval of the artworks and bypass the ALR's claims for covering its costs in the investigation altogether. It would be a good news story for (almost) everyone. In July 2003 Argentinian government officials therefore announced their intention to file criminal proceedings against Mr L in France. 'Interpol agent recovers stolen works of art' was a jubilant – if rather misleading – newspaper headline.[45] The gleeful museum director was cited in *La Nación*: 'I am jumping with joy at the recovery of the works without payment and will kiss the ears of the agent who found them.'[46] Kisses on the ears from an extravagantly bearded former conceptual artist were certainly not the kind of reward for which the ALR had been hoping.

Salvage operations

For the ALR, the press coverage portraying it as a ruthless bounty hunter beaten to the goalpost by the forces of law was very worrying. Neither the museum nor politicians had acknowledged the ALR's effort to retrieve the paintings. Was it time to walk away from the case with all its unpaid bills or plough on regardless? The ALR's legal partners in Buenos Aires considered that when the paintings were recovered (including the thirteen still in Mr L's possession), they could claim reimbursement of their expenses.

Under Argentinian law, it is illegal for a principal to cheat an agent out of their fees and expenses, even if the *mandato* is deliberately vague about financial details. Yet the ALR also realised Argentina was in the process of restructuring US$60 billion in government debts and expected bondholders to accept a 90 per cent cut in the net present value of their assets. Generosity was not the order of the day: the ALR would join the back of a long queue of frustrated creditors.

The ALR decided to proceed slowly while keeping costs to a minimum. The Taiwanese party had also got wind of the drama in Buenos Aires and lost interest in negotiating with the ALR. Emails to fine-tune the agreement to cede the paintings were still exchanged, but both sides dragged their feet. The ALR could not offer any incentive to Mr L without prior approval from Interpol, which was now fully involved in the case. But if the ALR reported on an impending breakthrough in the negotiation, Interpol would probably pass the details to Argentinian officials. If an agreement was imminent, they might swoop once again, either scuppering the deal or taking the pictures to Buenos Aires. This would leave the ALR without leverage in its negotiation with the government over reimbursement of its costs. In these difficult circumstances, constructive negotiations stalled.

An excellent reason to re-engage with the Argentinian Culture Secretary arose in November 2003. The deadline for the Argentine government to formally file its claim in the criminal court was approaching. The ALR's legal team in Buenos Aires therefore asked the minister to provide formal evidence of the theft and its judicial investigation. It also sent along a large file documenting the development of the case so far. The papers provided detailed evidence of the negotiations between the ALR and the previous office holders in the Culture Secretariat and the museum, as well as a breakdown of its costs. In addition to conveying the message about the massive expense of the operation so far, the documentation showed that a court case in Paris would be complex, costly and of uncertain outcome. It was not just a matter of an official breezing in to pick up the pictures. The bottom line was that the Argentinians still needed the ALR's help to recover their lost patrimony. The letter presented the officials with a simple choice: extend the *mandato* or risk losing the pictures.

There was no reply from the Culture Secretary and the start of the criminal case in Paris was postponed. The civil court process was therefore also put on hold. The judge expressed her dismay with the Argentinian government to the ALR's lawyer: first, for threatening to start a criminal court case without ever mentioning the ALR's long-running campaign in the civil court to retrieve the pictures on behalf of the museum; and second, for unceremoniously dropping the baton it had just wrested from the ALR. The judge's statement made it less likely that the civil court would hand over the paintings to an Argentinian government official without recognising the ALR's claim for reimbursement and the ALR took heart once again.

Proceeding with a criminal trial was not truly in Argentina's interest. The criminal proceedings would be focused on holding the consignor of the paintings to account, not on repatriating the artworks. It would take at least two or three years to decide whether Mr Y could be found guilty of a crime, which seemed unlikely. The civil procedure to settle the ownership of the paintings would take its course afterwards. In the meantime, the pictures would remain in Paris, racking up further storage and insurance bills. Whichever way the two cases were finally resolved in Paris, the ALR could still take the Argentine government to court in Buenos Aires over violating its *mandato*. The alternative was a speedy conclusion of the settlement agreement between Mr Y and the ALR, followed by the restitution of the artworks to the museum in exchange for a reasonable recovery fee, however that might be funded. By now the ALR needed US$150,000 to cover the out-of-pocket costs of conducting the recovery operation in Taiwan, Buenos Aires and Paris. Another US$200,000 would be required to compensate the ALR for time spent in trying to recover the paintings – sixty days in total so far – but realistically it expected reimbursement of only a percentage of these costs.

Blowing hot and cold

The Culture Secretariat seemed overwhelmed by the problem, driving a bizarre zigzag course. One week it was proactive, belatedly filing criminal proceedings against Mr Y in Paris, but then missed the next deadline for submitting the paperwork. The Culture Secretary refused to see the ALR's lawyers in Buenos Aires, but the Argentinian ambassador in Paris met with Radcliffe and his Paris lawyer. The ambassador was sympathetic regarding the ALR's predicament, but officials from the Culture Secretariat disputed that the ALR should receive any compensation for its work so far. They argued the museum was not a separate legal entity from the government and therefore its director did not have the authority to give a *mandato* in the first place. Thus, the Culture Secretary appointed his own lawyer in Paris to represent Argentina, but then failed to brief him. The only positive outcome of this confused flurry of activity was that Mr L in Taiwan was alarmed by the threat of a trial in the French criminal court. He offered to resume negotiations about giving back the missing thirteen paintings in return for dropping the criminal and customs charges and his nephew's complete rehabilitation with the French authorities.

With the Argentinian ambassador in Paris apparently supporting the ALR's request to be compensated for its expenses,

Radcliffe re-engaged with Mr L and Mr Y. As long as the ALR was demonstrably on track with negotiating a voluntary agreement to return all sixteen paintings, the Argentinian government was less likely to swoop into Paris to claim the three seized paintings. But the location of the missing pictures was still unknown, meaning the negotiation could easily be derailed. Therefore, a plan was made for Mr Y to bring the remaining artworks to Paris where they would be held in escrow during the negotiation. Once a deal was concluded (including the settlement of the ALR's fees), all sixteen pictures would be repatriated together. However, it was not just the Argentine government blowing hot and cold. Mr Y and Mr L, who had briefly been cooperative and had instructed their lawyer to negotiate and draft the escrow agreement, became evasive again.

Regardless, Radcliffe pressed on with negotiating a fee agreement with the embassy. The government's dire financial constraints limited its contribution to US$20,000. However, the ambassador had used his excellent personal connections to the Buenos Aires financial elite to great effect. He found a sponsor among the Friends of the Museum, but he could only ask for US$50,000. The ALR was disappointed about being left with a big loss on this recovery, but eventually accepted. It was agreed that a first payment of US$70,000 would be due when the first three pictures were released to Argentina. A further payment of US$20,000 would be conditional on the other thirteen paintings also being recovered, although the funding source for this remained unclear. After months of haggling, the contract was ready in October 2004. Unfortunately, it was never signed.

Stalemate

An unexpected calamity befell the judicial restitution process. On the morning of the day scheduled for the criminal court hearing, Mr Y's lawyer in Paris was arrested and imprisoned on charges of facilitating the smuggling of gold and money laundering on behalf of an African client. All court proceedings had to be postponed, as the defendant no longer had legal representation. However, Mr Y refused to appoint a new representative, maintaining that his lawyer continued to act for him despite his incarceration, even though he could no longer attend court hearings. Thus, a year later, in October 2005, there was still no progress with the legal proceedings or the ALR's fee agreement.

The commercial negotiations with the irascible Mr Y were not going well either. He maintained that his uncle had obtained the three paintings in good faith and he was upset about how the damage to his reputation had affected his business in France. As for Mr L's other thirteen paintings, with a total of only US$20,000 offered for their return, the real compensation would have to be in kind. Yet, any 'commercial preferment' of Mr L's companies would require the cooperation of the Argentine government, which was not part of the negotiation. Unable to make progress, Mr Y and Mr L once more cut off communications with the ALR. Having tried every possible avenue for making contact, everyone settled down to wait for Mr Y's lawyer's release from prison. When he finally resumed his work a year later, it turned out that his Taiwanese clients were no longer speaking to him either. Surely the time had come for the French judicial system to end this farce.

An 'unprecedented' resolution

Back in Buenos Aires a number of people realised that a window opportunity had opened. The Ministry of Culture decided to use diplomatic channels to obtain control of the pictures, bypassing all other claimants and taking full credit for the repatriation. In November 2005 the French court proceedings were summarily terminated. Friendly journalists informed Radcliffe that there was to be a glamorous reception at the Argentinian embassy on the day originally scheduled for the court hearing. Instead of holding a trial, the Palace of Justice would retrieve the paintings from the gallery and hand them over to an Argentinian judge, a representative of the Ministry of Culture and two Interpol officers, all jostling for publicity and advancement. The ALR's Paris lawyer was shocked about politicians overriding what should have been a lengthy judicial process. Without a court case, there was no opportunity to raise the issue of the ALR's costs. Gallingly, Radcliffe was not even invited to participate in the festivities. This would be the judge's, the minister's, the police officers' and the ambassador's day in the limelight. Rather than sharing a stage with the officials celebrating inside, Radcliffe therefore mingled with the journalists waiting outside the reception. The ALR still needed to ensure the best possible press coverage on a terribly disappointing day.

Once again, the Argentinian newspapers were jubilant: three important Impressionist pictures were coming home thanks to the amazing efforts of Argentina's government. If the ALR was mentioned in the coverage at all, it was only given credit for spotting the paintings in Paris. What about rumours of a fee agreement between the ALR and the government? Well, perhaps, but that was never signed. If anything, the ALR might receive some minimal financial recognition. As for the other thirteen artworks, they were presumed to be in Taiwan with whom Argentina does not have diplomatic relations. There was nothing anyone could do about them. As far as Argentinian public opinion was concerned, the case was closed. Would there be any payment at all?

Wash-up

When the paintings were put back on display in the Bellas Artes Museum, the Argentine ambassador – at least partially – kept his word. He managed to obtain US$25,000 for the ALR from a private sponsor. It was barely enough to cover the ALR's French lawyer's fees, who was still at a complete loss to explain the resolution of her case by the French judicial system. It had no basis in law or indeed a precedent. Thus, all other expenses related to the recovery had to be absorbed by the ALR and there was nothing for the lawyers in Buenos Aires either, not even a kiss from the museum director. But a further (tiny) carrot was dangled: if the ALR could retrieve the other thirteen paintings it would be paid US$75,000. This agreement was eventually signed by the ambassador on behalf of the Ministry of Culture. Whether it would be honoured was a different question.

The bizarre story of the Santamarina Impressionists has a fitting coda. Radcliffe went back to Buenos Aires one more time, to formally thank the ALR's benefactor and promote the ALR's work in a presentation to wealthy art collectors at the Bellas Artes Museum. One cannot bear grudges in this business. Treating Radcliffe to a large steak and copious amounts of red wine at one of the city's finest restaurants afterwards, his host nodded politely to a man dining at a neighbouring table. 'There is your thief', he whispered, 'this is the agent who stole the pictures for the government.'

Priceless national heritage

There are three big lessons from this highly unusual recovery story and the ALR learnt them all. First, it is essential to secure a contract with fees agreed at the outset. Throughout the case, the ALR knew that its contracts were weak and constantly struggled to obtain clear commitments and directions from the Argentinian government. Yet under pressure of time, it proceeded on the basis of vague terms dictated by stressed and otherwise preoccupied officials. The discovery of the Santamarina Impressionists in 2001 occurred when the ALR still needed to prove itself to a doubting art world. The ALR's search income was low and its business relied heavily on recovery fees. At the outset, retrieving the attractive Impressionist paintings for the Bellas Artes Museum seemed to promise income and positive global media coverage. There was obviously a risk that the Argentinian government would try to wriggle out of paying a recovery fee given the ambiguous commitments made in the negotiation of the *mandato*. However, the ALR trusted the French justice system to force the Argentinian government to honour and reward its honest work. That confidence was misplaced.

Second, regardless of whether you have a formal contract, dealing with a government is like conducting business with criminals in one important respect: there is no third-party enforcement when your counterparty cheats. If a government decides not to pay you for your services and you have nothing that today's politician values more than what they can gain by reneging on their (predecessor's) commitment, you will lose. The ALR is just one of the numerous creditors, investors and citizens let down by Argentina's government over the ages. Since gaining independence in 1816, this proud country has defaulted on its debt nine times.[47] Politically and financially unstable governments are a particular risk for enterprises such as the ALR. For politicians, national patrimony has little economic value (unless they can steal it), but great political value if they can take credit for saving or retrieving it. In periods of political turmoil, short-term benefits often outweigh long-term costs: three artworks were recovered, but thirteen were probably lost forever. The lesson is therefore that work for museums in poor and politically unpredictable countries is best undertaken on a *pro bono* basis from the outset, with affordability in mind and a clear PR strategy agreed beforehand.

Third, it is easy to be drawn into an exciting art recovery, especially one that seems straightforward at the start and has such a fascinating cast of characters. Truth is often stranger than fiction in the ALR's world. But the recoveries side of the business has to earn enough to cover its costs. Although it is psychologically difficult, sunk costs – that is, money that has already been spent and cannot be retrieved – should be ignored when making the decision about whether or not to continue in a business activity. Otherwise, it is more likely than not that good money will be thrown after bad. From the case files it can be seen that the ALR implemented ever more stringent cost controls as the case progressed, but this was still an expensive lesson. We know it was learnt though: the Argentinians' promise to pay US$75,000 for the remaining thirteen paintings did not tempt the ALR to resume negotiations with Mr L in Taiwan or his brother in Suriname.

There is another interesting observation in this story about art crime: it is rather short on criminals. The thief appears to have been a secret agent acting on government orders. Although Mr L did not exactly acquire the artworks in good faith, it seems that he obtained them in a consensual trade, even if it was an arms deal. The marvellously outré Mrs W was probably not aware she had been roped into facilitating a fraud. She had loved the glitz and drama of the art world but was entirely out of her depth in its murkier parts. Mr Y, our irascible smuggler and seller of art of questionable provenance, was just doing his uncle a favour. He did not want his business in France to be ruined or to be hounded out of the country. Mr Y's lawyer was given ample opportunity to reflect on the moral issues surrounding his shady clients' business during his spell in prison, but he was a peripheral character here. As for the politicians who eventually ended the odyssey of the three paintings through the French court system and took the credit for the recovery, they were opportunists rather than rogues. The real villains hover in the shadows. We will probably never know who decided to press a grieving widow to hand over her late husband's art collection to the national museum, to have it stolen, to blame and beat up the innocent security guards, and then use the artworks to buy weapons for a futile war.

5

A Find in the Attic:
The Missing Minutes of the
Royal Society

In February 2006, the auction house Bonhams landed a publicity coup: its glossy catalogue announced the auction of 'A Manuscript of Outstanding Importance, Encapsulating the Revolution in Scientific Understanding that Marks the Beginning of the Modern World – A Record of the Greatest Scientific Institution of the Age, Written by One of its Greatest Scientists'. But could the anonymous consignor in whose Hampshire country house the dusty manuscript had appeared really be its true owner? These documents had been prepared for the Royal Society and should have been committed to its archive. They had been missing for over 300 years. Could the Royal Society make a valid legal claim for their return or find another way of stopping the sale to a (foreign) private bidder? It would be a race against time.

An auctioneer's dream

Bonhams had sent its expert to a Hampshire country house to value the contents for a probate sale. After a long afternoon assessing furniture and artworks of varying quality, he was ready to leave when the executor appeared with a battered box full of papers from the back of a dusty cupboard. Already in his coat, the expert leafed unenthusiastically through old bills and some sheet music and found a leather-bound volume of manuscripts of some antiquity below. The calf-leather binding indicated it was probably eighteenth century. Intrigued, he opened the volume at random and deciphered some familiar names: Sir Isaac Newton, Robert Hooke, Sir Christopher Wren – the leading scientists of the late seventeenth century. This was rather interesting.

Manuscript experts and Royal Society scholars agreed, and the volume, or Folio, was soon described as the greatest scientific discovery of a generation. It contained notes taken during the meetings of the Royal Society in the late 1670s and early 1680s, plus transcripts of earlier meetings, mostly in Robert Hooke's own hand. The records of the meetings corresponded to a gap in the Society's archive at a time of major scientific advances. Hooke's candid asides and acerbic personal observations about skulduggery and power games at the top of the Society added further spice and really brought the characters back to life. The press loved the stories, too: headlines such as

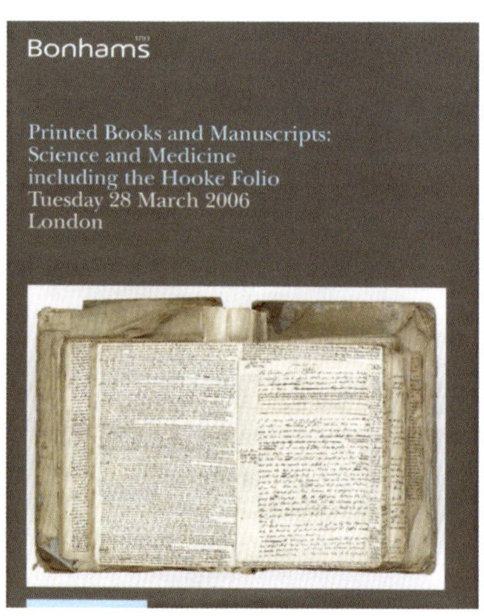

Bonhams catalogue for the auction of the Hooke Folio in March 2006.

'Scientific "gospel" of Newton's greatest rival'[48] and 'Eureka! Lost manuscript found in cupboard'[49] captured readers' imaginations. The BBC referred to Hooke as 'the unsung hero of science' and 'England's Leonardo'.[50] The auction house put an estimate of £1 million to £1.5 million in the auction catalogue. The Folio would go under the hammer on 28 March 2006. The auctioneers' dream continued with the media encouraging rumours that some West Coast billionaires might take a fancy to this unique piece of the history of science and bid its price into the stratosphere.

A rude awakening

But should this quintessentially British document be going abroad? And why was it in private hands and not in the Royal Society's archives? The Society would never have sold such important documents, so when did they go missing, how and why? If they had been stolen centuries ago, could the Society still lay claim to them? The Royal Society asked for permission for its experts to examine the manuscripts in detail. Having established their authenticity and importance, the Society's president launched a campaign for private donations to buy the papers. The acquisition would complete the Society's archive and make the manuscripts accessible to scholars. Bonhams fully appreciated the Society's desire to purchase the Folio and put it in touch with a number of wealthy clients to help out with fundraising.

However, the negotiations to buy the manuscript hit a roadblock. With the media hype and the interest expressed by wealthy private buyers, the vendors were not keen to arrange a private sale. Who knew where the price could go in frenzied bidding? With Bonhams' PR team whipping up buyer interest and a skilled auctioneer teasing bidders into competing over this unique object, a competitive auction would deliver the best price for the sellers and, of course, the highest commission for the auction house. In the unlikely event that the bidding was muted, the day was dull and the Folio failed to make its reserve, one could still sell it to the Society afterwards. There really was no downside to waiting and seeing what would happen at the auction.

Before offering an object for sale, auction houses require the sellers to formally state that they have good title and then perform a due diligence check with the ALR to ensure the object has not been registered as stolen. But auction houses generally do not make specific efforts to advertise problems with a provenance: the catalogue entry focuses on information likely to maximise the price. Under the caveat emptor (buyer beware) principle, buyers must discover adverse information for themselves. The Royal Society therefore decided to publicise its concerns about the Folio's origin. It planted an article in *The Times* on 23 February 2006: 'Royal Society wants £1m book back'.[51] It was clearly intended to warn off buyers with a set of worrying legal issues. Had

the volume of manuscripts been stolen? Did the vendors really have good title? Could a new buyer purchase the Folio in good faith and obtain good title in turn? Even if the Society could not prevent the sale, mooting the possibility of a future legal dispute would probably put off many high-calibre buyers. With reduced competition at auction, the Folio's price might become affordable for the Society.

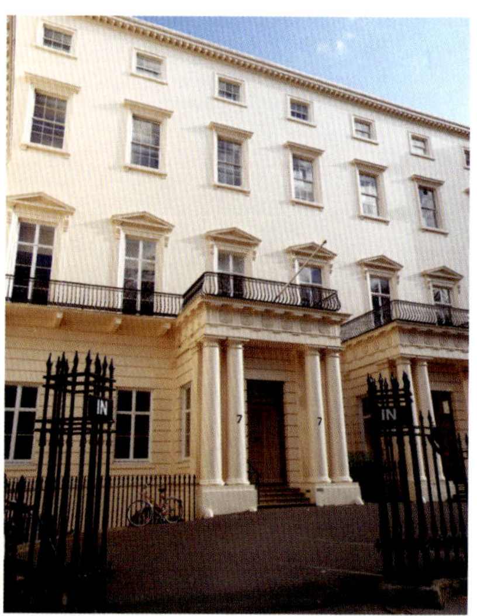

The Royal Society in London.

However, the vendors dug in. When the Society approached them with an offer of £1.5 million and after further negotiation offered to pay the full buyer's commission on top of this (20 per cent of the first £70,000 and 12 per cent thereafter) the vendors still prevaricated. The auction house suggested the Society might succeed with an offer of £1.8 million. Was it time for the Society's legal team to come up with an alternative?

A legal quagmire

The Royal Society's lawyers investigated the volume of manuscripts and its history in forensic detail. They found that – legally speaking – the Folio was not a single piece of work but should be considered in four different sections. The Society could at best lay claim to two parts of the Folio. In the first section were Hooke's copies of minutes from Royal Society meetings up to 1677. These he made for his personal use and the Society's lawyers could not see any basis for the Society claiming ownership of them. The next section, however, contained draft minutes prepared by Hooke in his capacity as the secretary of the Royal Society from 1677 to 1682. The Society's 'proper' minutes would have been created from these notes and it was the Society's practice to keep both the rough and the fair copy of the notes in its archive. But the Society's archive was missing all secretarial notes from 1676 to 1688. The Society's legal advisers therefore thought the Society might have title to these draft minutes.

For the years 1683–5, Hooke did not hold office in the Society but continued to make draft minutes that were gathered in the Folio. However useful these notes might be for the Society's records, as Hooke did not have an official position, these had to be considered his personal property. In the final section are rough minutes prepared by Hooke in 1691 on behalf of a new secretary of the Society: Richard Waller. Once again, such notes were missing from the archive and the Society could argue that, as these notes were taken for one of its officers, they should have been committed to the archives.

The 1663 statutes of the Society state that the secretary had charge and custody of the documents of the Royal Society but should return Society property 'as required'. However, from the personal nature of the comments on these manuscripts, which proved such a delight to scholars, it is clear Hooke had considered them as his personal records. He seems to have left his papers to a cousin, who later gave them to Waller, Hooke's biographer. Waller's heirs then probably handed down the manuscripts among their 'books and papers' without ever raising the issue of their origin.[52] At some stage in the eighteenth century somebody had the manuscripts bound together into the Folio. There is no record that the Society ever made a claim for the return of the manuscripts. If the manuscripts had passed down the family line, could the Society now 'require' them to be returned, 300 years later? Possibly, but certainly not if someone else had bought them in good faith in the meantime.

Apparently, the Folio had been sold at least once. In 1939 the Folio was sold among the other contents of Woolston Hall, in Chigwell, Essex, by its trustees. The date is important. The UK Limitation Act did not come into force until 1 July 1940. Thus, if the Folio went straight from Woolston Hall to the house in Hampshire where it was found, the Society probably still held the legal title. However, if there had been a further sale after 1 July 1940, the good faith buyer would then have obtained good title after the statute of limitation had expired. Nobody had come forward with evidence of such a sale. The lawyers therefore advised that, unless the anonymous vendor could provide information about a post-1940 sale to validate their title, the Society could request that those parts of the manuscript prepared while the author was taking minutes in an official capacity should be returned to its archive. The other parts of the Folio could go forward to auction uncontested, if anyone was still interested in buying the sadly diminished remains.

A letter to this effect was sent to the auction house on 21 March 2006, one week before the auction. The management's response was predictably apoplectic. The auctioneers pointed out that they had cooperated fully with the Society. They had allowed its officials to study the Folio and had even helped with identifying sponsors to buy it. The Royal Society had appeared genuinely desirous of purchasing the Folio implying that it was not its property. Only when the negotiations over a private sale had reached an impasse had the Society suddenly claimed ownership. The vendors were convinced they were the lawful owners of the Folio. The auction house was similarly satisfied of the vendors having good title. In short, the Society's 'last ditch attempt to prevent or upset the sale and/or obtain the papers for a lower price' was 'entirely unacceptable'.[53]

The Society already knew its legal position was not quite as strong as its letter had set out. Its legal counsel had spotted that the sale of the contents of Woolston Hall had occurred after the UK Limitation Act had been passed by Parliament in 1939, but before it came fully into effect on 1 July 1940. The Society's lawyers warned that a judge might take the view that the passing of the Act in 1939 was the 'watershed moment' for statutes of limitation rather than the date at which the law was formally implemented. In this case, the Society's title would have been extinguished six years after the Woolston Hall sale. Although there was a legal precedent where a further sale had been required to fully extinguish the former owner's title, the lawyers were doubtful this judgment would stand up to renewed scrutiny in court. In short, if the Society decided to take the case to court, it might well lose, and expensively. Although a million pounds' worth of documents was at stake, reading between the lines, the only real winners of a legal action would be the lawyers on both sides. The Society probably could not afford to sue and lose, and the auction house was calling the Society's bluff.

Threats need to be credible to be effective. If someone threatens to do something that would be very costly for them act upon, it is unlikely they will carry out that threat. How could the Royal Society persuade the vendors to come back to the negotiation table with reduced price expectations without wasting its resources on a legal action it did not actually want to pursue?

The ALR becomes involved

The Royal Society decided to approach Julian Radcliffe: was he prepared to use his negotiation experience and the ALR's position in the art market to bring about an amicable and affordable commercial resolution? This was not a stolen object and the Royal Society had never registered its missing rough notes with the ALR. The notes had been retained by their author and passed down the generations as Hooke's personal record. However, the ALR advised that it could register the Folio as 'in dispute' if the Society made a formal claim at the High Court. The 'in dispute' function alerts auction houses and buyers to a conflict between a vendor and other claimants. For example, in divorce proceedings the party that has left the marital home can use this ALR service to prevent the remaining spouse from secretly liquidating their joint art collection. The ALR will only issue a clear search certificate when the ownership of the artworks has been formally resolved.

Registering the Folio with the ALR as 'in dispute' was an inspired strategy from the point of view of creating publicity and credibility for the Society's position. If the ALR announced that the Folio was 'in dispute', no buyer could claim they had purchased it in good faith. Buyers could choose to ignore the warning, but their title might subsequently be challenged. The threat of legal action would put off most collectors and potential buyers would expect a discount. Radcliffe therefore had a powerful bargaining chip when he approached the auction house to discuss the issue.

The Society also asked Radcliffe to act as its agent in resolving the conflict. The agreement could be used as a textbook case for contract design. It included incentives for the agent to take on the case (with a down-payment of £10,000), to resolve the issue amicably (a further payment of £25,000 contingent on success) and to remain firm with the price. The last was achieved by offering a 15 per cent premium on any savings if Radcliffe pushed the overall cost of purchase to below £1 million. He thus had every incentive to produce a timely solution well within the Society's budget.

Securing a contract to recover the Hooke Folio was an excellent opportunity to raise the profile of provenance research and pre-sale due diligence in the art market. However, the ALR had to weigh up the PR gains from saving a unique piece of national heritage on behalf of the prestigious Royal Society against the cost of picking a fight with a highly respected auction house. Upsetting an important customer could undermine the ALR's future business in the art market. The Royal Society had offered £1.5 million plus buyer's commission in the first negotiation and now the ALR had been instructed to shift the purchase price towards £1 million. However, Radcliffe had thought of a way to reconcile the parties' positions. British inheritance tax law favours private treaty sales to a limited list of charities.[54] Although the Royal Society is not one of these, another charitable institution might acquire the Folio on the Society's behalf. In that case, the vendors' tax bill could be reduced significantly. The ALR's proposal would thus protect the vendors' profit and reduce the Royal Society's purchase price.

Radcliffe's brief email to the Royal Society on Friday 24 March sets out this negotiation strategy:

> I suggest that I send an email which states that we have been asked to enter [the Folio] as in dispute and before doing so we wanted to hear [Bonhams'] side of the question ... [We] have some ideas which may help a settlement. If he does not see us today, then on Monday we would have to warn the trade that [the Folio is] in dispute ... and this would complicate the sale. This puts the onus back on him and he would find it difficult to argue that he does not have an answer to our question.

Thus, the Royal Society prepared a writ claiming the Folio as its property. To further discourage super-rich foreign buyers from bidding, it also put together a request to the Arts Council to bar the Folio's export from the UK. As an object of outstanding significance in the history of science it might well be classed as a national treasure.[55] Finally, the Society drafted a press release, stressing the Society's moral rights over the manuscripts and the charity's earnest endeavours to save the Folio 'for the nation' that had been foiled by the vendors. Plan B was in place, but fingers were firmly crossed for plan A to succeed.

Drawing the battle lines

Having initially been told the chairman of the auction house could find only a tiny gap in his schedule for a late afternoon meeting on the day before the sale, Radcliffe put his plan into action. He sent an email to Bonhams threatening that the ALR would register the Folio as 'in dispute' and inform the trade on the morning of Monday 27 March: 'Before doing so we would like to have Bonhams' response. A meeting on Monday would be too late'. Radcliffe made himself available to talk for the rest of Friday and all day on Saturday. Two hours later an emailed response arrived. The Chairman was furious. The matter had nothing to do with the ALR, and Radcliffe should stay out of it. It was simply a ploy to exert commercial pressure on the flimsiest of pretexts. In fact, it was laughable. The chairman threatened the ALR and Radcliffe personally with legal action for substantial damages should the sale be foiled. But – importantly – the chairman also handed over the telephone number of a director who would be available to discuss the issue over the weekend, except, of course, all Radcliffe's calls went straight to answerphone.

The nominated director eventually returned Radcliffe's urgent calls on Saturday evening. The conversation did not start well. The auction house – speaking on behalf of the vendors – deeply resented the ALR's involvement and once again threatened Radcliffe with litigation. Being sued by one of its customers would clearly be problematic for the ALR. However, Radcliffe is sanguine about such threats: despite many similar warnings over the years, the ALR has yet to be sued. The costs and risks of this kind of litigation are so high that the threat lacks credibility. Radcliffe duly ignored it and the conversation swiftly moved on to negotiating a price, or a 'settlement', as this appeared to be the preferred term. The idea of discounting the price to reflect the potential tax savings from a sale to a charitable institution fell on stony ground. The vendors were numerate and would have done their own tax planning. They were only interested in a cash offer. The director suggested that the starting price in the negotiation should be above the Society's previous offer of £1.5 million plus the buyer's premium. If the Society put its offer in writing, Bonhams would submit it to the vendors.

Having made this somewhat unpromising first contact, Radcliffe returned to the Society with a number of suggestions. He advised the Society to discount the threat of litigation. The Society might also benefit from continuing to pursue the inheritance tax idea: the only reason for the vendors to brush away such an offer would be if they had already moved the asset offshore. In this instance, the Inland Revenue might be interested in investigating and the Society could claim the moral high ground in any further publicity surrounding the case. As for the Society's price offer, it should structure its proposal in line with its legal team's advice. It should make one offer for the important papers for which its ownership claim was strongest and the ALR could prevent their sale by registering them as 'in dispute'. The Society should also make an offer for the remainder of the manuscript that could go forward to auction unimpeded, should the vendor insist on doing so.

Radcliffe was fully aware the Society wanted to obtain the whole Folio and reassured it that the suggested separation of the Folio was an unlikely outcome. Who would be interested in purchasing the 'less important' papers? Few UK citizens would bid against the Royal Society. Foreigners might be put off by the object's potential status as a national treasure, making it more difficult to obtain an export licence or perhaps preventing its export altogether. Moreover, changing the lot at the last minute would be an administrative and publicity nightmare for the auction house. By being reasonable and cautious in stating its claim, the Society would probably achieve its ultimate aim at a lower overall cost. Yet Radcliffe also counselled that Bonhams should not be pushed too far: the total offer should be at or above the minimum estimate in the catalogue (for face-saving reasons) and the auction house should earn a significant buyer's premium.

Hardening positions

If Bonhams had expected to resume negotiations at above £1.5 million, Radcliffe's next email would have come as a shock. The Royal Society made an offer of just £600,000 for that portion of the papers which it claimed as its moral and legal property. The buyer's premium on this portion would be subject to negotiation. Adding in the proposed inheritance tax relief scheme, however, the Society's offer would be worth up to £900,000 to the vendors. As for Hooke's 'private papers', its offer would be £250,000 plus the standard buyer's premium. Unless there was significant progress by 9.30am on Monday, the Royal Society would issue legal proceedings to claim title of those parts of the Folio compiled by Hooke and Waller in their official capacity as secretaries to the Royal Society. The ALR would then immediately register them as 'in dispute'.

When Radcliffe next phoned the director – ostensibly to check his email had arrived – the call was taken and he was greeted 'quite warmly'. There would be a negotiation and for the entire Folio rather than its component parts. And yes, the vendors were UK taxpayers and interested in the tax relief scheme. This was a massive step forward, except that the price was far too low. On Sunday evening the director reverted with further details. The vendors' expectations had been shaped by the Society's previous offer of £1.5 million plus buyer's premium. Ten days prior to this, the Society had been able to afford £1,680,000. The vendors were therefore 'ballsy' and demanded a clean deal independent of its eventual tax treatment. While they would cooperate with a tax relief scheme supporting the Society's acquisition of the papers, any financial risk of this not working out would have to be borne by the Royal Society.

Radcliffe felt the vendors did not take the threat of legal action sufficiently seriously. On Monday morning he would need to be ready for battle: with 'the claim form in one hand and a stick in the other to beat them down on the headline figure.'[56] The Royal Society therefore officially informed Bonhams of its intention to claim legal title in the High Court on Monday morning, with the relevant parts of the Folio being immediately registered on the ALR database. At this point the chairman of Bonhams re-entered the fray. He felt aggrieved and misunderstood: his team had worked towards an amicable solution ever since Bonhams had notified the Society about the auctioning of the Folio. It was the Society's fault that the negotiations had broken down. The Society had blown hot and cold: first offering to buy the papers, then breaking off negotiations, then restarting them at the last minute with a third-party representative and finally threatening litigation. Such behaviour was intolerable – was it worthy of the Royal Society? Certainly, Bonhams would continue to work very hard to resolve the issue, as it had all along. There was no need for litigation.

Early on Monday morning, the Royal Society circulated a draft contract among its team. Bonhams would be asked to withdraw the Folio from the auction with immediate effect. The agreed sale price would be £1.2 million, but the buyer's commission payable to Bonhams would be the same as for a sale price of £1.5 million. Everybody would undertake their best endeavours to proceed with a tax-saving private treaty sale, with the British Library stepping in to officially purchase the manuscripts. There was agreement that a commission giving Bonhams the previously offered premium income (reflecting a price of £1.5 million) was a good idea. Decoupling the commission from the sale price would reduce the financial incentive of the auction house to push up the sale price. However, offering the full commission on £1.5 million straight away would make the strategy very transparent and reduce the space for give and take in the negotiation. Better to leave it open, start low and end up at this level. The vendors had still not disclosed how they (or the owner of the house) had come into possession of the Folio, and this suggested their legal claim was potentially quite weak. To test this, the cash offer was reduced to £1.1 million, with a significant proportion coming from the expected inheritance tax relief.

Just as this offer was ready to be made, new information arrived from Bonhams. The tax relief would be considerably lower than initially expected. One of the two vendors was not a UK taxpayer, but, even so, the cited figure did not make sense under the inheritance tax regime. It was not clear what was behind this, but it suggested an inconsistency with the vendors' original story about how they acquired the Folio. The team therefore decided to drop the offer to £1 million. The reasoning is interesting: it felt that the vendors' decision to proceed with the sale and their creation of an arbitrary deadline to resolve the matter now worked against them. The team judged that Bonhams could not go ahead with the sale if the Royal Society served its claim and the ALR registered the papers. But cancelling the auction at such a late hour would also look bad for Bonhams. If the vendors decided to withdraw the Folio, Bonhams would lose its commission. At this stage, a successful last-minute sale to the Royal Society was the best option for Bonhams, shifting bargaining power to the Society and the offer price downwards.

In a classic good cop/bad cop tactic, Radcliffe dangled the carrot of £125,000 plus VAT in buyer's commission, while the Royal Society issued its claim at the High Court. Bonhams received a curt fax, informing its chairman of the Society's intent to pursue its claim against the purchaser, vendor and Bonhams in court should the Folio be sold at auction. However, the Society was still willing to find a compromise solution. Importantly, the claim had been issued but not yet served, giving an option to further ramp up the pressure later. From this point onwards the negotiation intensified. The director responded very positively to the idea of decoupling Bonhams' commission from the sale price but proposed an even higher commission for the auction house. He asked for the offer of £1 million to be put in writing for consideration by the vendors, while the Society's team suggested imposing a time limit on the offer and threatening further price drops.

The next piece of information further bolstered the Society's confidence: apparently the vendors had received the Folio as a gift in 1993. The disappointing tax relief was thereby explained: the UK vendor only had to pay capital gains tax on the gift. The information made it less likely that evidence of a post-1940 sale would come to light to undermine the Society's legal claim. Moreover, with one eye on a potential trial by public opinion in the media, this new development was helpful as it contradicted the vendors' original media story. How did the fortuitous discovery of the manuscript in a dusty old cupboard fit with a fully documented gift? The PR advantage was moving in the Society's favour and the Society's negotiating position hardened at £1 million.

Against a tight deadline

Predictably, the Bonhams director was disappointed by the Society's offer of £1 million: auction houses must guard their reputation for acting in their vendors' best interest. The director complained about the short deadline to avert the serving of the claim, the fact that the offer was so far below the previously rejected offer of £1.5 million and the prominence of the (irrelevant) tax issue as an explanation for the revised offer. Yet, he had no choice but to submit the offer to the vendors for consideration. Time was running short: it was late afternoon on the day before the auction and the Royal Society would serve its claim the next morning. Late on Monday evening the director got back in touch. The vendors' preferred plan of action was to sell to the Royal Society. However, he claimed they were also considering selling to another (mystery) buyer who had scented a bargain and was willing to risk being sued. The director then helpfully spelled out the significant financial risk of legal action to the Society. Should it not revert to an offer close to £1.5 million and do a deal?

Radcliffe was not impressed with the bluster, reporting in his team update: 'He tried not to sound desperate, but I detected a hint of please help.' While Radcliffe did not discount entirely the idea of a rich gambler coming in, the purchase price would have to be really low to make this gamble worthwhile. The offer of £1 million was therefore reaffirmed, plus a £125,000 commission for Bonhams. Moreover, the Society's claim was ready to be served at 9.30am the next day with a press release to be published shortly thereafter. Yet, as Radcliffe put it in his email: 'I very much hope that this can be avoided and that we can work on the announcement of a historic find by Bonhams and a major addition to our national heritage through your expert skill.' Another carrot was being dangled enticingly.

Nothing was heard from Bonhams until the next morning. At 9.54am Radcliffe wrote to the director to state that the Society was ready to serve the claim and that its PR machine was on standby with a press release to be issued at 11.00am. At 10.01am Radcliffe was told that a call from the director was imminent. There was no resolution yet, but Bonhams was awaiting the clients' instructions.

If serving the claim was unavoidable, so be it, but its publication in the press would probably antagonise the vendors and make a deal less likely. The Society decided to wait, while fine-tuning the press release and publication strategy, just in case.

At 10.42am Radcliffe proposed that Bonhams withdraw the Folio from the auction to give them more time to find a solution. He received a reply instantly. Although there was no new development at this stage, there was no need for anyone to make helpful suggestions. Nonetheless, the Royal Society's team were on the alert in case the withdrawal was done quietly to keep the pressure up in the negotiation. Waiting was tense. As the 11.00am deadline passed, Radcliffe put forward a quid pro quo: withdrawal of the Folio from the auction in exchange for delaying the press statement. At 11.11am Bonhams finally asked for the Society's draft purchase agreement for the Hooke papers for the vendors' consideration.

Another flurry of activity in the Society's legal team followed, to finalise the draft agreement, make it watertight and ensure that each side would be responsible for its own legal costs. At 12.40pm the contract reached the auction house and the PR team turned its attention to drafting a press release announcing the last-minute private purchase of the Hooke Folio by the Royal Society. With the auction due to start at 2.00pm all eyes were on the clock. At 1.20pm the manuscript still had not been withdrawn from the sale and the director ominously predicted an 'action-packed afternoon'.[57] Radcliffe resolved to install himself at the Bonhams reception, so as to be on hand should there be some paperwork to sign.

At 2.00pm the auction started, but the vendors still refused to be rushed into a decision. The Folio was lot number 189 and it would take some time to sell the first 188 lots. Finally, with the auction in full swing, there was a call from the director. The purchase price of £1 million had been accepted by the vendors, while Bonhams assented to the buyer's premium of £125,000. But there were a few desired clarifications and amendments to the draft contract. As lot after lot came under the hammer, both sides' legal teams scrutinised each other's amendments and came up with further improvements. At 3.30pm it was agreed there was simply not enough time to fine-tune the official contract. Instead, the director sent three printed copies of the email with the latest agreed terms downstairs to Radcliffe's 'present resting place in the Bonhams reception' for his signature on behalf of the Royal Society.[58] The director's polite 'Thank you for your help in resolving this matter' sounds a little hollow, but as the bidding for lot 145 was underway, the last signature was placed on the paper. It could finally be announced that the Hooke Folio had been sold to the Royal Society in a private sale. Lot 189 was withdrawn from the auction.

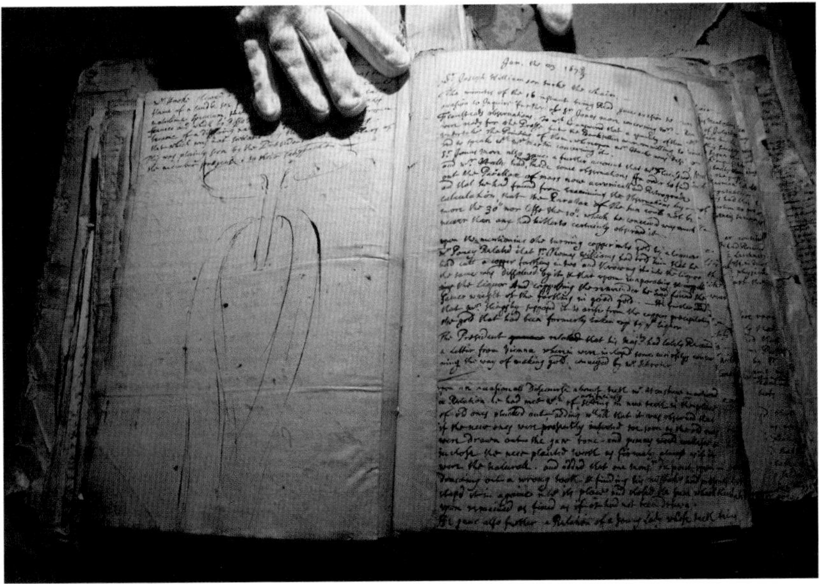

Robert Hooke's Manuscript of the Minutes of the Royal Society for 1661–82.

A last-minute reprieve indeed, but there was no time to rest: there was a press release to be put out. At this point the ALR's priority shifted to securing positive publicity for everyone involved, including the auction house and the vendors. There is no hint of tension in the Society's effusive thank you to the vendors for preserving the Hooke papers over the centuries, and to Bonhams for identifying them and facilitating their return to the Society's archives. Scientists were jubilant, as were the many private donors who had pledged the funds for the private acquisition. And, of course, the ALR was given due credit for its role in saving the Hooke Folio for the nation. All is well that ends well.

Conclusion

It is difficult to set a 'fair' price for a unique piece of national heritage. One might argue that auctions ensure objects go to the highest bidder and therefore to the person or institution that values them most. On the other hand, one might want to balance the interest of the wider community against the immense purchasing power of today's multibillionaire collectors, who can easily outbid any charitable institution serving the public interest. The Hooke Folio negotiation was about finding a mutually agreeable price between the Royal Society and the vendors, with the added complications of the Folio's uncertain legal status and the vendors withholding important information from potential buyers. Initially, the vendors' hopes for a competitive auction propelled their price expectations into the stratosphere. The Royal Society's financial constraints and its resentment of the vendors' attempt to extract every last penny from a cash-strapped public institution drove the two sides apart rather than towards compromise.

This is an unusual recovery story for the ALR. In most recoveries the parties take their time to work out a mutually acceptable compromise. In this negotiation the vendors created an artificial deadline by insisting the Folio would be auctioned at a specific point in time. This turned what could have been a civilised (if lengthy) conversation about a fair division into a game of brinkmanship. Economists often describe situations where two parties have to resolve irreconcilable differences in a short space of time as a 'game of chicken'. The opponents are racing at top speed towards a head-on collision. Neither party wants a crash, but whoever swerves first loses the game.

If we apply the 'chicken' analogy to the Folio case, the threatened court action would be the 'car crash' that both sides would prefer to avoid. Indeed, the only thing that was predictable about the outcome of a legal battle was the immense financial and reputational cost to both sides. The winning strategy in a 'chicken' game is to convince your opponent that you are unable to take action to avoid the crash, and therefore they have to. The Royal Society used two strategies to commit itself to sticking to its position. First, it employed a third party to negotiate the deal and gave it a contract that rewarded a purchase price below £1 million. Second, the Society put in motion a process that would inevitably lead to a High Court action unless the other side conceded. By issuing the claim, registering the Folio with the ALR and finally serving the claim on the auction house, the Royal Society made commitments that could not be reversed easily.

By comparison, the vendors' threat to sell the Folio at public auction lacked credibility once legal proceedings were demonstrably under way. Nothing compelled Bonhams to put lot 189 under the hammer on Tuesday 28 March 2006 and every rational counsel would have advised them against doing so. Could the vendors convince their opposition that they would find a wealthy buyer despite the legal uncertainty over the Folio's ownership? They certainly tried to do so by blithely letting every single Society deadline pass. Yet when Radcliffe strolled into the Bonhams reception on the afternoon of the auction day it was clear the time for negotiating a rise had passed: it was 'take it or leave it'. The vendors avoided the head-on collision in the final approach, printing out a hastily drafted agreement and rushing it downstairs to reception for signing a few minutes before the auction.

From the moment the price was agreed, amicable cooperation was restored. The press briefings focused on saving a unique cultural treasure for the British nation, the venerable Royal Society and the global scientific community. Everyone involved was given due credit. For Bonhams, the outcome was more favourable than a potential public outcry over selling off a national treasure to a foreign billionaire. The ALR had also made sure that none of Bonhams' red lines were crossed: its income had been protected, its customers' anonymity and reputation were preserved, and its price estimate had been validated. Thus, although the negotiation was tough and emotions occasionally ran high, the result was moderate and even-handed. The ALR did not pursue its own financial interest but brokered an acceptable compromise between Bonhams and the Royal Society instead. Radcliffe himself had suggested that Bonhams' premium should be based on the upper price estimate in the auction catalogue even though this eroded the ALR's bonus for keeping the acquisition costs to below £1 million. Once the tax scheme was implemented, the Society's overall costs were probably still below this threshold. However, the ALR presented a bill to the Royal Society charging only the registration and agreement fee, stating that 'the enclosed fee is fair to us'.[59] For the ALR, building a reputation as a fair mediator in art disputes is far more valuable than a one-off profit from driving a hard bargain.

6

Sleeping Beauty: From Grubby Seascape to Saleroom Glory?

Here is a four-million-dollar question: are we looking at a lost masterpiece by J.M.W. Turner or a better than average copy? It is one the art world has been puzzling over for some time, with people coming to radically different answers.

Pro	Contra
'I here propose that this painting is an autograph work by Turner.'	'like hundreds of other "Turners" produced in the nineteenth century'
'probably genuine'	'unusual to the point of oddity'
'beautifully executed'	'less fluent and more studied … limp and ineffectively realised'
'Almost certainly by Turner'	'no merit at all'
'A demonstrable connection to Turner's hand'	'The artist has been able to recreate aspects of the appearance of a Turner'

But the pattern of responses is not random. Only two Turner connoisseurs categorically made up their mind: one in favour and one (more senior voice) decidedly against. The large majority of Turner experts' opinions crucially depended on what they (thought they) knew about the provenance of the painting. But would the evidence documenting the painting's history impress the ALR experts?

Fakes, forgeries and financial crime in the art market

With stolen masterpieces near-impossible to sell on the open market, crooks have turned to other ways of supplying desirable artworks to investors and collectors desperate to acquire them. Forgers and conmen have been incredibly creative in their efforts to smuggle additional artworks into the oeuvre of famous artists. Therefore, the art world is justifiably sceptical about accepting unknown paintings found in random attics as bona fide works of great masters. To succeed, forgers have to clear three hurdles.

First, they must provide a credible provenance for the artwork. Genuine works of great masters should leave a trail in the historical record. Any painting or sculpture in the style of a renowned artist that appears from nowhere is deeply suspicious. One would expect autograph works to be referred to in the artist's diaries, work-shop records or their estates. They should be mentioned in the catalogues of museums or

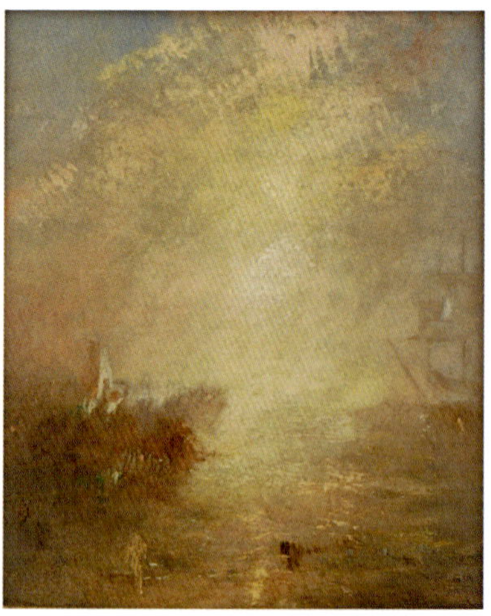

A seascape painting in search of its author.

inventories of stately homes, or recorded in well-known private collections. They would – perhaps repeatedly – have been sold at auction over the years. But a good provenance is not a guarantee of authenticity. Several major art world scandals involved forgeries with fake provenances. Famously, the British fraudster John Drewe sold mediocre paintings by his accomplice John Myatt on the strength of bogus provenances generated by introducing false information into the archives of major collections.[60] The German forger Wolfgang Beltracchi faked an elaborate photographic record for a fictitious pre-Second World War art collection that he used as a vehicle for selling millions of dollars' worth of his own counterfeit paintings.[61] Alternatively, forgers can try to recreate a long-lost masterpiece and take advantage of its existing provenance, or – as Ely Sakhai famously did – create a copy of an artwork and sell the copy with the provenance of the original and then sell the original artwork on its own merits.[62]

Second, the work must convince the art world's key experts on the artist's oeuvre to accept it as their autograph work. Art historians will check whether the work fits the artist's style, techniques, colour choice and subject matter of the proposed period of the painting. Connoisseurs are deeply familiar with the artist's work and look for subtle clues that allow them to recognise the painter's hand. Sceptical outsiders are often unconvinced when intuition is invoked to identify genuine works in statements like 'it's like recognising a friend's voice on the telephone' or 'you can just feel his presence in the room'. Indeed, many respected connoisseurs have been fooled by artworks that were later exposed as deliberate forgeries or mere copies. The market therefore increasingly looks for a consensus of expert opinion rather than a single endorsement.

Third, the object will be put under the microscope. Unless an artwork literally has the maker's fingerprints all over it, forensic scientists cannot identify who painted a picture. However, they can tell whether the materials would have been available to the artist at the time and whether they are similar to those known to have been used by the artist. Many later copies of artworks and outright forgeries were exposed by scientists as being 'of the wrong period' entirely. Forgers therefore put considerable effort into sourcing old canvases, pigments and stretchers. An easier alternative is to find contemporary copies or pastiches that will pass the scientific test and – suitably 'restored' (that is, enhanced) – will fool the connoisseurs into accepting them as a work of a master. Scientists also employ imaging techniques to study any underdrawings and identify changes in the composition as the pictures developed. Copying a painting is a very different process from producing an original artwork. Once again, this is something a determined and well-informed forger could take into account.

Each of the three tests is therefore flawed and can be circumvented. But it is very difficult to pass all three tests at once. For anyone who is convinced they have discovered a genuine masterpiece in a junk shop or at a flea market, the process of rehabilitating it will probably be time-consuming, expensive and often deeply frustrating. However, discovering a so-called 'sleeper' can be hugely lucrative. A dark and dusty canvas picked up for a few hundred pounds might eventually fetch millions or even tens or hundreds of millions in the world's most glamorous auctions, as the painting *Salvator Mundi* proved. The picture dates to around 1500, but is it by Leonardo da Vinci? For centuries it had been considered the work of a follower or at best a workshop copy. Yet, after a highly skilled restorer brought out (or arguably filled in) the features the Leonardo experts would be looking for, a provenance researcher staked her reputation by linking it to a royal collection and a few key experts endorsed its inclusion in a major exhibition, it was sold as 'the last Leonardo' for US$450.3 million in 2017.[63]

This is a business model that would not only suit enthusiastic (and well-heeled) amateur art historians and bargain hunters, but also fraudsters. An attractive painting in a fashionable style and of the correct period can be tweaked into a condition likely to deceive.

There is yet another way to multiply the supply of masterpieces: by selling stakes in or securing loans against valuable artworks. As long as investors do not ask to take actual possession of the artworks but permit the crooks to store them on their behalf, the same object may be offered to several parties. One example is Inigo Philbrick, who stands accused of selling overlapping stakes in several artworks, so that the sum total of the shareholders' interests exceeded 100 per cent. His disappointed investors are now engaged in lawsuits over who owns the objects.[64] If all the buyers had registered their financial interest with the ALR, the competing claims on the artworks would have quickly raised the alarm and Philbrick might have been caught much earlier. And perhaps further irregularities would have come to light, as they did in the case of Frank Faryab.

Fake or Fortune?

Like most 'sleeper' stories, we start with an old, dark, grubby painting and a rumour that it might be a long-lost masterpiece, by J.M.W. Turner. Frank Faryab, an art and antiques dealer, acted on a tip-off, acquired it and took it to a restorer. Once the thick layer of degraded varnish, surface dirt and areas of previous infill were removed, the subject matter became much clearer. It was a seascape bathed in warm sunlight with an indistinct shape on the left and a ship approaching from the right. Having consolidated the wooden panels, the restorer filled in the losses and retouched and corrected any 'blemishes, cracks and unsightly accretions'.[65]

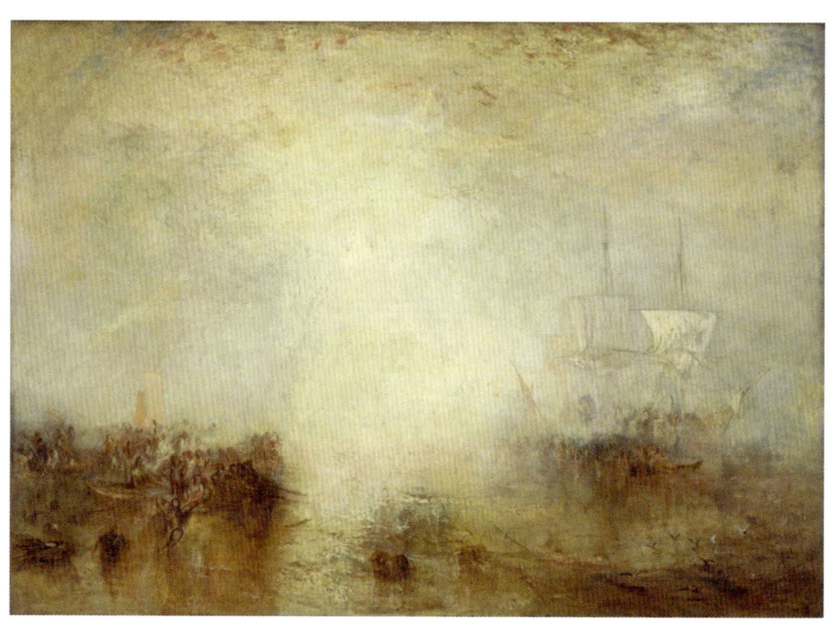

Joseph Mallord William Turner (1775–1851) *'Hurrah! for the Whaler Erebus! Another Fish!'* (c. 1846), Tate.

They also discovered a thumbprint on the canvas: someone – presumably the artist – had accidentally touched it when it was still wet. Faryab then researched his 'Ships at Sea'. He thought it looked very similar to the central portion of a famous Turner painting, the clumsily titled *'Hurrah! for the Whaler Erebus! Another Fish!'* (*c.* 1846; Tate). The picture was certainly attractive in its golden period frame, but could Faryab convince the art world that he had found a genuine Turner painting?

When somebody comes forward with a sleeper, they encounter a wide variety of responses. There is always a demand for works by famous artists. For many collectors the name of the artist is at least as important as the quality of the artwork. As even minor pictures by well-known artists can sell for millions, dealers and auction houses tend to be positive about new masterpieces entering the market. Museum curators are at the other end of the spectrum: they are charged with protecting the integrity of the historical record and the painter's reputation. They have nothing to gain from diluting the master's oeuvre by supporting the inclusion of indifferent works in the canon. For private experts – connoisseurs and art historians – there are two countervailing incentives. On the one hand, making an important discovery raises their prestige in the art world. On the other hand, they risk ridicule when their peers fail to endorse their opinion, or it is later revealed they have been taken in by a fake or forgery. Most experts therefore carefully hedge their bets by weighing up all the available evidence as well as their peers' reactions before issuing their verdicts, for a fee payable regardless of the outcome.

Faryab knew he faced an expensive uphill battle to have his seascape accepted as Turner's work. He decided to approach friends and colleagues with an offer to share both risks and rewards. Mrs D, one of his business partners, took a gamble and bought a share in the picture. She and Faryab elected to investigate along four lines. First, if the thumbprint on the canvas was Turner's it would be highly convincing evidence. They therefore commissioned an eminent fingerprint specialist to examine it. Second, they would show it to some Turner experts – starting with the all-important curator at the Tate Gallery – to check whether the painting would pass the Turner test on stylistic grounds. Third, they would commission scientific tests to exclude the possibility that the artwork was a later copy or a recent forgery. Fourth, one of Mrs D's friends, a former librarian and amateur historian, would check auction records to establish a provenance for the painting. Mrs D paid for the fingerprint analysis and Faryab gave her a handwritten receipt to document her 30 per cent share 'in return for monies transferred to Frank Faryab'.

Gathering evidence

In late 2008 Faryab showed his trophy to the curator at the Tate for some free advice. What would the senior specialist in charge of the largest collection of Turner paintings in the world think of this painting? Was there any chance it might be a 'version' of or a 'study' for Turner's whaling pictures? Britain's major museums are all engaged in research about their collections. It is part of their public service to examine relevant objects brought in by members of the public. Predictably, they have a lot of experience in gently letting down the high hopes of people who come in with poor copies to spare them the expense and trouble of further investigations.

Although the curator thought the painting was of a higher quality than most of the copies people brought into the Tate, he expressed his reservations clearly when he wrote to Faryab. The seascape was atypical of Turner's work in many respects.

Faryab's picture appeared to be a 'near-replica' of the central part of a painting, something that was unknown in Turner's work. When Turner made preparatory oil sketches for his larger compositions, they were always of the whole picture and tended to be less finished and more fluid. Turner almost always worked on canvas, but this painting was on a wooden panel. This was the sort of material an art student might have used to make a copy of an artwork. The *Erebus* painting had been exhibited at the Royal Academy of Arts in London and in Edinburgh so there were opportunities for contemporaries to produce high-fidelity copies.

The curator further opined that even if the thumbprint discovered by the restorer turned out to be Turner's it would still not prove he was the painter. Turner could easily have touched someone else's work while it was wet, most likely that of his studio assistant Francis Sherrell, who took art lessons from Turner.[66] And last but definitely not least: why was there no provenance at all for the seascape? Without a credible paper trail, this painting would really struggle to be accepted in the market. Although the curator did not completely dismiss the possibility that it could be a Turner painting, reading between the lines his opinion was that it was far from investment grade. Yet, as Faryab seemed absolutely determined to devote more resources to his quest, the curator suggested the names of four key experts. For this unprovenanced painting to be exhibited or sold as an autograph work of Turner, Faryab would need the support of at least three of them.

Scientists to the fore

In late March 2009 Faryab and Mrs D read the fingerprint analyst's report with mounting excitement. The expert had made a very detailed study of fingerprint impressions in Turner's output and had found 3,000 examples: around 10 per cent of Turner's paintings have fingerprints on them. However, the 'overwhelming majority' of fingerprints are on his watercolours. They are used intentionally and with artistic purpose, such as creating soft transitions between darker and lighter areas. The thumbprint on the seascape, however, was an (unparalleled) accident. The only other left thumbprint in the entirety of Turner's oeuvre was on the artist's paintbox. The expert had studied the two images in great detail and concluded that '[the] two impressions compare in ten characteristics'. His baseline verdict seemed very encouraging: 'The examination of the Faryab painting reveals a demonstrable connection to Turner's hand in terms of contact evidence.' However, one needs to read between the lines again: a 'demonstrable connection' is far from incontrovertible proof.

Faryab and Mrs D took the result at face value and commissioned a laboratory highly respected for art analysis to date the painting and place it in the context of Turner's workshop. The investigation was extremely comprehensive. The forensic scientist identified fifteen different colours in the painting in areas that were unlikely to have been restored. He sampled and analysed each of them and compared them to pigments known to be in use in Turner's time. His report of 27 March 2009 concludes that '[t]here are no counterindications for a nineteenth century origin for the Seascape'. Moreover, '[none] of the pigments falls overtly outside Turner's known choices'. Thus, '[t]here is no basis … to reject such an attribution'. However, he continues 'that said, [Turner] appears to have exploited a very wide range of pigments generally and that therefore there is some correspondence is not so surprising.' Unfortunately, 'none of the more unusual pigments Turner is known to have at times employed or have access to were found on the Seascape such as indigo or iodine scarlet.'

Not only was there nothing that would have permitted a positive identification, but the forensic expert was also highly suspicious of the pine panel. Although wooden panels are rare in Turner's oeuvre, a few of his early works were painted on pine panels. They were a cheap option readily derived from furniture, coach or interior panelling. The knot in the wood in one of the boards found and later carefully stabilised by the restorer points to such a lowly origin. But Faryab's seascape was not an early work, when Turner might have economised on his materials. The pigment analysis established 1828 as the earliest date at which the seascape could have been painted: the year in which synthetic ultramarine blue first became available. Turner was a famous artist at this time and when he painted on wood it was of the highest quality, that is, mahogany. The picture's background was thus completely different from 'the prepared panels found in some of his works from the 1830s, such as those from Davy, which are of hardwood and were seemingly grounded using "gesso" or an "absorbent Flemish ground". The only comfort Faryab and Mrs D could draw from this report was that the painting was of the right period.

The fine art dealers that Faryab and Mrs D consulted were cautiously optimistic, but so far they were a long way away from making a profit. One of them sent the following valuation in September 2010: 'I have a Client for the above painting. The offer is in the sum of £40,000 … once authentication is complete the offer would be substantially more. In my opinion the above painting is by Turner as I have personally examined the x-rays. We are now awaiting further authentications.'[67]

A perfect provenance

Then the provenance researchers came back with a very exciting result. There had been a painting called *Whalers* in the famous Woolner sale in June 1875 at Christie's that had exactly the right measurements: 45.7 × 61 cm (18 × 24 in.). The painting's similarities to the central section of Turner's picture of the whaler *Erebus* made it possible that it could have been sold under this title in 1875. Thomas Woolner had been a Royal Academician and had owned several artworks by Turner. If Faryab's seascape had been in the Woolner sale, it had an impeccable provenance. It was finally time to introduce the painting to the connoisseurs. Faryab took his picture to the Freeport in Geneva and arranged for the key gatekeepers to view it there. There was a major breakthrough: a famous dealer in Turner's watercolours – and one of the Tate curator's list of 'big four' – was very happy to endorse the painting in a letter to Faryab dated 13 October 2010: 'I am led to the conclusion that this work is almost certainly by Turner rather than being derived from his work. Undoubtedly this is a picture which deserves to be taken seriously.'

The next expert, an eminent art historian, was unconvinced. Although he thought the painting had some aesthetic merit and he took the fingerprint evidence at face value, he 'found the portrait format for this type of work unusual to the point of oddity.' When Turner painted landscapes, he used the landscape format. The art historian confirmed it 'would be extremely persuasive if one could prove that the Faryab picture was the work mentioned in the Woolner sale.' However, he noted that the dimensions of the *Whalers* at the Woolner sale were reported as 18 × 24 inches, indicating the painting was in a landscape format. At such a major public event it was unlikely the numbers had been reversed in error. The real *Whalers* must be somewhere else. With doubts about the provenance Faryab was back at square one. The art historian counselled:

> My overall feeling is that it is important to build up a consensus regarding the picture which means getting the opinions of a wider range of scholars, including [A] and [B], who both worked for the Tate, have impressive skills of connoisseurship and a deep knowledge of Turner, but are no longer (I assume) bound by Tate restrictions on curatorial attributions.

Faryab decided to follow up on this recommendation. Unfortunately, the first senior specialist dismissed Faryab's seascape outright. The second specialist seemed positive, but did not write an endorsement letter. However, James Hamilton – an art historian and a biographer of Turner – was completely smitten with the seascape: 'It is as if you can feel Turner coming out of the painting'.[68] Ignoring all the warning signs, he decided to stake his reputation on helping Faryab establish it as a bona fide Turner painting.[69] In 2011 he wrote a detailed report for Faryab entitled: 'A Study for the Arrival of King Louis-Philippe in Portsmouth October 1844'. Hamilton had examined the painting closely. After 'prolonged looking' the shape on the right of Faryab's seascape resolved itself into a ship with an exceptionally long bowsprit. This was not a whaler: Hamilton recognised it as that of the *Gomer*, the royal yacht of the King of the French. Turner and Louis-Philippe had been friends in the early 1800s, when the king lived in exile in Twickenham. Turner had gone to Portsmouth to witness the arrival of Louis-Philippe in 1844 on his subsequent visit to Britain. Turner's watercolours and an ink drawing done at or near the time clearly show that he had noted the characteristic shape of the *Gomer*'s bowsprit.

Hamilton therefore thought the seascape was a stepping

stone between the watercolour sketches and the Tate's two large oil paintings of the king's arrival. Although the study was quite different from these paintings, it could have contributed to the evolution of Turner's ideas for the later whaling pictures: its 'compositional ideas emerging most markedly in *'Hurrah! for the Whaler Erebus! Another Fish!'*. Hamilton was so convinced by his own bright ideas that he brushed off all the objections other scholars had raised. Turner painted on wood occasionally, he painted vertical landscapes occasionally, there is no reason he should not have done both at once. As for the artwork's shaky provenance, Hamilton did not care. He claimed that a number of bona fide Turner paintings had come out of the artist's workshop without the artist's knowledge or permission. Hamilton was certain that Daniel Pound – the son of Turner's last mistress, Mrs Booth – had privately disposed of this group of Turners: '[M]uch advantage was taken of the elderly artist, with or without his knowledge … It seems quite possible that the small panel painting under discussion here, with its authenticated Turner fingerprint into wet paint, is just another of the artist's late works that was somehow removed from the studio before the executors could start an inventory.'

Faryab was finally ready to approach Sotheby's about a potential sale. In these circumstances the seller can sift carefully through the accumulated evidence and present the work in the best possible light. There was no need to include any letters raising the unhelpful questions about the Woolner provenance in the file. Luckily for Faryab, the Sotheby's experts and management liked what they saw in Geneva. Possibly they were at least partially seduced by the hope of a significant commission. Faryab was delighted to receive a draft letter on Sotheby's headed notepaper:

Estuary with vessels by J.M.W. Turner

I am writing to confirm that in our opinion, the painting owned by [gap] which we saw last week in [gap] is by J.M.W. Turner. We would advise a saleroom estimate of £4,000,000 to £6,000,000.

At the pawnbrokers

Rather than rushing into a sale, however, Faryab used the estimate from Sotheby's, his bundle of supportive letters from the experts and the scientific evidence to raise a loan. He approached a lender specialising in short-term asset finance who (at the time) offered loans of up to a £1 million without a credit check. Instead, the loans were secured against valuable assets. Effectively, the company was an upmarket pawnbroker. This was ideal for Faryab: his credit history was chequered to say the least.

Faryab probably did not realise the lender would check the painting's title with the ALR or that the ALR already had his name on file. The ALR had helped the police identify several stolen items seized from Faryab's business in the 1990s. It had taken the police nearly ten years to put the case together, but in 1998 Faryab had been convicted of handling stolen goods. He served an eleven-month prison sentence before his conviction was quashed on a technicality. As Faryab had already served most of his prison term, it was deemed too late to order a retrial and he was released.[70] However, five years later the ALR's contacts were once more on the lookout for a man named Frank Faryab. It seemed that perhaps he had not left prison as a completely reformed character.

'All the hallmarks of a scam'

The ALR's database search for the Turner painting came back clear, but when the experts looked at its provenance things did not quite add up. Faryab had learnt that his picture needed a plausible history, so he had submitted three pieces of information to the lender.

The first part of the provenance located Faryab's seascape in the Woolner sale of 1875 at Christie's, despite the concerns raised by the art historians. Indeed, the ALR art historians found *Whalers* in the 1875 auction catalogue, but it was not sold at the auction: Christie's brokered an aftersale to a Mr Ellis for £325.10. However, the picture did not disappear into obscurity afterwards. It was sold at public auction a number of times before it was finally bought by the Metropolitan Museum in New York in 1896. It has resided there ever since.[71] The provenance of *Whalers* was indeed impeccable, but it was not available to be used for Faryab's painting.

The second part of the provenance gave the painting a nice aristocratic touch. Faryab claimed it had been in the possession of a Viscount Lisburne at Hafod House in Wales. This Viscount Lisburne had allegedly sold the painting to a Sir John Latter in the 1940s, but Faryab offered no evidence for this sale. Hafod House would be a credible abode for a Turner painting: built in 1785, it was widely renowned for its picturesque landscape gardens.[72] The politically active Vaughan family were plausible owners of a Turner painting, too. Wilmot Vaughan, who acquired the title 'Earl of Lisburne' in 1776, held high political office in London in the late eighteenth century and several of his descendants served as Members of Parliament for Cardiganshire.[73] However, as the ALR quickly established, the Hafod estate was never owned by the Vaughan family, who in fact lived at Trawsgoed House across the river Ystwyth from the Hafod estate. Trawsgoed House was sold into public ownership in 1947 and some of the Lisburnes' chattels were offered at a public auction. It so happened that Julian Radcliffe's in-laws had attended this sale and the family had kept a copy of the catalogue. The ALR team checked it carefully several times over, but there was no record of a painting that could conceivably have been the seascape in question. The second part of the provenance provided was therefore also problematic. At best, it confused names, sales and houses. At worst, it was a complete fabrication.

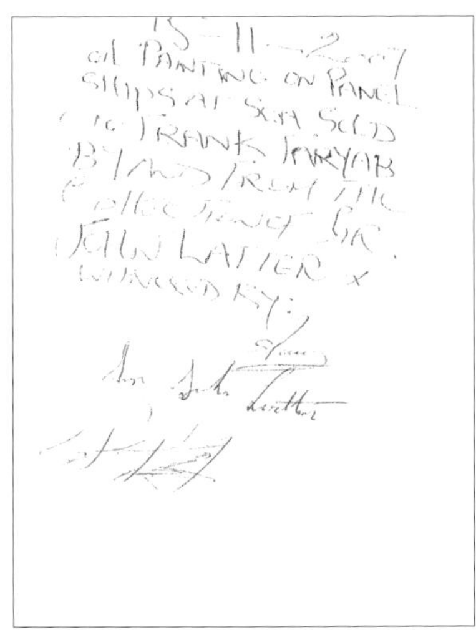

The 'provenance' of Frank Faryab's seascape: '15-11-2007, Oil painting on panel Ships at Sea, sold to Frank Faryab by and from the collection of Sir John Latter & witnessed by Sir John Latter'.

The third part of the provenance was documented by a receipt from 'Sir John Latter' confirming the sale to Faryab, albeit without a price. It was an odd document written in shaky capitals suggesting a person of severe disability or infirmity, or a right-handed person writing with their left hand. Yet, the signature – presumably written by the same person – is much firmer. The ALR staff thought it looked wrong in every way. Normally, a peer of the realm would use headed notepaper and such a document would be typewritten. And apropos peer of the realm, there is no Sir John Latter in Burke's Peerage or in Debrett's, nor a Sir John Luter, Lutter, Lather, Luther or Later. With no evidence that the seller existed, the ALR could not provide a certificate. Its summary of the evidence was devastating: 'The provenance for the work in question is … elaborately researched, but false.'[74]

On 6 June 2011 the ALR gave a very strong warning to the lender: the provenance was weak or discredited and Faryab had served time in prison for art crimes. But the deal seemed like a big opportunity and the management was keen to proceed regardless. The ALR arranged a joint meeting with Faryab and the lender so that it could ask him to provide a fuller picture of the painting's provenance, as well as all the information and permissions needed for the ALR to verify it independently. The meeting went ahead on 8 June. Faryab could give no evidence to dispel the ALR's doubts regarding the object's provenance. He described himself 'as a ducker and diver wheeler dealer in silver, furniture, etc', and talked at length about his successful efforts to build consensus for his Turner in the art world. Yet, he remained suspiciously evasive when pressed for evidence that Sir John Latter existed and that a payment had been made for the painting. The ALR representatives walked away from the meeting thinking 'It had all the hallmarks of a scam.'[75]

Nonetheless, the company executives seemed impressed with Faryab's determination and his (supposedly) massive financial investment in the painting. Even if his background was a little troubling, that did not mean he could not discover a sleeper. Sotheby's had estimated the picture would sell for at least £4 million. Faryab asked for a loan of only £1 million, so the loan-to-value ratio looked excellent. After the meeting, the ALR sent a letter urging the lender to invest in a full provenance analysis, at a price reflecting the ALR's considerable research effort. Disappointingly, the report was never commissioned. The conversation ceased, but the ALR kept the Turner(?) seascape/whaler/royal arrival on its database marked with a red flag. If the painting resurfaced on the market, the next client would be informed of the provenance problems, and any further 'improvements' in the documentation would be noted and cross-checked.

In the summer of 2011 Faryab went back to the Tate to reacquaint the curator with the picture as a study for Louis-Philippe's arrival at Portsmouth in 1844. As the ALR had scuppered Faryab's attempt to claim the Woolner provenance for his painting, he decided to test out a new idea. Perhaps the work had been in the Pound sale at Christie's in 1865? Once more the curator equivocated, writing: 'I was never convinced that all the elements of the picture's provenance had fallen into place. Even now the history might be a work in progress. But it is interesting that James Hamilton, and as you say […] as well, have identified the picture as lot 200 in the Pound Sale at Christie's'. The Tate had already identified several paintings by Turner's studio assistant Francis Sherrell in the Pound sale, so this was not a first-rate provenance. Accordingly, anything from the Pound sale stands or falls by the visual evidence, and pictures with unusual characteristics face a particularly steep uphill battle for acceptance.[76] In terms of the endorsements Faryab had produced, the curator considered the letter from the Turner dealer – one of his original 'big four' – as the biggest step forward: 'you seem to have strengthened your position considerably. Some questions remain, but then in some cases they always will.' As a curator at the Tate he had to remain non-committal, but he ended the letter on a mildly positive note: 'You must now have quite a file of encouraging material, should you need it.'

A high price for fifteen minutes of fame

In spring 2012 Faryab was ready to test the market. The media love sleeper stories, and on 29 April there was a big splash in the newspapers. The *Sunday Times* hailed the formerly 'Grubby seascape' as 'a lost Turner'.[77] Having dazzled the lenders with his expenditure on the research, Faryab foregrounded his massive investment in the press interviews. The *Daily Mail* expressed astonishment: 'Art dealer spends £2million proving obscure oil painting he bought "on a hunch" is lost Turner masterpiece.'[78] However, he had probably gone too far: insiders were immediately suspicious of this figure. How could anyone possibly spend this amount of money on authentication? And why would you if you can get an undisputed Turner painting for less?[79]

Noting that the *Sunday Times* article featuring the triumphant Faryab mentioned a potential Sotheby's sale, the ALR sent a warning to the auction house. Preventing Sotheby's from inadvertently selling a fake would strengthen the ALR's reputation for provenance research and general vigilance. 'In the article of last Sunday, it states that Mr Faryab is in discussions with Sotheby's about a sale and, if so, you might wish to contact us about the provenance.'[80] Genuinely alarmed, Sotheby's got in touch almost immediately. The ALR's research on the picture's provenance raised serious concerns. Of course, the auction house was keen to sell (and collect the commissions on) a multimillion-pound Turner painting. However, the first line of the sales catalogue containing the painter's name is under a warranty. If a buyer realises the auction house has not done its due diligence properly and the attribution is false, it is customary for the sale to be cancelled.[81] If Sotheby's wanted to sell Faryab's seascape as an autograph work of Turner despite its poor provenance, it needed expert consensus on the attribution. Otherwise, its reputation and money would be at stake if the buyer pulled out afterwards.

On 28 May 2012 senior staff from Sotheby's met six Turner experts at the Tate to compare the seascape with *'Hurrah! for the Whaler Erebus! Another Fish!'*. Now they finally had the opportunity to talk directly to each other, rather than being fed positive half-truths about each other's opinions. Unfortunately, only one of the six was convinced the seascape was by Turner: James Hamilton remained a steadfast champion in the face of adversity. Sotheby's conveyed the disappointing news to Faryab, who shared the letter with Mrs D: 'While [A] privately admitted a more positive view of the picture, he was reticent in doing so at the meeting and presumably would be reluctant in public.' This is hardly surprising as there was stiff opposition to the painting: 'At the other end of the spectrum [B] can see no merit at all in the painting.' The other three experts also refused to endorse the painting: '[C] took a measured approach but could not conclude this work was by J.M.W. Turner. [D] and [E] concurred with that view.'[82]

Faryab's hopes for making a fortune were dashed to the ground as Sotheby's stepped back from the sale: 'in the light of the opinions mentioned, amongst others by some leading experts on Turner, I do not think we could offer the painting at auction as a work by the artist.'[83] It was a devastating verdict. It would have been a good time to give up on the painting: there was little hope of ever recovering the costs sunk into its rehabilitation. Any additional spending would be a high-stakes gamble, but Faryab pressed on. He was deeply involved emotionally, but he was also gambling with borrowed money. His debts were mounting fast and 30 per cent of the sale price belonged to his long-suffering business partner Mrs D. There was no way that a mere copy would cover his liabilities. The painting just had to be sold as a Turner.

Trying again

So far, the most objective evidence for the attribution to Turner was the thumbprint found by the restorer and positively identified by the fingerprint expert in 2009. But even this proved impossible to corroborate. When Faryab and Mrs D commissioned a second fingerprint specialist to examine the picture in 2013, his report was much more cautious. Although there were ten areas of similarity between the two available thumbprints, 'these marks would not be seen as acceptable for presentation in court.' The British National Fingerprint standard requires there to be a minimum of sixteen ridge characteristics in sequence of agreement between the crime-scene mark and the suspect: 'This interim report must therefore conclude that although there is strong circumstantial evidence … that they were made by the same person, as a fingerprint expert I simply cannot prove it at this stage.'[84]

In September 2013 Faryab's creditors finally lost patience. They sent in the bailiffs to seize some of his stock, including items that belonged to Mrs D.[85] As she struggled to retrieve her property, Mrs D realised her trust had been betrayed in more than one way. She contacted the ALR on 17 April 2014 to register the painting as 'in dispute': 'Mr Faryab used it as security on a loan with a company called […] without my knowledge … I would like to protect my interest in this painting as at this point I am afraid it may be sold without my knowledge.' Having checked her paperwork thoroughly, Mrs D's claim was officially registered on the ALR database and the ALR put her in touch with the pawnbrokers' lawyers to inform them of her claim and hopefully resolve it.

A jigsaw puzzle with missing pieces

Even now, the various stakeholders hold out the hope that their seascape will eventually be sold as a Turner. The great and the good in the art world still come to radically different assessments of the painting. Provenance plays a fascinating role in the formation of connoisseurly opinion. When the Pound sale provenance of 1865 is taken at face value, we might well be looking at a Turner painting. One expert who had been very hard to pin down previously, wrote a tentative endorsement for Faryab in September 2014 on the assumption that the painting had been in the Pound sale: 'the small work is almost startling in its rough, heavily impasted texture … The impasto of this picture is exceptionally heavy, though not conclusively implausible as Turner's own.' Yet apparently 'the whole picture is convincingly Turnerian' and '[t]his sense of coherence and the absence of any seriously jarring features effectively persuades me that the picture is probably genuine.'

But the Pound provenance cannot be verified. The next expert, writing in January 2015, doubted that the picture had been in the sale of 1865: 'This seems unlikely to me, as I have recently finished an article on that sale for which I am able to account for all but one of the works sold – all of which were on canvas. None of the sizes as given in the catalogue relate to the dimensions of this panel.' And out come all the usual objections: the inadequately prepared pine board, the painting being too developed for a study, the unusual portrait format and an assessment that it is stylistically wrong:

> '…the paint is applied with much smaller brushes than those generally used by Turner himself. … [M]any of the details are less fluent, and more studied in the panel than they are in the original. … Though the artist has been able to recreate aspects of the appearance of Turner's style, a close comparison of the two works demonstrates that the layering of the paint on the panel is an approximation rather than a directly comparable method of building up the image.'

And once again, the dreaded words at the bottom of the letter: 'I regret to say that I cannot support the attribution of this work to J.M.W. Turner.'

And thus, Sotheby's stays on the fence. Even though at least one of the directors remained outwardly positive until 2015, the auction house will not take the risk of the sale having to be rescinded, especially as it is clear that it will not be able to go back to the seller for its money afterwards. Therefore, it advises revisiting the usual gatekeepers: 'I understand that in the past both [X] and [Y] had seen the paintings first-hand. Both have said that they did not believe its authenticity. … Before reacquainting them with the picture I think you need to build up a bigger consensus of positive critical support … I would recommend [Z]'. So round and round it goes. The key will be to finally pin down the painting's provenance such that – as Mrs D's friend the librarian wrote – it 'leaves no gaps for [X] and [Y] to come back with'.

Beauty is in the eye of the beholder

The saga of Faryab's seascape illustrates the importance of provenance in the attribution of paintings. At first sight the system looks like it is based on three equal pillars: science, art historical and connoisseurly expertise, and provenance. But in some cases, provenance is key. Many great masters' pictures were heavily copied during their lifetime: by artisans employed for that very purpose in their own workshops, by freelance copyists, and by students honing their skills through in-depth study of the celebrated artworks of the day. This means that the scientists come back with an open verdict, and the connoisseurs can find it very difficult to make up their minds, unless they get a strong steer from the provenance research. The provenance provided by the owner is not necessarily an unbiased, academic weighing-up of possibilities, however. A freelance provenance researcher employed by the painting's owner may be trying to please their customer (or friend) with the most helpful interpretation of the historical record. This story has shown how tempting it is to embellish or borrow a provenance to ease an artwork past the sternest of gatekeepers into the realms of glory.

The ALR's art historians do not have a financial interest in maximising the sale price of artworks. They have to protect their company's reputation for providing honest and objective opinions on whatever documents are supplied by the seller. Obtaining an outsider's opinion can prevent expensive mistakes, but buyers, lenders, dealers and auction houses may choose to ignore a missing or problematic provenance. If there is credible scholarly support for an artwork and a sufficiently high commission in the offing, an auction house may decide to take the risk of endorsing its authenticity. As illustrated by the upmarket pawnbroker in this case, some companies prefer not to spend money on research that could scupper a promising deal.

With debated attributions, a lot of money can be at stake. It is therefore tempting to bury bad news. Many vendors select the most positive endorsements. Negative opinions have to be inferred from the absence of a key expert's support. Crooks may fill in awkward gaps with plausible fake documents. If we want to protect the integrity of artists' oeuvres, we need a change in norms in the art world: towards the full disclosure of all the available evidence and its independent verification by a neutral third party. Experts who spot fakes or forgeries on the market mostly use gossip and informal warnings to deter the sale of disputed works. Researchers often worry that they might be sued by super-rich art investors if they publish negative opinions. A formal register of disputed works and outright fakes and forgeries, bringing together (positive and negative) peer-reviewed evidence, would therefore be a useful institution for the art market as a whole, even though some would prefer it not to exist.

For Frank Faryab's, Mrs D's and the pawnbroker's 'Turner' the door is still open to eventual rehabilitation, although one fears the possibilities for objectively linking it to the master's hand may by now have been exhausted. Even if the painting is eventually established as a Turner, there is a further hurdle before it can be sold in the open market. To obtain the all-clear from the ALR, Faryab would need to remember from whom he acquired it and provide credible evidence that he did so in good faith.

7

Justice v the Law: Restitution of Holocaust-era Looted Art

Around 600,000 art objects have a peculiarly grim and melancholy history. During the Third Reich an estimated six million Jews were murdered by the Nazis (or their collaborators) and their property was confiscated. Several hundred thousand Jews managed to flee from Nazi-occupied European countries. Some Jewish families had owned notable works of art, antiques, jewellery, musical instruments and antiquities. A few could sell their treasured possessions at fire sale prices, many more had their property confiscated, while others left everything behind as they fled their homes in fear for their lives. Jewish art dealers were forced to abandon their entire trading stock or sell it to their German employees for a pittance. Elite Nazi officials usually took the first pick from famous collections: for public museums, as their private spoils, as gifts to their family and friends, or to reward their collaborators. Whatever was not stolen was auctioned off for the benefit of the Nazi regime.

Over the years, many Nazi-looted objects have been resold multiple times without the issue of their troublesome provenance ever being raised. In most jurisdictions, people who buy something in good faith – meaning they are unaware of a theft – become lawful owners: sometimes immediately on taking possession and sometimes after a three- to ten-year statute of limitation period. Yet, lobbies for the victims of the Nazi regime argue that the wrongs of that dark period should be acknowledged and righted by the restitution of former family property to survivors or their heirs. How are these cases resolved in practice? This chapter shows how private resolutions can trump official legal channels, and how the ALR can help both current and former owners to find just and fair solutions.

The politics of restitution

The moral case for restitution has been made eloquently by people such as Maria Altmann, fighting for the return of Gustav Klimt's painting of her aunt Adele Bloch-Bauer: 'When people see the famous portrait, they see a masterpiece by one of Austria's finest artist. But I see a picture of my Aunt.'[86] Art restitution is about the emotional connection families feel to objects associated with lost or murdered family members and about having the victims' suffering and grief acknowledged publicly. The increasing use of the internet in marketing art objects to an international clientele and the digitisation of public art collections has made it easier for former owners to track down their possessions. Yet when they do, numerous claims for restitution or compensation hit a legal brick wall. Many people perceive this as unfair: the grave historical wrongs perpetrated by the Nazi regime against the Jewish people can and should still be addressed when the opportunity arises to do so.

This is – at least superficially – reflected in political commitments. Forty-four governments participated in the 1998 Washington Conference on Holocaust-Era Assets. They endorsed a series of (non-binding) principles to take steps to identify Nazi-looted art and resolve their ownership in a 'just and fair' manner on a case-by-case basis.[87] However, government commitments apply primarily to art in public collections and restitution is far from assured. Some governments have set up commissions and advisory bodies to adjudicate restitution claims.[88] These weigh up the claims of the former owners against any previously paid compensation and may also consider the public interest in keeping iconic artworks openly accessible to researchers and museum visitors. Even if museum directors are sympathetic, they have a responsibility to protect their collections. Laws and museum statutes often explicitly prevent public collections from deaccessioning objects. The public process of restitution is thus slow and unpredictable. In the first twenty years after Germany and the UK signed up to the Washington principles, only fifteen and twenty-two cases respectively were resolved through the official channels.[89] For example, the legal team toiling for the restitution of the beautiful medieval Guelph Treasure bought by Hermann Göring from a consortium of Jewish dealers in 1935 accuses Germany of 'pretending to care about the issue of Nazi-looted art while doing everything it can to stand in victims' and heirs' way and run down the clock until another generation passes away.'[90]

Some former owners or their heirs have therefore pursued legal cases for restitution of their possessions in the United States. However, this is not a panacea. US law – and particularly the law of New York – is relatively favourable for theft victims, but there needs to be a clear link between the artwork and America for US courts to take jurisdiction. Even then, it may not be appropriate to apply US law, or the courts may not be able to enforce a judgment if the property is located abroad. The US judge ruling on the restitution claim of the Cassirer family for a looted Camille Pissarro painting held by the Spanish Thyssen-Bornemisza Collection reluctantly concluded that 'the Court has no alternative but to apply Spanish law and cannot force the Kingdom of Spain … to comply with its moral commitments'.[91] We thus have a strong moral principle in favour of the restitution of art in public collections but limited legal means of enforcing it, even if governments are broadly supportive.

Looted art in private collections

What about looted art in private collections? How does the art market deal with this minefield of competing claims? Most former owners do not rediscover their artworks until long after their first post-war sale, meaning the statutory periods have long since expired. It is therefore rare for former owners to win court cases for restitution or compensation.[92] But the current holders are seldom immune from the heartache and tragedy that are the basis of every restitution claim. The current laws are clearly unfair, just as mandatory uncompensated restitution would be. Can the private sector improve on the legal process? For many years, holocaust survivors had privately petitioned the people in possession of their family's former treasures for compensation. Sometimes they received a sympathetic hearing, but more often they were sent away empty-handed or offered a derisory payout.[93] Many Jewish families were in dire need of funds and had no choice but to accept whatever paltry sum was suggested. But in the late 1990s the situation began to change. The Washington Conference principles reflected and reinforced a shift in public attitudes towards buying and owning looted art: a property right could be legally watertight yet morally tainted.

Collectors, dealers and auction houses became increasingly concerned about their reputations should their trading of looted art be exposed. As one lawyer put it: 'Yes, we could win this case in a court of law – but what would it look like in the court of public opinion?'[94] Media exposure is a two-edged sword, however. Even if restitution is supported in principle, journalists may well take the side of a sympathetic good faith purchaser. Prominent public figures – such as the curator and art historian Sir Norman Rosenthal – have led a backlash against restitution to Holocaust victims' grand- and great-grandchildren by arguing that 'each person should invent him or herself creatively in the present, and not on the back of the lost wealth of ancestors'.[95] Bernd Schultz, the former director of Berlin's Villa Grisebach auction house, put it even more bluntly: 'When people say "Holocaust", he wrote, 'they mean money.'[96] The threat of adverse media exposure can thus bring both sides to the negotiating table to cut a confidential deal to clear the moral taint from looted art.

With buyers sensitised to the issue of Holocaust-era art and valuations for Impressionist and pre-war modern art shooting into the stratosphere, a business opportunity emerged: offering provenance research and art dispute resolution services to Holocaust survivors and their families. Identifying and mediating competing claims on expensive objects can add considerable value, creating profit opportunities for provenance researchers, negotiators and lawyers. Dealers and auction houses benefit too: many families who regain control of former possessions sell them straight away to share the proceeds among the heirs, as do collectors who have to raise funds for a compensation payment. Traders who ignored the problem or were insufficiently vigilant found that selling looted art could easily turn into a PR and legal nightmare.[97] Predicting that the art market would throw its weight behind resolving restitution and compensation claims, the ALR decided in the late 1990s to make a major investment in building a credible database of historic art losses. By refusing to issue clean search certificates for European artworks with gaps or suspicious names in their provenance during the Nazi period, the ALR could encourage legal owners to engage with the claimants and help broker amicable settlements.

Creating the historic claims database

Historic claims are a very different business model from searching for stolen art, where theft victims provide clear evidence of their ownership and the crime at the time of registration. In the case of Holocaust-era looted art, many former owners perished, and survivors often remained silent about their traumatic experiences. Thus, their heirs might not even be aware of their family's losses. Even if people know of their lost inheritance, proving their claim can be extremely difficult. Many personal documents were lost. Although Nazi Germany's bureaucracy was famously efficient in recording its art crimes, the documents are stored in archives that are (or were) extremely difficult to access and retrieve information from, especially if you do not know exactly what you are looking for. Sometimes it is impossible to prove the precise circumstances of a wartime loss: was the object stolen, looted, confiscated, sold, given away or lent to someone for safekeeping? If there was a sale, was the object sold involuntarily and for a fraction of its value? There is also the possibility that looted objects were returned to their former owners after the war and are back on the art market legitimately. A museum, collector or dealer approached by a Holocaust survivor or their heirs is therefore likely to ask for proof that the claim is legitimate.

Providing commercial services to identify Holocaust-era loot on the art market is a risky undertaking. For the ALR, collecting the information for a database for such art required a large initial investment. Registrations of Holocaust-era losses were offered without charge, as the ALR was in competition with multiple charitable and government-sponsored databases. The ALR also had to make difficult decisions on what exactly should be registered. First, what proof would be required to register a missing object? What happens when survivors and heirs have gathered only limited evidence to support their claims? Nobody has an incentive to carry out the complex research until the missing heirlooms appear on the market and the current holders demand to see proof of ownership. Second, what about registering artworks that had been reported as looted during the war but for which nobody was actively looking? Should they be part of a comprehensive database creation effort, too? On the one hand, setting high barriers for registration lowers the probability of finding Holocaust-tainted objects and earning location or settlement fees. On the other hand, the cost of investigating claims that fall apart after many hours of hunting down information or where the new owners resisted making a settlement could easily outweigh the returns from the successful cases. Moreover, if the ALR made claims for compensation that turned out to be spurious on closer inspection, it could easily undermine the reputation of the entire enterprise. The ALR had to tread very carefully. The two cases below illustrate the problems, opportunities and immense satisfaction of working on the restitution of Nazi-looted art.

Femme en Blanc

In 2001 the ALR received a search request for Pablo Picasso's 1922 *Femme en Blanc* from a German dealer. Its provenance information, 'Private Collection, Paris', seemed vague and might be queried by sophisticated art buyers. Paris was known as a major centre for trading Nazi-looted art during the Second World War. It would be risky to buy a major painting without checking out its former owners. The ALR's search came up clear: nobody had registered this Picasso on the ALR database. However, as Holocaust survivors and their heirs were only just beginning to register their losses with the ALR, this was not a clean bill of health. The ALR advised its client that this multimillion-dollar painting should not be acquired without a full provenance. It offered to do the research at an hourly rate, but the dealer was reluctant to make that investment and drew back on the warning. Over the next year, the ALR's Historic Claims Division steadily added new registrations and information from public sources to its database. One key source was a reference list of valuable paintings and antiques looted in France between 1939 and 1945.[98] In early 2002 a Parisian dealer expressed an interest in *Femme en Blanc*. He had been given more reassuring provenance information: 'Artist's Family ca 1960; Eugene Thaw; Stephen Hahn; Private Collection, Chicago since 1966'. But the ALR now found a match on its database: Picasso's *Femme en Blanc* had been reported as stolen from the private apartment of the well-known gallery owner Justin Thannhauser shortly after the German troops arrived in Paris in 1940.

The ALR informed the dealer of the potential issue and immediately began to look for the (heirs of the) former owners. Thannhauser had fled from Paris to Switzerland and had subsequently emigrated to the USA, where he resumed his trade. He had died in 1976 having donated most of his famous art collection to major museums in Switzerland and the USA.[99] As there were no surviving children, his second wife, Hilde Thannhauser, created the Silva-Casa Foundation to distribute the couple's remaining estate among Swiss arts charities after her death (in 1991).[100] Undoubtedly, Silva-Casa was the legal heir of the Thannhausers. But if the foundation wanted to make a compensation claim it would have to prove three things. First, that the painting had belonged to the Thannhausers. Second, that it had been looted by the Germans rather than having been sold or given away. Third, that there had been no settlement or a restitution in the post-war period. The ALR also needed to find out the identity of the current holder and investigate the strength of their title claim. Its main lead was the dealer in Paris who had

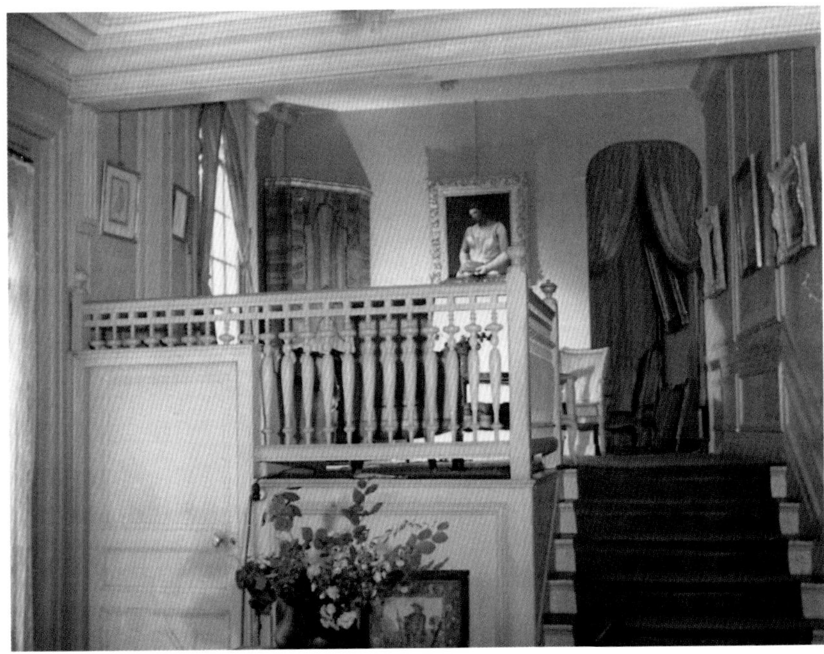

Photograph of Justin Thannhauser's apartment in Paris taken before the German invasion with *Femme en Blanc* (1922) by Pablo Picasso (1881–1973) in the background.

made the search request, but he did not know the identity of the owner. He was keen to buy the painting and – if necessary – clean its tainted title before resale. He therefore offered to contribute to the cost of the ALR's next round of provenance research.

The ALR's first step was to make an appointment with the Silva-Casa Foundation in Berne. Sarah Jackson (now Lavington), the ALR's historic claims director, was shown a treasure trove of documents relating to the Thannhausers' historic art losses. Silva-Casa's archivist had already sifted through the papers and had put together a file on Picasso's *Femme en Blanc*. She had found a photograph showing the painting prominently displayed in the Thannhausers' Paris flat. The photograph had been included in a large file reporting the wartime loss of precious antiques to the French and German authorities to facilitate their restitution. A close-up shot of the painting was annotated on the reverse in

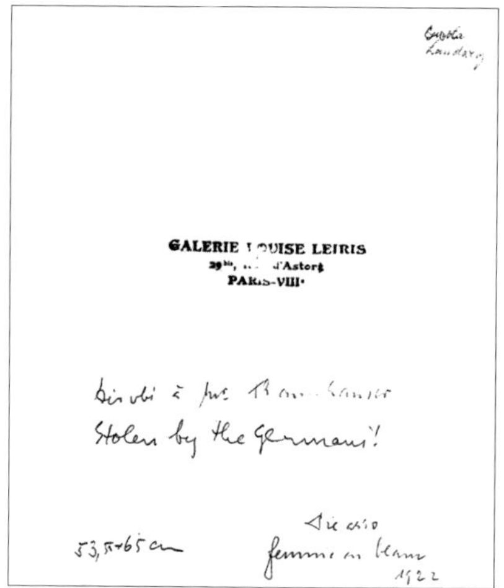

Reverse of Justin Thannhauser's photograph of the lost Picasso *Femme en Blanc*, annotated with the name 'Carlota Landsberg' and 'Stolen by the Germans!'.

Justin Thannhauser's own handwriting as 'stolen by the Germans'. With this poignant evidence in hand, the Silva-Casa board members decided they should try to pursue a claim and distribute the proceeds to the charities favoured by the Thannhausers. The foundation asked the ALR to continue the provenance search and start a negotiation with the current holder.

In the meantime, the Parisian dealer had divulged the name of the gallery representing the owner of the painting: David Tunkl Fine Art in Los Angeles. The ALR asked David Tunkl to forward a letter to the owner. In late April 2002 a reply came from a Mrs Marilynn Alsdorf, the widow of a Chicago magnate and a well-known patron of the city's arts scene. The Alsdorfs had amassed a collection of fine Impressionist paintings including several Picassos from the 1950s onwards.[101] Alsdorf identified herself as the owner of *Femme en Blanc*, appending her purchase receipt to the letter. Alsdorf was a co-founder and a generous benefactor of the Chicago Contemporary Art Museum,[102] and widely known as 'the queen of the Chicago arts community'.[103] She asked the ALR to negotiate a resolution of its claim with her attorney. Her lawyer's response was guarded, however. Alsdorf had bought the painting in 1975 in good faith. She was absolutely certain she had good title. As for a 'moral' claim based on Nazi-era looting, very little had been proved so far. There would be no negotiation without further evidence.

Alsdorf's purchase receipt showed the painting had been exported from France in 1975. The ALR therefore decided to obtain a copy of the export certificate. When a copy was retrieved from the archive, it indicated the Picasso had come from a gallery called Renou and Colle. This firm is included on the 'Red Flag' list of the post-war Art Looting Intelligence Unit of 1945/6 for its close contacts with the notorious dealers in Nazi-looted art, Albert Skira and Hildebrand Gurlitt.[104] When confronted with a second piece of evidence of a Holocaust taint Aldorf's lawyer tentatively began a tough negotiation. His client had stated that the heirs could at most hope for a few hundred thousand dollars as a full and final settlement. Even if the painting had been looted in 1940, the ALR had not proven that the Thannhausers had not been reunited with their Picasso or been compensated in the meantime.

A flying changeover

To strengthen the Thannhausers' claim, the painting needed a full provenance from the date of its creation in 1922. When had Thannhauser acquired *Femme en Blanc* and from whom? The ALR found a reference in a 1927 book identifying a Robert Landsberg as the previous owner of the painting.[105] This matched up with the name 'Carlota Landsberg' written by Thannhauser in the top right-hand corner on the reverse of the close-up photograph of *Femme en Blanc* in the archive. The ALR's further research revealed that Robert Landsberg was a prominent member of the Berlin arts scene in the 1920s. He had owned an arts bookshop-cum-gallery very close to Thannhauser's own, but no information could be found to verify the sale of the Picasso to Thannhauser. The ALR obtained power of attorney from the Silva-Casa Foundation so that it could request a (manual) search of the vast German archives detailing post-war compensation and restitution claims.[106] It was in for a surprise. Thannhauser had never claimed compensation for the Picasso looted from his apartment in Paris. Although he had initially submitted a claim for the entire contents of the flat, he had later struck *Femme en Blanc* off the list. He wrote a letter to the German authorities to explain the painting had been sent to him by Charlotte Landsberg from Berlin for safekeeping in 1938 or 1939. So who and where was Charlotte – or Carlota – Landsberg? It seemed unlikely she had survived until 2002, but were there any living heirs? The ALR went back to the Silva-Casa Foundation with the disappointing news but gained its wholehearted support for tracking down the true owner. Yet, when it informed Alsdorf's lawyer of the unexpected complication it received a threatening letter by return of post. The attorney claimed the ALR had no right to interfere with the sale of the painting if it did not even know the identity of the former owner. Alsdorf would sue the ALR unless it immediately removed the painting from its database and let the sale proceed.

The ALR had to find Charlotte Landsberg fast, but it could not search the German archives for her documents unless it represented her (unknown) heirs. More genealogical research was urgently required. Sarah Jackson found that Robert Landsberg had died in 1932. There were rumours his widow had emigrated to Palestine, Paris or perhaps to Argentina in the late 1930s. The ALR contacted every

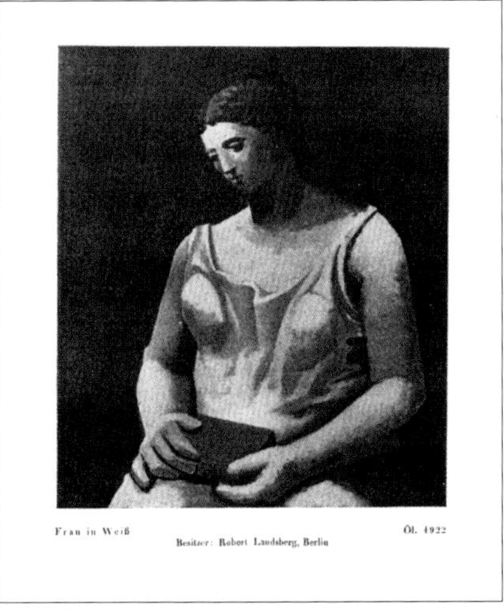

Photocopy of the entry for *Femme en Blanc* in Oscar Schürer's 1927 book obtained by the ALR, which mentions Robert Landsberg as the painting's owner.

organisation in the world tracking Jewish refugees to help it trace Charlotte Landsberg. Silva-Casa could not find any post-war correspondence between her and Thannhauser in its archive. However, archivists in the Wiedergutmachungsämter[107] in Berlin unearthed a copy of a letter from Thannhauser to Landsberg about the stolen Picasso. Writing to her at an exclusive residential hotel in New York in 1958, Thannhauser confirmed Landsberg's ownership of the painting to enable her to make a compensation claim. Jackson gave the hotel a call, but no one in the office knew of a Mrs Landsberg. When she sent someone to make enquiries in person, however, one of the doormen remembered the old lady, saying she had passed away in the early 1990s. He also recalled she had been visited frequently by her grandson. The search therefore moved on to the death registers of New York. Indeed, a Carlotta Landsberg had passed away in Manhattan in 1994 and her death was reported by her grandson, a Mr Thomas Bennigson from Ohio.

The ALR traced Bennigson across the USA to California, where he was studying for a law degree at Berkeley. The ALR's initial approach was met with scepticism.[108] Here was a foreign company proposing to negotiate a seven-figure compensation claim for a painting Bennigson knew nothing about. He had been very close to his grandmother, but she had never mentioned *Femme en Blanc* to him. Was this a scam? As the ALR asked for a percentage recovery fee rather than a down payment, he decided to give it a try. Bennigson provided the ALR with documents proving he was Carlotta Landsberg's only living descendant and heir. He appointed the ALR as his proxy, so it could once more search the German archives for the correspondence detailing Landsberg's efforts to recover her artwork(s) after the war. This time it struck gold: Landsberg had never given up the search for her missing Picasso. Even though she had accepted some money from the German government in compensation in 1969, it was on the understanding that both sides would keep looking for the painting. The transaction would be reversed as soon as the picture was restored to her. Even in advanced old age Landsberg had kept up a regular correspondence with the German authorities to confirm her search was ongoing, but unfortunately it had remained fruitless.

Back to the negotiation table

Nobody could now deny the moral case for compensation of Landsberg's heir: it must be worth more than the 'few hundred thousand dollars' Alsdorf's lawyer had put on the table for the Silva-Casa Foundation. The negotiation resumed: the ALR was aiming for a swift settlement with a compensation payment between US\$2 million and US\$3 million. Although the painting was worth around US\$10 million, Alsdorf would have to pay capital gains tax if she sold it, leaving her with around US\$6.5 million. Bennigson was asking for less than half of this money. He also offered Alsdorf an alternative option: she could pay US\$5 million to a charity of his choice and take advantage of the tax break. However, Alsdorf's lawyer dug in: his client had bought the Picasso in good faith in 1975 from a dealer who had obtained good title under French law. This formidable woman would not bow to pressure and she was certainly not afraid of the media exposure a court case might bring. She and her husband were known as scrupulous collectors. Indeed, the couple had been among the first subscriber-members of the International Foundation for Art Research (IFAR) that collated and published information on stolen art. Marilynn Alsdorf's charity made regular donations to IFAR and she had personally invited its staff to give a talk in Chicago on 'The tension between law and ethics in the restitution of WW2-era looted art'.

As Alsdorf's attorney appeared to be heading towards a legal stand-off, the ALR recommended Bennigson should engage a legal expert, too. It suggested several attorneys, including the young lawyer E. Randol Schoenberg who was creating a furore in the art world with his campaign to retrieve five Klimt paintings from the government of Austria on behalf of Maria Altmann.[109] Being of Austrian Jewish descent himself, he connected deeply with the grievances of Holocaust victims and their desire for justice. When Bennigson was first told about his (largely moral) claim on the Picasso, he wanted a swift and amicable resolution. The ALR's recovery contract reflected this: Bennigson would pay a percentage fee on the first US\$500,000 of his net gain to the ALR, a reduced percentage on the next million dollars and an even lower one beyond US$1.5 million. In addition, the ALR's percentages decreased over time, with the contract terminating after five years. But Alsdorf's attorney had antagonised Bennigson with his condescension and the haggling over the compensation. Schoenberg sympathised. He had a completely different objective from the ALR: to make legal history and turn the tables on the owners of looted art. He encouraged Bennigson to demand the outright restitution of his grandmother's looted Picasso. It looked like a long shot, but a new law was coming into effect in California on 1 January 2003 extending the statute of limitation on Nazi-looted art. This made it considerably easier for Holocaust victims to claim restitutions from museums and galleries, although not necessarily from private collectors. Nonetheless, Schoenberg offered to take on the case on a no-win-no-fee basis. Bennigson would receive his legal expertise for free and only pay for out-of-pocket expenses. In return, Schoenberg would take a hefty cut of winnings, but only if they exceeded US$2 million.

Playing hardball

Alsdorf's lawyer was in for a shock. He had bragged to colleagues about the ALR being a 'pushover' and suddenly he was facing a strident young attorney ratcheting up the pressure on his client. When Alsdorf was told of the restitution demand in mid-December 2002, she was not at all pleased. She had slowly come to accept she would not get the full value of the Picasso on the open market unless she paid some compensation. However, if Bennigson wanted to be difficult, she could just keep this painting and sell another object from her collection instead. She asked her dealer to return the picture to her. When Schoenberg next called Alsdorf's lawyer on 18 December, he was informed gleefully that 'all offers are off the table' and that the painting was 'on its way to Chicago'. Both lawyers knew that if the artwork left California Bennigson's legal claim faced an even steeper uphill battle. Under Illinois law, Aldorf's title was probably secure. Bennigson thus hastily filed suit against Alsdorf in Los Angeles for US$10 million and applied for a temporary restraining order against the painting being removed from California. It was a race against time. On 19 December 2002 Schoenberg was granted an injunction hearing for the very next day and was told to notify Alsdorf's lawyer of this. The advance warning gave the dealer the chance to finalise the shipping arrangements. On 20 December 2002 at 6.36am – just a few hours before the scheduled hearing – the picture left Los Angeles. By the time the restraining order was granted, the plane had already landed in Chicago. As Schoenberg remarked in an email to the ALR, the case was becoming 'more and more like a crime novel'. Was this the end of Bennigson's claim?

Schoenberg did not think the setback was insurmountable. Bennigson could still pursue every legal avenue to have the case tried in California. He would assert the painting had been moved deliberately to evade California's new stance on Holocaust-era art claims. Alsdorf's lawyers countered that the presence of the picture in California had been 'fleeting and transitory'. The Picasso had been bought in New York and was displayed in the Alsdorfs' home in Chicago for decades. Although Marilynn Alsdorf's dealer's gallery was located in California, he had aimed to sell *Femme en Blanc* in Europe. The following years would be spent in a grim struggle to decide whether the case should be tried under Illinois or Californian law. As the story unfolded in the court rooms, the media became fascinated by the battle between the Berkeley law student and the Chicago philanthropist. Although Bennigson worked hard on presenting his side of the story, he failed to land a knockout blow. Alsdorf refused to be drawn into a trial by public opinion and maintained a dignified silence. Her lawyer just repeated that his client was defending her legal rights as a good faith purchaser.

Courtroom dramas

The court cases did not go well for Bennigson. The California Superior Court decided in June 2003 that it did not have jurisdiction over Alsdorf, as 'the wrong in this case did not occur in California, regardless of whose perspective is used'.[110] Schoenberg was 'completely disgusted' by this judgment and encouraged his client to appeal. But the California Court of Appeal confirmed the decision in May 2004. There was only one more chance to keep the case in California: would the California Supreme Court review the case? Schoenberg filed a petition for review arguing that the state of California should protect the right of its citizens to recover Nazi-looted art. The painting had been sent purposely into the state for exhibition and sale. California should not allow foreign defendants to avoid prosecution by simply whisking the disputed property from the state a few hours before a temporary injunction hearing. The Supreme Court agreed unanimously to review the judgment in July 2004, but it would be a lengthy process. In August 2004 Bennigson and Alsdorf finally met in person, although not in auspicious circumstances. When Schoenberg went to Chicago to take Alsdorf's deposition, Bennigson, who had just completed his law degree, accompanied him as a third-party observer.

If the intention had been to normalise or defuse the situation, the plan backfired. The legal war of attrition escalated. In September 2004 Alsdorf's lawyers filed a claim to 'quiet title' in Chicago. There was little doubt the dealer who had sold the painting to Alsdorf in 1975 had obtained it in (what passed as) good faith in France at the time. Under French law, the former owner then had just three years to reclaim their former property from the date the purchaser took possession. Clearly, that period had long expired. In October 2004 Bennigson struck back by applying for a stay in the proceedings in Chicago until the question of jurisdiction was settled in California. But Schoenberg had another ace up his sleeve. Regardless of how the issue of jurisdiction was settled between California and Illinois, moving stolen property across state lines is a federal offence. Having received the ALR's dossier on *Femme en Blanc* that had the words 'stolen' and 'looted' all over it, Alsdorf should have realised the painting was 'hot'. In late October 2004 the US government filed a forfeiture suit against Alsdorf for transporting the artwork in interstate commerce knowing it was stolen, and for receiving, storing, concealing or possessing a stolen object after it had crossed a state boundary.

The Feds come for tea

Accordingly, the FBI called on Alsdorf at her sumptuous residence in Chicago to serve a seizure order. Their surprise visit almost sent the old lady into hysterics, but eventually she calmed down sufficiently to offer them a drink. She explained that she had never seen the ALR's report: the case had been handled entirely by her staff. But henceforward it would certainly receive her personal attention. The officers left the painting in Alsdorf's apartment with strict instructions not to move it again until its ownership was settled. The FBI's call proved a turning point for the case. Alsdorf decided she wanted to put the dispute behind her, ideally with her reputation intact. She expressed her willingness to pay compensation to Bennigson if he formally acknowledged she was the rightful and legal owner of *Femme en Blanc*. The amount was up to negotiation, a process Schoenberg described as 'to use an understatement, arduous'.[111] Although Alsdorf's legal team kept up the pressure in the courts, there was movement behind the scenes. Unlike many other Holocaust cases where ageing claimants were worn down by legal expenses and delays, here the holder was a 79-year-old woman who wanted to put her house in order. Her opponent was young, extremely media-savvy and clearly not intimidated by the expense and risk of multiple lawsuits. If Alsdorf wanted to be remembered as a discerning and scrupulous art collector and a generous philanthropist, she had to end the press fixation with *Femme en Blanc*, at almost any cost.

In June 2005 the parties were finally ready to participate in a formal settlement conference in Los Angeles. Alsdorf was awarded legal title to the Picasso in exchange for a US$6.5 million compensation payment. This outcome was highly favourable to Bennigson: it represented 100 per cent of the painting's total after-tax sale value to Alsdorf. If Tunkl's gallery in Los Angeles was to sell *Femme en Blanc* within the next three years, Tunkl would have to pass 10 per cent of his commission to Bennigson, too. All outstanding lawsuits were dismissed and in November 2005 the case of *Femme en* Blanc was resolved at last. Alsdorf must have deeply regretted refusing the initially proposed US$3 million claim. For Bennigson, Schoenberg and the ALR the two years in court and in the media spotlight paid off handsomely, but it had been a nerve-racking process. Bennigson had invested a six-figure sum in legal costs, while the ALR and Schoenberg had worked hundreds of hours for an uncertain return. All is well that ends well though. The settlement was widely reported, giving other claimants and good faith owners more information about what just and fair solutions might look like.

Resolutions in the (European) mid-market

Most Second World War art losses are in a completely different league from *Femme en Blanc*. Unless one is arguing over a multimillion-dollar asset, it is in no one's interest to engage in expensive and protracted legal action. In any case, many looted artworks remained in Europe, where the law favours good faith purchasers. Unless the current owners take the artwork to the USA for sale, there is no hope of a legal remedy when looted art is discovered in a private collection. However, the same moral arguments and reputational concerns apply. Some collectors are horrified when a Holocaust-era taint is brought to their attention and immediately want to put matters right. Others will also be encouraged to do so by art fairs, dealers and auction houses. Reputable traders would rather reject an artwork with a dubious provenance than risk being exposed publicly as dealing in looted art. Private sales are of course a possibility, but prices are unlikely to match those on the open market. There are therefore both moral and economic incentives to resolve title issues amicably. Landmark legal cases and out-of-court settlements in the USA and restitutions from European museum collections have also contributed to a shift in social attitudes towards accommodating rather than fighting restitution claims, especially if compensation claims are perceived as reasonable. The higher the value at stake, the more commercial options become available for owners and claimants to negotiate a bespoke compensation claim. But many people look for quick resolutions and want to avoid unseemly haggling. An experienced third party that is perceived to be neutral may be able to suggest a solution satisfactory to both sides. The case of *Deer Family* by Friedrich Gauermann is an example of this.

An Austrian family collection

In 2003 the sons of Albert Benbassat instructed their lawyer to register their father's art collection on the ALR database. Benbassat had been a successful banker in Vienna who owned several properties as well as a decent art collection. In 1938 the Benbassats – a Sephardic Jewish family – were forced to flee from their home in Vienna, initially to Warsaw and from there to Romania. Thanks to a close friendship with Hermann Göring's younger brother Albert, the family eventually managed to escape to Switzerland.[112] Their lives were saved, but the family's houses and their contents were confiscated by the Nazis. After the war, the family engaged in a lengthy correspondence with the Bundesdenkmalamt in Vienna to locate its missing art collection.[113] But it had been dispersed long ago: the Nazis had auctioned off the paintings among other pieces of looted art. The Benbassats were able to identify twenty paintings from their art collection in an auction at the Dorotheum in 1939, but nobody could help them trace the buyers or the current owners. By sheer luck, Albert Benbassat's wife Ella found one painting on display at the Hotel Sacher in Vienna and negotiated some compensation.[114] The other pictures remained hidden. Instructing the ALR to monitor the art market was the family's final attempt to make a physical connection with their stolen past.

By the time Albert and Ella Benbassat's sons passed away in 2011 and 2012, the family had made no further progress. Only one painting had surfaced briefly in an Austrian auction catalogue in 2009, where it was spotted by the ALR and two Austrian provenance researchers. The artwork was immediately withdrawn from sale. However, the family's attempt to negotiate an amicable resolution failed and the consignor took it off the market. Despite the media pressure on the owner to settle, the painting never reappeared.[115] After this disappointment, the next generation of Benbassats gave up hope. Thus, when the ALR found *Deer Family* by the nineteenth-century artist Friedrich Gauermann offered for auction in Vienna in April 2017 and got in touch with the family's lawyer, it drew a blank. The lawyer wrote back that he no longer represented the family. His clients had passed away. All he knew was that there were some heirs living in Switzerland, but he had no contact details for them. Once again, it was up to the ALR to engage in genealogical detective work to track them down.

As usual, the ALR asked the auction house to withdraw the painting from sale. It also politely asked the sales team to keep the painting in-house until its status was resolved rather than risking a repeat of the 2009 fiasco when the family's hopes were raised and then dashed. The auction house complied, with the consignor's explicit permission. Here was a golden opportunity for a claim, if only the Benbassats' heirs could be located. Thankfully, Benbassat is a rare name and a Swiss company's entry on Bloomberg led the ALR to one of Albert's grandsons in May 2017, and another awkward cold call. However, in this case the heir had worked with his father for more than twenty years to retrieve the missing paintings. He was not optimistic. So much time had passed, and his generation of the family held out little hope of recovering their grandparents' inheritance.

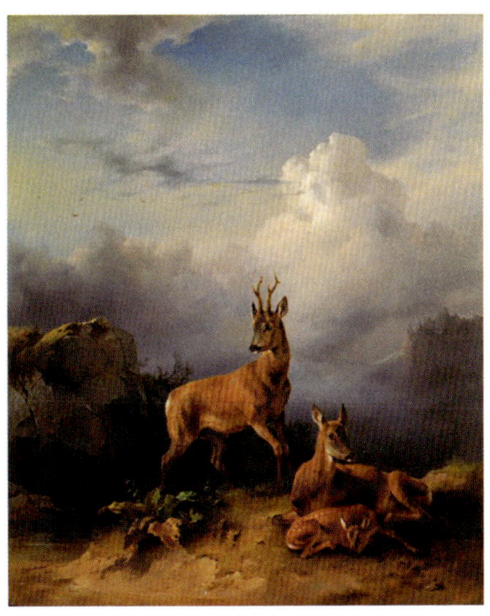

Friedrich Gauermann (1807–1862), *Deer Family* (nineteenth century), confiscated by the Nazis and auctioned at the Dorotheum in 1939.

Clearly, they were unlikely to win a court case. Was there a realistic possibility of receiving anything?

The ALR agreed there was no legal case for a restitution under Austrian law, but an amicable settlement with the legal owner would facilitate the sale of the painting with a full and unsullied provenance. The size of the compensation would depend on a number of factors: the circumstances of the loss, whether the victims had already received some form of compensation, and when and how the current owner acquired the painting. Equally important was the legal owner's goodwill and how their social circle viewed restitution claims. The heirs had three options: sign a release to take the paintings off the database, take the case forward themselves and pay the ALR the location fee, or employ the ALR to represent them and pay a recovery fee of 20 per cent of the ultimate benefit.

Six weeks and several prompts later, the grandson replied at the beginning of July. There were three living heirs, and they had all been 'ready to give up' on the family art collection. They did not want to buy the painting and neither did they want to incur out-of-pocket costs to claim compensation for an artwork with an estimated value of just €25,000–€50,000. The ALR's offer to represent their interests was therefore attractive to them, as long as the ALR did all the footwork. In September 2017 they instructed the ALR 'to manage this as you think fit'. The ALR could finally get back to the auction house. It was told that the consignor had inherited the painting, which had been purchased in the 1960s without any knowledge of its problematic provenance. She was willing to make a financial settlement but was increasingly unhappy about the lengthy delay. As the current owner clearly had legal title, the ALR thought that securing a share of the sale proceeds for the Benbassat heirs would be a fair outcome, to which the heirs agreed.

Before initiating a negotiation, ALR staff completed the set of documents required to make a credible case on the heirs' behalf. Most importantly, they had to prove the Gauermann painting in question was indeed the one confiscated from the Benbassat family. The family had registered a list of paintings but had been unable to produce photographs. Deer had been one of the artist's favourite subjects and there was every possibility that a number of works featuring deer families existed. However, the ALR managed to obtain a copy of the catalogue of the 1939 looted art auction at the Dorotheum in Vienna. By sheer luck, *Deer Family* was one of the few paintings reproduced in the catalogue and the two paintings were identical. Next, the ALR needed to demonstrate that the Benbassats had not received any of the proceeds from this sale. As the Benbassats had left Vienna in 1938, they had been in exile for more than six months at the time their collection was auctioned off. It was clear that in these circumstances they would not have benefited from the sale. The ALR already had the evidence that the Benbassats had made an attempt to reclaim the painting after 1945: the extensive early post-war correspondence between the Benbassats and the Austrian authorities. This showed that the family had left *Deer Family* in Vienna and searched for it directly after the war. The ALR thus had a sound basis for the Benbassats' claim, but it would be weighed against a good faith purchase around fifty years ago.

The ALR approached the auction house's lawyer with an offer in December 2017. Acknowledging the legal owner's cooperation and patience, it proposed dividing the sales proceeds with the Benbassat family. A day later the lawyer got back to the ALR. The consignor had immediately accepted the suggested split. Moreover, the lawyer was prepared to act as a trustee for the transaction, without charging either party. The ALR returned to the heirs with the agreed settlement figure and the lawyer's generous offer. The heirs were delighted and signed the release, so that the auction house was able to re-advertise the painting for an auction in April 2018. This time the artwork had a complete provenance and a note saying that it was on sale with the full agreement of the Benbassat heirs. The heirs' reticence to invest their own money and effort in their claim was vindicated, however. The painting failed to sell at the April auction or in a private sale afterwards. The auction house tried again the following October with a lower reserve. The picture sold for just €18,500. It is a shame the painting came onto the market too late for Albert and Ella Benbassat and their sons, who had tried so hard to find their family's former possessions. Even if the compensation paid to their grandchildren was not huge in monetary terms, the constructive and cooperative attitude of the owner and the auction house left them very content with the outcome.

These two cases illustrate both the commercial opportunities and the risks of art restitution. Both involved painstaking research to piece together the provenance of the paintings, to trace the heirs and document their claim, plus the time spent in agreeing a settlement. The high-value Picasso case became very antagonistic. The ALR could easily have made a loss if Alsdorf had continued on the court route. The positive outcome was down to factors largely beyond the ALR's control. For Bennigson it was important to know that the ALR would plough its windfall gains from *Femme en Blanc* back into restitution cases for Jewish families in a less fortunate position than himself. Doing the research necessary to resolve title issues is not commercially viable for paintings like *Deer Family*. However, cross-subsidising between cases allows the ALR to consider cases on the basis of merit rather than purely on profitability.

Just and fair solutions

The law is adversarial in nature. Court cases create winners and losers. The process of obtaining a judgment pits the parties against each other. In many cases this is counterproductive and particularly so in the highly emotional area of Nazi-era restitutions. Most victims of the Nazi regime primarily wanted to receive an acknowledgement of their families' suffering and some compensation for the treasures stolen from them. Often survivors were in dire need of funds to make a new life for themselves far from their original homes. The legal system told them they were either entitled to outright restitution or nothing at all. In practice, the legal system's many financial and bureaucratic hurdles meant most survivors had no chance to even begin to make a case. Similarly, for legal owners who could not afford to magnanimously hand back objects from their collections, the 'all or nothing' legal system stands in the way of doing what they feel to be right.

Private resolutions open a third way: discreet, just and fair settlements. When I first heard about 'amicable' resolutions between complete strangers I was surprised. But in the case of *Deer Family*, the heirs' expectations were at rock bottom and the ALR's reasonable suggestion for a financial settlement met a generous and sympathetic current owner. The split proposed by the ALR exceeded the hopes of the claimants but was not perceived as extortionate by the owner. Haggling would have felt demeaning to both sides and was avoided entirely. The ALR's long-term commercial relationship with dealers and auction houses is important in explaining its negotiation strategy. Although the ALR formally represents former owners, it also has an interest in serving the market by avoiding acrimonious and lengthy negotiations. The percentage recovery fee encourages the ALR to ask for the maximum compensation that would be perceived appropriate and acceptable in a given circumstance. If it settled too low, it would lose business to more assertive competitors. If it asked for too much, it would upset current owners and scupper or delay sales. The market would soon look elsewhere for Holocaust-era provenance information. It is therefore in the ALR's best interest to cultivate a reputation as an honest broker, putting forward genuine claims and resolving them with the minimum of fuss and publicity.

For people who want to avoid the emotional roller-coaster ride of a court-case and its attendant media circus, as well as the expense of lawyers and mediators, the ALR offers an attractive resolution service. The great advantage of the ALR's historic claims database is that it is generally consulted when a sale is imminent. At this stage, the legal owners have already decided to part with the object. They are less likely to be emotionally attached than when a restitution request comes out of the blue. The owners are not being asked to give up something that brings joy into their daily lives or has pride of place in their personal collection. At the point of sale, they are thinking of the object in monetary terms. If the object has gone up in value since they bought it or they inherited it, they may well be prepared to share the gain with former owners or their heirs, and begin to restore their faith in humankind. If not, they can keep the looted object as a reminder of the anguish of its former owners: a memento mori of a different sort. I can see why most people decide that an amicable and fair resolution is a better outcome.

8

A Convenient Grey Zone: 'Restoring' Antique Furniture

On 28 In January 2000 a fairly standard transaction took place in the Dublin antiques trade. The buyer of a major London-based firm had flown into the city early that morning and was met by two charming and loquacious antiques dealers. They had been shown an 'interesting' red lacquer bureau at a restorer's workshop in the city, but it was in poor condition and would need lots of attention to bring it back to its former glory. The owner knew the piece was special and offered it for £50,000. The Dublin dealers could not afford the significant financial outlay of buying and restoring the bureau themselves, but knew that a high-powered antiques trader with the right connections could make a neat profit on this. They therefore sent a few pictures to colleagues in London to see who might bite.

The buyer at a top London antiques store immediately realised the bureau was a rare gem, if it was not dilapidated beyond rescue. He would have to see it for himself. Thus, he found himself standing in a cold Dublin workshop with his Irish colleagues and – despite the undoubted restoration challenge – he was impressed. The deal was done in the car outside the workshop. The London dealer agreed to pay £80,000 to his Dublin scouts. They went back to the owner and bought the piece at his asking price of £50,000. A few weeks later, the bureau arrived in London for restoration. Everyone was happy: the restorers had bought the piece for £20,000 and had resold it for £50,000; their buyers had immediately flipped it for £80,000. After restoration, the London dealer would offer it at the world's most glamorous antiques fairs for £450,000. This was good business as long as nobody bothered to ask where the bureau had come from.

A troubling history

If somebody asked about the object's provenance, there were two answers. The first was brief and straightforward. The bureau had come from the damp cellar of a Georgian house. This had satisfied everyone in the antiques trade so far: it explained the substantial damage to its fabric. But there was a second, darker answer that takes us into the ganglands of Northern Ireland's paramilitary organisations. The red lacquer bureau had been stolen in an aggravated burglary from the 9th Earl of Roden in County Down in February 1990 along with a range of other treasures. The distinguished elderly homeowner had confronted the burglars, but they beat him up and tied him to a chair. He watched in helpless fury as the gang members pocketed silverware and miniature family portraits and carried off paintings and furniture that had been in the family for centuries. The Earl of Roden never recovered from this terrible ordeal and died a few years afterwards. It was one of several high-profile burglaries in the region at the time, including the infamous raid on Sir Alfred Beit's home in County Wicklow in 1986. There, the thieves stole eighteen Old Master paintings including works by Francisco Goya, Johannes Vermeer and Peter Paul Rubens. It was the world's biggest art heist at the time.

The raids were masterminded by Martin Cahill – sometimes referred to as the 'the General' or the 'godfather of the Irish criminal underworld'[116] – and his occasional partner Pat Shanahan. For Cahill, who had grown up in abject poverty, burgling stately homes was not just about money. It was part of a private vendetta against state institutions and the country's elite. Cahill often deliberately provoked the police (for example by vandalising the Garda golf course[117]), obstructed the law (by instructing his gang to set fire to the Central Criminal Court in Dublin) and killed and maimed those who tried to bring him to justice. Just to show they could, Cahill's gang even supplied themselves with arms from the police's own weapons stores. Although Cahill's gang was primarily a criminal enterprise, they occasionally worked with the Protestant paramilitary Ulster Volunteer Force.[118] The middle-class Shanahan was attracted by the 'glamorous' image of Cahill's outlaws and loved the buzz of participating in dangerous and violent raids. But he was also a shrewd entrepreneur with excellent business contacts. Shanahan proposed a bold plan to the General. Why not employ his gang to supply the burgeoning market for antiques with family heirlooms from Ireland's country houses? The scheme held unique appeal for Cahill. He jumped at the chance to make millions, humiliate the privileged and embarrass the police. His victims could expect no mercy.

Indeed, it was Pat Shanahan who turned up at a restorer's workshop in Dublin with the late Earl of Roden's red lacquer bureau and a Dutch marquetry bookcase in 1993. He had become a property developer: a career offering great money laundering opportunities at the time. It also meant he now had a legitimate interest in fine furniture. He explained that he had acquired the bureau and bookcase 'in England'. Unfortunately, they had got damp in storage and were now falling apart. The restorer agreed to take in both pieces but decided he would subcontract the work to others. He sent them off to two of his associates, but in October 1994, before meaningful work could commence, Shanahan was shot dead. The shocked restorer tried to return the two pieces of crumbling but undoubtedly fine furniture to Shanahan's widow, but she reacted angrily and shouted at him to leave. She wanted nothing to do with him or anything her husband might have left. Rather concerned, the restorer laid low for a while. He later moved the Dutch bookcase to a friend's place and offered the lacquer bureau to a dealer in Dublin with a larger restoration business. The Dublin firm spotted the bureau's potential and had it valued by Sotheby's to confirm its hunch. The auctioneers did not request to see any paperwork and gave an estimate in the range of £15,000 to £20,000 despite the bureau's sorry current state. On the back of this valuation the dealer in Dublin paid £20,000 to Shanahan's furniture restorer. A few months and two highly advantageous sales later, the bureau was on its way to London.

Changing attitudes

As this ten-year odyssey through the antiques market shows, Shanahan's original business idea was completely sound. Stealing fine antiques was good business because provenance was perceived as irrelevant in the trade. There is a good reason for this. Furniture is rarely unique: even the most exclusive furniture makers made multiple objects of each design, or at least they could have done. Therefore, dealers felt safe in the knowledge that it would be impossible to prove a specific object had been stolen. The case of the red lacquer bureau would eventually convince them otherwise.

There were three parties who wanted to track down the bureau. The police were keen to bring the perpetrators of this particularly unpleasant aggravated burglary to justice. They advertised the theft with a reward advert in *The Burlington Magazine*. The victim and his successors were also determined to recover their heirlooms. The antiques had been in the family for generations; some of them were gifts from historic figures to their ancestors and they were of great sentimental value. In addition to mourning the death of their father, the family had sustained a massive financial loss in the burglary. Like many country homeowners, the Earl of Roden had bought fairly standard insurance cover. His belongings had not been valued since he had first taken out the policy in the 1970s. The payout for the entirety of the stolen family silver, paintings and the best of the furniture came to just over £14,000, a small fraction of the value of the red lacquer bureau alone. Even so, the insurer wanted its money back. When the ALR was formed in 1991, the family logged the missing objects on the database and two years later their insurer followed suit. Therefore, we arrive back at the basic question: can you uniquely identify items of (antique) furniture?

If you look closely, wooden furniture is distinctive from day one even if multiple copies of a design exist: the grain of the wood is as unique as a finger-print. Handmade decoration is never perfectly identical even

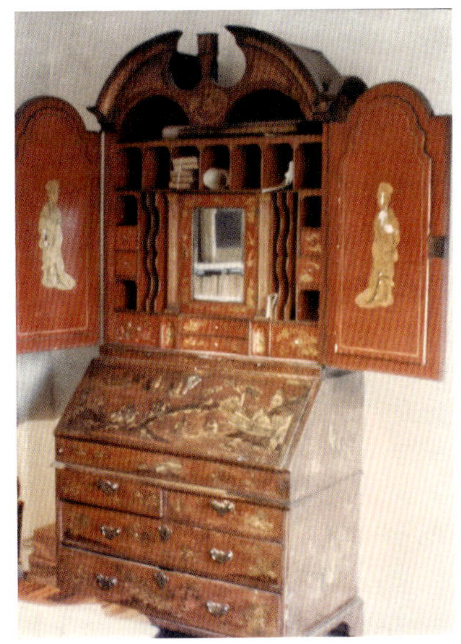

Pre-theft photograph of the Queen Anne lacquer bureau in Lord Roden's residence.

when the maker tries their best to create a match. With the passage of time antiques become ever more recognisable, even without a high-resolution photograph. Objects develop a particular patina, as polishing, smoke, sunlight and humidity leave their marks, corners are scuffed, surfaces get scratched and carved details are knocked off. The mends and patches applied by generations of appreciative owners as well as the ministrations of careful restorers can give antiques additional charm. Therefore, if the owners keep good records, it is often possible to prove beyond reasonable doubt that a family's stolen heirloom is the same object as the one now on offer in a glitzy showroom or at an antiques fair. However, it is neither easy nor cheap to track down a specific piece if multiple copies (could) exist and hence it is only worthwhile for truly exceptional objects. Can the ALR convince the antiques trade to change its business practices and pay attention to provenance?

As the ALR built its reputation for tracking down stolen paintings, antiques dealers started checking the artworks in their stock and requesting ALR searches for valuable paintings before buying. But most dealers remained unconvinced that the ALR could identify stolen furniture. Extensive restorations are common in the antiques trade. The moneyed elite and their interior designers mostly just want a hint of patina on their antiques. Restoration does not mean conservation: if something has worn out, restorers will replace or retouch it, and they are often liberal in their interpretation of 'worn out'. Many objects destined for the top end of the market leave the restorer's workshop completely transformed and hence unrecognisable to their former owners. Nonetheless, the ubiquity of paintings on the walls of antique dealers' sale stalls at high-end art fairs gave the ALR a (grudging) entry to these events. While not exactly welcomed with open arms, it was increasingly given the chance to vet the goods on offer and thereby lend greater respectability to the events. Although the fees the ALR could charge for doing so rarely covered its costs, it considered it as a loss-leader. Being at the fairs gave it the opportunity to talk to dealers in the hope of eventually signing them on as customers.

What the ALR really needed was a high-profile proof of concept. Thus, in June 2001, the ALR's art historians were beavering away on their laptops at the prestigious Grosvenor House antiques fair in London. They had been admitted on the first day of the fair, which was reserved for the press. It did not leave them much time to prove their mettle. Moreover, they had been given a desk space right at the back of the vetting office, so they had to use their coffee breaks to start conversations with the dealers and explain their work and the database to them.

An uncertain match

As the ALR furniture expert worked her way through the fair catalogue at top speed, a gloriously shiny red lacquer bureau offered by Mallett's caught her attention. She started a search for an eighteenth-century Queen Anne red lacquer bureau with raised gilt chinoiserie figures. The ALR database came up with three possible matches. On closer inspection they all turned out to be the same item: the bureau had been logged by the family and the insurer, and ALR staff had picked up the reward advert in *The Burlington Magazine*. But was the item on the database the same as that on Mallett's stall at the fair? The latter was perfect, with a price tag to match: £450,000. It looked quite different from the picture of the ancient bureau on the ALR database that had been stolen from the Roden family in County Down. The overall shape and the gilt figures were very similar though. Just how rare was this kind of bureau and was the one from County Down still missing?

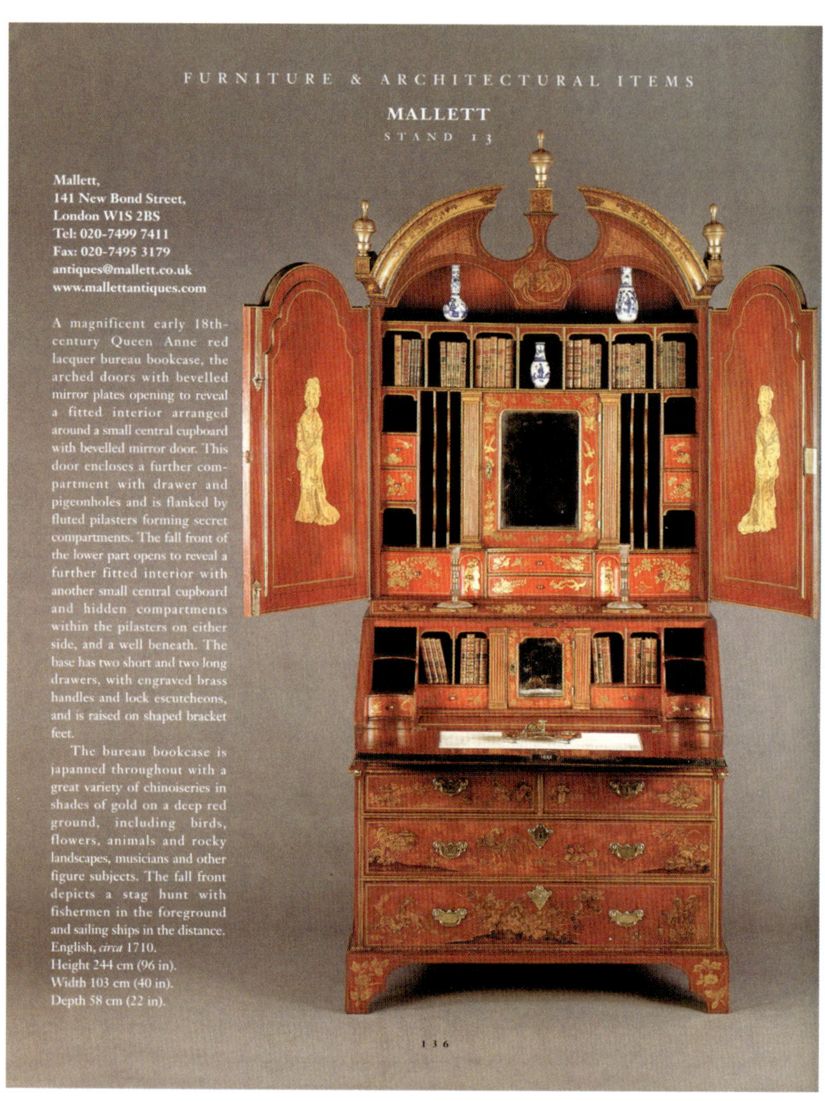

Mallett,
141 New Bond Street,
London W1S 2BS
Tel: 020-7499 7411
Fax: 020-7495 3179
antiques@mallett.co.uk
www.mallettantiques.com

A magnificent early 18th-century Queen Anne red lacquer bureau bookcase, the arched doors with bevelled mirror plates opening to reveal a fitted interior arranged around a small central cupboard with bevelled mirror door. This door encloses a further compartment with drawer and pigeonholes and is flanked by fluted pilasters forming secret compartments. The fall front of the lower part opens to reveal a further fitted interior with another small central cupboard and hidden compartments within the pilasters on either side, and a well beneath. The base has two short and two long drawers, with engraved brass handles and lock escutcheons, and is raised on shaped bracket feet.

The bureau bookcase is japanned throughout with a great variety of chinoiseries in shades of gold on a deep red ground, including birds, flowers, animals and rocky landscapes, musicians and other figure subjects. The fall front depicts a stag hunt with fishermen in the foreground and sailing ships in the distance. English, *circa* 1710.
Height 244 cm (96 in).
Width 103 cm (40 in).
Depth 58 cm (22 in).

The bureau looking its best in the Grosvenor House Art & Antiques Fair Handbook 2001.

The ALR had to tread extremely carefully here. This was not the time to rush in and cry foul play. First, its business proposition that antique furniture was unique had yet to be proven to its sceptical audience. It would be very embarrassing to raise the alarm and retract it afterwards. Second, if it looked like it was accusing its future customers of being crooks that handle stolen goods it would do more harm than good to its commercial relationship with the antiques trade and fair organisers. Yet, on the other hand, the buyers were expected at the Grosvenor House fair on the very next morning and the stunning red lacquer bureau was likely to arouse somebody's interest. Back-up from head office was urgently needed. Could someone please come over to the fair with the highest-quality photo available and confirm this was a match? Could someone else phone the police in County Down and confirm whether they had retrieved the late Earl of Roden's lacquer bureau in the meantime? Could they also get hold of the current Lord Roden and confirm whether the family's red bureau might be on the market legitimately? But even if the bureau was still missing, this could well be one of several remnants of a popular eighteenth-century interior design craze. Could the family remember any unique identifying feature that could have survived the restorers' attention?

The second ALR expert agreed with the first that it was a match, but the police in County Down were sorry to say that the case files from ten years ago were in storage some 35 miles away. They would do what they could (and when they could) and call back. When the ALR finally got through to Lord Roden's residence, his Lordship was out and a message had to be left. But by the time he received it, it could be too late. Julian Radcliffe cautiously approached the fair organiser with what were so far only suspicious circumstances. Would it be appropriate for him to speak to Mallett's about the provenance of this piece? Hopefully, the dealer could immediately put everyone's mind at rest with an impeccable trail of purchase receipts. The fair organisers were fascinated and horrified. They suddenly realised how the ALR's work could enhance (or ruin) their fair's reputation, and also that the ALR needed more time to do its job properly. Bringing the ALR in on press day was clearly too late. Mallett's red lacquer bureau had been given pride of place in the fair's glossy catalogue. Some explanation would be needed if it disappeared from the stall. Yet if it was left on display despite the question marks over its provenance and the former owner successfully claimed it back afterwards, the press would have a field day reporting on stolen goods for sale at the Grosvenor House fair. The organisers therefore gave Radcliffe their blessing to talk to Mallett's and, having made an urgent appointment, he set off for Bond Street.

The finance director at Mallett's had all the paperwork to hand when Radcliffe arrived. It was immediately obvious that, now he had been put on the spot, he was far from confident about the object's provenance. While the director was quite happy to discuss the expensive restoration work his firm had undertaken on the bureau, he clammed up about its origins. 'From an Irish dealer' was all he was prepared to divulge at that stage, claiming his buyer had purchased the bureau in good faith. He then launched a counter-attack. Whatever the origins of the bureau, eleven years had passed since the theft. Surely a previous owner would have acquired good title when the limitation period had expired. Were the ALR experts completely sure that this was the Earl of Roden's bureau? Could they prove it? And why had they not picked up the problem at Maastricht or the Armoury Fair in the USA where the piece had also been exhibited? Radcliffe explained that these fairs had not yet contracted the ALR to check furniture and it was up to individual dealers to search all of their objects against the database, as Mallett's already routinely did with its paintings.

Presumably after an incident like this, the fairs' organisers would be more careful, and dealers would realise it was better to check before buying and investing in expensive restorations.

Although perfectly polite and presumably hugely instructive, this conversation failed to resolve the fate of the bureau at Grosvenor House. Radcliffe returned to the fair's organising committee with three more pieces of intelligence. First, the dealer did not have a credible provenance for the piece, but it had come from Ireland. Second, in the meantime the police had confirmed that lacquer bureau was still missing. And third, Lord Roden himself had examined the pictures. He thought it might be the stolen family heirloom, but he knew there were other, similar pieces in circulation. The family had had a few near misses in the past, so he offered to come to London to check if this bureau had certain unique features that only the family knew about. Based on this information, the fair organisers requested that Mallett's remove the bureau from its stall. Leaving it on display would contravene the fair's rule of only exhibiting pieces that were definitely for sale. Mallett's complied immediately.

The bureau's precipitate departure did not go unnoticed by the press. The *Art Newspaper* reported: 'If you had wanted to take a second look at the magnificent Queen Anne scarlet lacquer bureau bookcase on Mallett's stand, priced at £450,000, you had to be quick: by the second day it had gone, "on approval" according to the dealer.'[119] With the dealer implying it had sold its star piece on press day, the ALR would have to rely on gossip to spread the real story among antiques traders. Radcliffe would certainly allude to this case in discussions with the fair organisers in Maastricht and in New York, and any other opportunity where the question of vetting furniture arose.

A family's long quest

The very next day, Lord Roden arrived at Mallett's premises to look at the bureau and he was not pleased. In May 1995 Mallett's had offered a very similar cabinet to the one the Roden family was searching for. Lord Roden had phoned the managing director to enquire, but it was not the missing heirloom. Afterwards, the disappointed family sent photographs of all the stolen objects to the dealer with a polite request to keep their eyes open should they ever appear on the market. The letter had been addressed to the very man who had bought the red lacquer wreck in the restorer's workshop in Dublin five years later. Why had no one bothered to contact the original owner?

Lord Roden also brought along two fine furniture experts from Sotheby's to compare the bureau with the pictures taken before the theft. The construction and form of the bureau were consistent with the photographs, but as the senior expert's later statement to the police made clear: 'there had been so much restoration that it was impossible to identify any common features'.[120] The areas of pre-theft damage that would have permitted a positive identification had been erased comprehensively. The expert also lamented that on the inside the figures 'had been repainted entirely and were not to the standard I would have expected'.[121] The matter would have rested there had it not been for a set of high-resolution pre-restoration photographs supplied by Mallett's. On these, the furniture specialists identified several areas that matched the pre-1990 damage. In addition, there was the damage sustained during the ten years when the bureau was dragged around Ireland and stored in unsuitable hiding places. But the senior expert had no doubt at all in his police interview: 'It is my professional opinion that they are the same.'[122] His junior colleague could only agree: 'there is no doubt in my mind that the cabinet in the photographs shown to me pre-theft and pre-restoration are the same, i.e. the cabinet examined at Mallett's was the stolen one'.[123]

But how would the ownership question be resolved? On the one hand, Mallett's had spent £80,000 on the bureau and a further £31,000 on its restoration. It might be sold for as much as £450,000, which is a lot of money to walk away from. Mallett's could make a legal case that it had acquired ownership of the bureau by transforming it from a crumbling wreck into a fine antique.[124] On

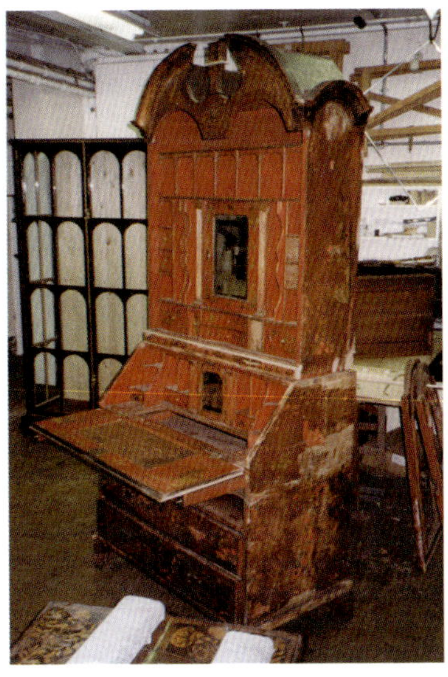

The dilapidated lacquer bureau at the restorer's workshop.

the other hand, Lord Roden was in no mood to reimburse the firm's expenses. As far as he was concerned, he had 'put them on notice' in 1995, and it was the company's problem if it spent money on buying and restoring stolen furniture. In fact, he fumed, Mallett's should probably take a good look at all the Irish furniture it had sold in the last decade or two. It was time for some ALR diplomacy to soothe ruffled feathers and suggest a solution that would serve everyone's interest.

'Amicably and without litigation or publicity'

While the ALR's sympathy lay with Lord Roden and other innocent victims of crime, one thing was clear: the furniture side of its business would only succeed if the industry accepted it as a trusted partner and service provider. Very few items of antique furniture are as valuable as the asking price of the red lacquer bureau at the Grosvenor House fair, and that valuation was very subjective. Most of the cashflow for the furniture database would have to be generated from routine trade searches and contracts with the major fairs. It was therefore not in anyone's interest for the ALR's customers to be drawn into an acrimonious dispute and to drag the reputation of the antiques trade through the mud in the process.

Thankfully, the Roden Trust accepted Radcliffe's offer to mediate, and he had a plan. If Mallett's gave in early and gracefully and handed over the bureau to the Roden Trust, the ALR would help Mallett's to recover its expenses from its Dublin suppliers. After all, the Irish wheeler-dealers should have suspected they did not have good title to give. The buyer from Mallett's had told them specifically that his firm would have to spend a significant amount of money on the restoration before the bureau could be sold. Hopefully, the suppliers could therefore be made liable for that expense, too. If they had any sense they should settle very quickly if threatened with an expensive lawsuit. Ideally, each dealer would then ask for reimbursement further up their own supply chain to make their losses more manageable. Thus, the warning about dealing in furniture of dubious provenance would spread in an important source country.

In the event of a successful free-of-charge recovery, the Roden Trust agreed the ALR should have the £10,000 reward originally posted after the theft. The ALR team thus started unravelling the ownership issue: to whom should Mallett's deliver the bureau? The insurance company had paid compensation to the family and would have to release its interest in the bureau. The insurance payout to cover the entirety of the theft had been only £14,000. Formally, the £500 paid out for the bureau transferred ownership to the insurer, but clearly it would be an unfair outcome for the theft victims if they lost their heirloom a second time. Indeed, the insurer offered to step back, but before the bureau could be returned to the family, the Earl of Roden's heirs had to settle an inheritance tax bill. Agreeing a fair valuation for the cabinet at the time of the late Earl of Roden's death would take a long time, but Lord Roden proposed a lovely interim solution. The bureau was be taken to the Royal Hospital Chelsea for its residents to enjoy until all the financial issues were resolved.[125]

In the meantime, Mallett's had decided to recoup the purchase price from its Irish suppliers, but it was far from confident that these had sufficient money to reimburse the firm. Therefore, the director requested that the Roden family should contribute the cost of restoring the cabinet. However, Lord Roden was still fuming about the ease with which the stolen property had circulated in the antiques trade and was in no mood to make concessions. Thus, Radcliffe drafted a pointed letter to Mallett's. It started by stating that 'all parties are keen that we should resolve the case amicably and without litigation or publicity' and then laid out the reasons why Mallett's might wish to avoid the latter option. But, officially, the letter was never sent.

Instead, Radcliffe phoned Mallett's director again. As he explained to Lord Roden's lawyer: 'I propose to speak to [the director] and to explain that if he does not withdraw the request we will have to write, and he probably would not wish to have our letter on file.'[126] It was a potent threat. The director asked to see an unsigned draft of the letter and one can just picture him turning paler with each line. Radcliffe argued that Mallett's legal claim was weak, but – equally importantly – that it was morally problematic to sue the heirs for compensation. Having failed to search the ALR database, a court was unlikely to accept Mallet's had purchased and restored the bureau in good faith. It would also be a PR disaster for the firm if the media got hold of the story of Mallett's pursuing the innocent victims of a nasty, aggravated burglary for money. Moreover, its reputation as a purveyor of legitimate fine antiques would suffer. Finally, if Mallett's wanted to make a successful claim against its supplier, it would need the ALR's active support. The firm would be highly unlikely to retrieve the £80,000 from its supplier if this letter was disclosed. After briefly considering the letter with its lawyers, Mallett's decided never to mention the issue of the restoration costs to the Roden Trust again.

Up the supply chain

Unfortunately for Mallett's, its Dublin supplier did not give in equally early and gracefully. Three years later, in January 2004, the ALR received notification that the case would to go court in Dublin. The lawyers for Mallett's argued the supplier did not have good title to give and therefore the purchase was void and the £80,000 should be returned. Mallett's also claimed a further £31,153 in damages, as the restoration costs were a consequence of the initial breach of contract. However, the supplier countered that this was a case of caveat emptor. Both buyer and seller were innocent victims of a robbery and both had acted in good faith. As for the restoration costs, if Mallett's had exercised reasonable care after the sale it would not have proceeded with the restoration and the further £31,153 in costs would not have been incurred. Having had heated arguments with Mallett's about the appropriate level of due diligence, would the ALR and Lord Roden make convincing witnesses for the prosecution? As is customary with court cases, there would be many months to think about it.

In the gentlemen's agreement of early 2001, the ALR had promised to help Mallett's to recoup its loss. Moreover, in the meantime Mallett's had changed its due diligence procedure and searched furniture of questionable provenance against the database. Radcliffe therefore offered his services as an expert witness, while gently encouraging Lord Roden to send another representative of the family Trust to give evidence. It was doubtful that Lord Roden had fully forgiven and forgotten, not least because he was still engaged in his campaign to retrieve further stolen objects from an opaque and uncooperative market. The police then interviewed everyone in the supply chain to piece together the bureau's winding path through the Irish antiques market. The painstaking research showed that nobody had ever acquired good title to the bureau. Shanahan's restorer had not bought the bureau but had accidentally and informally 'inherited' it. Since then, even if subsequent purchases were (at a very minimal level) in good faith, nobody had kept the bureau for long enough to acquire good title via the statute of limitation.

The judge therefore concluded that the sale had failed and Mallett's was entitled to have the sale price refunded. Regarding whether Mallett's had exercised sufficient caution before commissioning the restoration the judge was more doubtful, but was won over by Radcliffe's testimony: 'having considered … in particular the evidence of Mr Julian Radcliffe who is the proprietor of the Art Loss Register, I am satisfied that in January 2000 it was not the practice of reputable dealers in antique furniture and paintings to consult the Art Loss Register before purchasing furniture.'[127] Although stressing that by 2005 expectations regarding due diligence in the antiques trade had increased markedly, he awarded the restoration costs to Mallett's, too. Radcliffe had kept his promise while firing a broadside against the grey antiques market in Ireland.

Not every recovery generates value

Some more good news for the Roden family emerged from the evidence the dealers gave to the police. The Dutch marquetry bookcase that had been in the family for more than 200 years and was stolen alongside the lacquer bureau was found languishing in a shed in County Galway. Shanahan's restorer had asked a friend if he could keep a few items of furniture for him. The friend had agreed but said he had never looked or made enquiries as to what they were or from where they had come. Once again, the tenacious Lord Roden went to identify his property. This time there was not even a moment of doubt. He recalled how his mother had repaired the bookcase in the 1950s. She had lined one of the shelves with a damask fabric and it was still in place. However, it was a brief and bittersweet reunion.

Even though the holder had no basis for claiming ownership as he had not purchased the bookcase, it took five years of legal wrangling before the Roden Trust was awarded the title. Thankfully, one of the Roden trustees is a lawyer, which kept the family's litigation costs manageable. Even so, the law courts delivered justice at a snail's pace, further compounding the injury of the victims. When the family finally retrieved its stolen heirloom, it had deteriorated so badly that it had only emotional rather than commercial value. Nonetheless, the Roden Trust wrote a cheque for £500 to thank the ALR for its role in locating the bookcase, once more urging it to remain vigilant. The Trust had heard a rumour that a brass-bound lacquer cabinet – given to the Roden family by Queen Mary herself – had been spotted at the house of Cahill's widow. Lord Roden's family and the ALR are still diligently searching for it, as well as the family silver and several portrait miniatures.

The business and politics of provenance

The Roden family's loss and the recovery of just two of its missing heirlooms once again raises interesting questions about the effectiveness of public law enforcement. Martin Cahill and Pat Shanahan were widely known as criminals, but they ran circles round the police and were never formally brought to justice. Their families lived in comparative luxury even though the men were not declaring incomes to the tax authorities. Shanahan eventually invested his underworld income in legitimate enterprises to become openly wealthy. Both criminals' lives ended in gangland shootings, but it would have been far preferable for justice to have been carried out through the proper legal process.

When the victims of crime looked to obtain justice from the legal system, they had to wait a very long time for a trial and a judgment. Mallett's was awarded its money back plus costs after four years, and who knows how long it took to actually get paid after that. For the Roden family fighting for the return of the Dutch marquetry bookcase, there was not just one trial but a further two rounds of expense, stress and anxiety. The obstinate holder gave up only when he had exhausted the possibilities of first appealing the verdict and then appealing against the appeal before the family could recover its property, almost seventeen years after the theft.

The next question is to what extent private businesses can address the shortcomings of formal law enforcement. Private security and insurance are thriving in the conditions created by lax law enforcement, and usually in combination. To obtain insurance for a precious collection one needs to install a technologically advanced security system. Even so, insurance for valuable objects can be eye-wateringly expensive. Many families have therefore sold their valuables, stashed them away in safes, or lent or donated them to museums rather than paying insurance premiums. Some people still take the risk of living with their treasures. If they are targeted by thieves, they have three options: rely on the overstretched police and legal system, become amateur sleuths, or employ others to search for their property, such as the ALR. Lord Roden pursued all three options at once. But does the ALR have a viable business here?

The case of Lord Roden's antiques clearly demonstrates the challenges of changing the attitudes of a sceptical – if not outright hostile – market. Rescuing and restoring promising wrecks from the grey market was excellent business when the market was booming. If Mallett's had sold the lacquer cabinet for £450,000 its outlay of £111,153 would have been handsomely rewarded, even with significant further marketing costs. For dealers, the status quo was perfect. Understandably, many of them did not ask for the service the ALR insisted on offering to them. If occasionally an irate former owner identified and demanded something back from their stock of furniture, this could be absorbed into the cost of doing business. For the risk averse, there is insurance for defective title, although only if due diligence has been undertaken and for limited amounts. However, one can put up additional barriers to prevent retrievals. If the red lacquer bureau's pre-restoration photographs had conveniently disappeared, nobody would have been able to make a definitive match. When antiques buyers like their antiques to look 'perfect' and do not ask questions about their previous owners, an object's history can be completely erased. Plus, if antiques dealers wait for former owners to take them to court it would put most claimants off, even if they have a good case.

Unlike the top end of the fine arts business, there is not enough valuable furniture to build a profitable business around location and recovery fees. Lord Roden is exceptional among burglary victims. Most people consider furniture as replaceable and few would spend as much as the Roden family to retrieve their stolen heirlooms. If holders prove uncooperative, the cost of litigation can easily exceed the value of the objects under dispute. Thus, a private furniture loss register business would have to be mainly funded by insurers' subscriptions and dealers' search fees. However, underinsurance of furniture is common. Insurers have less of an incentive to fund a private initiative to change norms around provenance in the antiques business than they have in the art market. Losses from theft are also spread among numerous (home) insurers, making it more difficult to find a collective solution to the problem. Many dealers like the status quo. The current laissez-faire approach creates a perverse 'value chain'. It can be very profitable to buy stolen prestige goods and recycle them back into wealthy clients' homes. It is easy to see why the market ended up in a bad equilibrium.

From a public policy point of view, it is desirable to change market norms regarding provenance. Due diligence checks reduce the returns to crime and therefore victimisation rates. It would be relatively simple for governments in developed antiques markets to put in place rules and regulations that required dealers and market makers to research the provenance of objects valued above a certain threshold, for example, £10,000. Some rules would not be particularly onerous to monitor and enforce. For instance, export licences should only be granted with a credible provenance or a clear search certificate from a reputable database of stolen furniture. The red lacquer bureau would not have made it to the Armoury Fair in New York and back to Europe (for the Maastricht and Grosvenor House fairs) if that rule had been in place. Fairs and auction houses could be compelled to vet and to do so thoroughly. When demonstrating appropriate due diligence becomes essential for proving a good faith purchase in court, buyers will demand good provenance before making expensive purchases. This in turn would encourage dealers, fairs and auction houses to build reputations for creating significant barriers to the sale of objects from the grey market.

Pat Shanahan spotted a genuine business opportunity when he proposed that the Dublin mobsters supply the antiques market with the heirlooms of the aristocracy in the late 1980s. Fortunately, over the last fifteen years that calculation has begun to change. However, criminal profit opportunities will not disappear unless the rules governing the antiques market are amended and enforced by law enforcement, as well as by private companies.

9

Outfoxed: The Table with the Hairy Hocks

They came in the dead of night. The raid on Warneford Place, in Sevenhampton, Wiltshire, in June 2004 had been carefully planned. The multimillionaire owner was out, and the nearest village is half a mile away down a private drive. Nobody heard when the burglars removed the heavy steel bars from the drawing-room windows and dropped them into the lake. Soon they were ready to ransack the owner's exquisite collection of ceramics, clocks, silver and fine furniture. But, fortunately, one of the gang tripped an alarm. As the police raced towards Sevenhampton from nearby Swindon, the criminals grabbed what they could, carrying away the smaller pieces in a precious antique peat basket. When the police arrived twenty minutes later, the thieves had disappeared with loot of an estimated value of £750,000.

Compared to other country house owners in the region the owner of Warneford Place – Paddy McNally – could count himself lucky. Between 2004 and 2006 there was a string of break-ins at country houses in Oxfordshire, Berkshire, Gloucestershire, Worcestershire and Wiltshire with total losses estimated at up to £80 million. The most audacious of these raids targeted the property magnate and connoisseur collector Harry Hyams. Thieves looted possessions worth £23 million from his country home Ramsbury Manor in Wiltshire. Police officers investigating these burglaries noticed strong similarities between them. Eventually, police forces from five counties – Gloucestershire, Wiltshire, Thames Valley, Warwickshire and West Mercia – pooled their resources and mounted Operation Haul to track down the gang responsible.

Their investigations led them to a makeshift caravan site near Evesham, in Worcestershire, the home of the Johnson family. They are part of a group of travellers with a lifestyle that seems to hark back to a different era, and who resent the prejudice and rules imposed on them by the rest of society. As for the people on whose lands they live – and who keep trying to push them on and out – they express an explosive mixture of anger and contempt. They see taking from the rich as a form of retribution for past wrongs.[128] This puts them in fundamental conflict with British law. Indeed, several of the men have a string of criminal convictions and cautions: for theft, fraud, affray and attempted murder. They spend their lives under frequent police surveillance and in and out of prison.

When the Operation Haul case came to court in 2008, five members of the Johnson family were found guilty of conspiracy to burgle and were jailed for between eight and eleven years. The judge told them 'You have no respect for people's property or the law, so I have no alternative but to impose severe sentences.'[129]

Prison was the only sanction available. In 2009 there was a further court hearing to decide on financial penalties for the Johnson gang. Despite having made off with valuables worth many millions, the burglars did not seem to have any money. They lived a 'hand-to-mouth' existence, selling off the stolen treasures for a fraction of their value. The gang members claimed their fence had paid them a mere £76,000 for the loot from the £23 million Ramsbury Manor raid. Even though they admitted they had made tens of thousands of pounds each from their crimes, they claimed they had no assets. As in previous encounters, the judge could impose only nominal fines, as well as threatening the confiscation of future incomes or assets. However, given the family's lifestyle it seems highly unlikely the police will ever find a possession worth seizing. Indeed, the gang members were pleased with the verdict, giving the judge the 'thumbs up' on the way out of court.[130]

Therefore, even if policing is excellent, the law has no power when dealing with people who have a completely different value system and already consider themselves apart from society. The many repeat offenders and 'career criminals' in the British crime statistics show that in some sections of the population legal sanctions fail to deter crime. For law-abiding citizens, the pragmatic answer to this type of perennial problem is household insurance that covers the financial risks of burglary. For the rich, the super-rich and collectors of art or other valuables, high net worth insurers offer both higher limits and in-depth advice on how to keep their houses and collections safe. People have thus learnt to live with the constant background threat of thefts and burglaries by mitigating the financial impact of crime.

But can law enforcement do better with the businesses that make massive profits from buying loot at rock-bottom prices in the illicit market and selling it to (often unsuspecting) collectors? Dealers have a stake in the legal economy and assets that can be seized. Do we have the right sanctions and do we have the resources to pursue the fences? This chapter shows that the system works well enough for shady dealers to go to extreme lengths to disguise the true nature of their business. Retrieving loot from such savvy merchants requires significant public/private cooperation and a surprising amount of patience and tenacity.

A unique piece of furniture

Among the items the Johnson gang bundled out of Warneford Place before the police arrived was a beautifully carved Irish eighteenth-century card table. Made from mahogany, it has a deeply and elaborately carved edge with a scroll and foliage pattern. Its curved legs end in unusually hairy paws. It is a particularly fine collectors' item and attracted considerable interest at the Christie's auction where Paddy McNally had bought it in 2004. The loss adjusters for the Warneford Place burglary valued it at £70,000. When the insurer compensated McNally for his loss, it became the legal owner of the stolen goods. All unique objects from the theft were registered on the ALR database: successful recoveries reduce the cost of providing insurance. The loss adjusters also advertised the theft in the *Antiques Trade Gazette* in November 2005 offering a 'substantial reward' for information leading to the recovery of any of the silver, porcelain, clocks and furniture stolen from McNally. The key pieces were illustrated with high-quality images and their exact measurements to aid identification.

This system appears to be effective in driving stolen objects away from reputable dealers and sometimes quite literally underground. The Johnson gang routinely stashed away its loot in the surrounding countryside. The police found £2.3 million worth of items from the Ramsbury Manor burglary in an underground

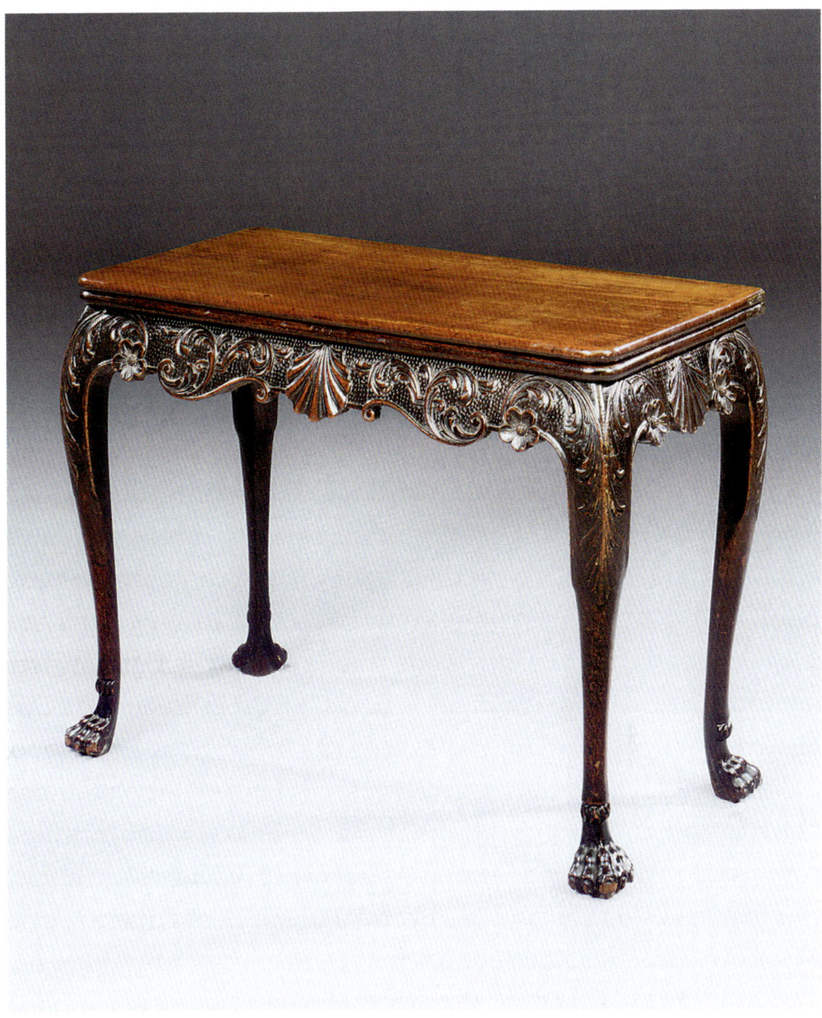

The George III mahogany card table with its distinctively hairy claw feet, *c.* 1765, Irish School.

bunker in a field owned by one of the Johnson gang's associates. Later, the imprisoned gang leader revealed the whereabouts of another £643,000 worth of loot in the hope of receiving a more lenient sentence.[131] Even the objects that are passed on to fences tend to take a while to re-emerge in the antiques trade.

Hide and seek

It took more than four years before the mahogany card table surfaced again. Just before Christmas 2009, the ALR heard a rumour that it was for sale in Ireland. Unfortunately, the table was not on display in a public showroom but on private premises, where it was believed to have been shown to select buyers only. The dealer was said to operate in the volatile borderlands between Northern Ireland and the Republic of Ireland, an area famous for smuggling and extralegal punishments. He was also known to have close connections to the paramilitaries. Therefore, not only could the table be spirited away at a moment's notice, but anyone who became involved had to avoid incurring the wrath of local armed gangs. The ALR took this sketchy and somewhat alarming information to the insurance company that had registered the theft, as well as to the theft victim. As the legal owner, the insurer instructed the ALR to attempt a retrieval on the usual no-win-no-fee basis.

Julian Radcliffe thus travelled to Ireland to gather more information and established that the table was with Mohune Antiques.[132] An internet search reveals surprisingly little about this business. You can find its address and it is marked on Google Maps. An upmarket boutique B&B references them as a source for its period furniture. Other than that, all you can find is a mobile telephone number. There is no website and no online catalogue to browse. There is no email address, but you can make enquiries through a third-party website. There are no regular opening hours: viewings are by appointment only. Presumably, there would be a further vetting process before customers were invited from the showroom into the house. Individually, none of these business practices is unusual or suspicious. Taken together with an address in County Monaghan – a few minutes' drive from the Northern

Ireland border where policing is tricky, to say the least – it looks like an ideal set-up for shifting stolen goods.[133] Given the local situation and the dealer's disturbing past, the ALR decided to move very cautiously.

The first step was to track down the table in the shady dealer's inner sanctum without arousing his suspicion. The ALR team therefore created an imaginative cover story for Radcliffe and an email address with a false name. 'Mr Psmith' was a wealthy individual who had just purchased a beautiful Georgian property for his son and his bride. He would be travelling in Ireland in early March 2010 and was interested in buying some fireplaces and good-quality period furniture for the happy couple. One member of the ALR team phoned Mohune Antiques to make an appointment for her 'father'. They were delighted to help and could open their showroom at any time. So, Radcliffe went off to Ireland again, this time for a secret reconnaissance mission.

Under cover

Mr Mohune was charmed by the wealthy and affable Psmith who picked out a number of items in the main warehouse. But Psmith was still looking for one or two 'very special' pieces. He showed the dealer the estate agent's details and floorplans. Could Mohune suggest something for the alcove in the front parlour, at a price in the region of £15,000 to £20,000? The dimensions were the perfect fit for the card table. The dealer took him into the basement of the warehouse, but nothing took Psmith's fancy there. They walked across the yard to the next building. There were a few clocks and tables and Psmith expressed a mild interest in one of them. It was not quite special enough, but perhaps … Mohune rose to the bait and moved on to his 'museum building', which was full of beautiful Irish furniture. Psmith was delighted but overwhelmed. After almost two hours of looking at antiques his enthusiasm for fine furniture was waning visibly. At long last, Mohune decided to invite his promising client into his house for a restorative cup of tea in the hope of closing a deal.

After a quick tour of the impressive ground-floor reception rooms, Psmith was ushered into the kitchen to meet the family. Tea was served in the tastefully furnished main room. In one corner stood the stolen table with the unmistakable hairy hocks. As Mohune had hoped, the genial beverage revived Psmith's interest in buying antiques. What about the card table over there? Might that fit into his alcove? Mohune was dismissive. 'It is too good for you,' he claimed, 'it is a museum piece.' Pushed a little further he said it was well out of Psmith's budget at £50,000. He brushed off an offer of £25,000 but thought he could source something similar in the London antiques trade. After two and a half hours, Psmith left with a list of the pieces he had picked out. Mohune would send him photos so he could get his wife's approval. Psmith promised to be in touch as soon as he arrived home.

X marks the spot

Back in the car, the delighted Radcliffe drew a detailed map showing the location of the table. But how could the table best be retrieved? Would the police be interested in a criminal investigation, or should the ALR attempt a civil recovery? Talking to an Irish lawyer, it soon became clear that a civil action would be very costly and cumbersome. If Mohune refused to surrender the table and claimed he had bought it in good faith, the ALR might have to negotiate a compromise settlement to avoid litigation. It would probably be hardly worth the effort. Radcliffe thus

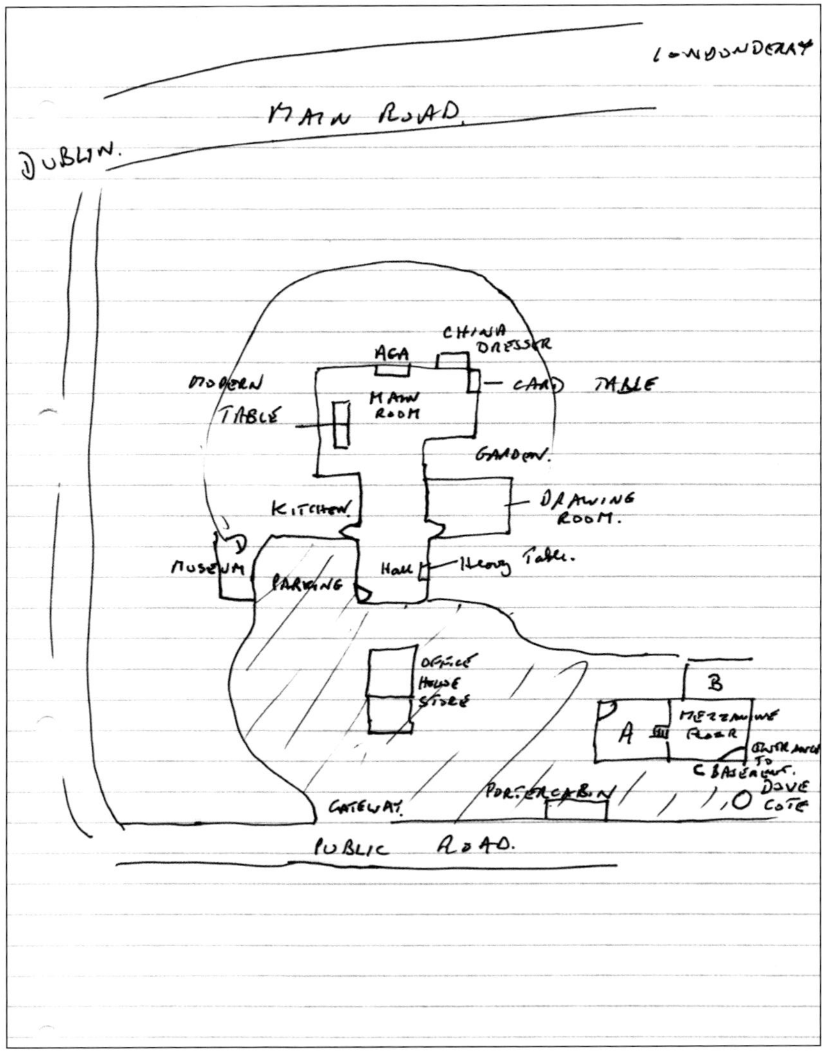

Hand-drawn map of the Mohune business premises showing the
location of the table.

approached the Wiltshire police who remembered the Warneford
Place burglary and Operation Haul only too well. As well as
providing them with the map, the ALR offered to have a team on

standby to check the entire stock of Mohune Antiques against the ALR database. It would be easy to establish whether the card table was a singular lapse in due diligence, or whether Mohune Antiques was a more sinister operation altogether.

While the Wiltshire police were keen to help, everyone appreciated that policing in the Irish borderlands was complex. The border is criss-crossed by hundreds of rural roads and paths. Some farms even straddle the boundary line, making it impossible to monitor or prevent travel between countries. Smuggling was rife and powerful paramilitary movements made it very risky for police and the military to patrol the region. Although matters had improved greatly within the European Union and especially since the Good Friday Agreement of 1998, the legacy of lawlessness lingers. Respect for rules is often limited in areas near customs borders where the arbitrariness of different countries' policies, procedures and laws is exposed by direct comparison. Rule breakers can make a handsome profit from exploiting differences in taxes, benefits and regulations. Certainly, the Mohunes had no qualms – but rather a degree of pride – when they told Psmith about how they used to 'smuggle anything that moved' in the olden days. Everyone knew about the family's IRA (Irish Republican Army) connections. Would the Garda be interested in seizing the card table and fully investigating Mohune Antiques?[134]

Having handed over the information to the Wiltshire police, the ALR heard nothing further for a month. But Mohune kept emailing: he wanted to close the deal over the furniture Psmith had picked out for his son. Radcliffe continued the conversation, asking about progress with sourcing a table for the alcove and even offering to reciprocate the Mohunes' warm Irish hospitality when the dealer came to visit London. In mid-April the Wiltshire police reported they had sent the information to the Garda and in mid-May 2010 Radcliffe found himself in Ireland for the third time: in a border town police station discussing Mohune Antiques with the local sergeants.

The theft victims – the McNally family – had originally come from Monaghan and the police were keen to help them. The officers also thought that Mohune was 'on the wrong side of the line'. The business had already received some police visits, 'and they were not social calls'.[135] Although nothing had come to court, the company was suspected of having links to a fence dealing in stolen antiques. Radcliffe thus made a formal statement of how he had personally identified the stolen table and its location. Just over a week later, the Garda informed the ALR that McNally's table had been seized and was in the possession of the police. Would Radcliffe come over to Ireland and formally identify it?

Radcliffe boarded the plane to Ireland for a fourth time ten days later, on this occasion in the company of McNally's antiques expert who had purchased the table for his client at Christie's in 2004. The expert still had his notes and a picture from the pre-sale inspection, on which he had marked a number of minor blemishes. On seeing the table, he had no hesitation in identifying it as the stolen item from Warneford Place. Radcliffe regretted that the police had seized only the table without giving the ALR a chance to inspect the rest of Mohune Antiques' stock, but he understood they had to tread carefully in the circumstances. The insurance company would be pleased with this recovery, although the table with the hairy hocks remained in police custody.

The long wait

As the lawyers had expected, Mohune did not surrender the table, but claimed he had bought it in good faith. However, the police thought they had a strong case against him and spent several months deliberating whether to prosecute. In February 2011 the ALR decided to gently rattle their cage. It pointed out that a police storage facility was probably not the ideal place for keeping fine antiques that require proper humidity and temperature controls. Was there any chance the prosecutor could release the table and substitute photographic evidence to prevent damage and any liability issues arising from improper storage? The Garda acknowledged receipt of the letter a month later, but said they needed a further few weeks to make a decision.

In May 2011, a year after the table had been seized, McNally sent a witness statement to the Garda. He urged them to release the table to the ALR, which was acting on behalf of the insurer. He was told that the Office of the Director of Public Prosecutions was still considering the matter. He was welcome to send an expert to inspect the table for damage at any time, but it would need to stay with the police. Another year later the ALR heard that its contact at the Garda had retired. In October 2012 an exasperated ALR employee tried once again to have the table restored to the victim: surely a two-and-a-half-year delay since the seizure was 'bordering on the absurd'?[136] Why would the table be needed in court? The superintendent refused to engage. The ALR received a two-line reply: the case would come to court in mid-January 2013.

A further request for an update in late January 2013 produced an equally terse reply: the matter had been adjourned until mid-June 2013. June came and went, as did the rest of the summer. In late September another ALR employee took over the case and sent an email to the Garda. It would be absolutely wonderful to have an update on the case. Perhaps they could manage to make contact by the end of October? On 3 October the Garda called, somewhat apologetically. There would be a court hearing on 9 October and both Radcliffe and McNally's antiques expert were required to attend. Sorry about the late notice, but the officer in charge had been ill. Radcliffe's schedule was hastily rearranged so he could give evidence in person.

Two days before the October trial, the ALR received the expert witness report submitted by Mohune. The dealer claimed he had bought the table at a reputable antiques fair for between £2,000 and £3,000, in cash as is customary in the trade. Unfortunately, he could not remember the supplier or the date and there was no paperwork to document the transaction. The dealer's expert witness opined that any transaction at a fair would have been a good faith purchase because antiques fairs are very closely policed. His main task was to explain the awkward price discrepancy between the £70,000 the table fetched at Christie's in 2004 and the £2,000 to £3,000 for which it changed hands a few years later. Such a significant discount should have made any buyer suspicious about its origins. Mohune's expert witness had an interesting explanation. He argued that the Christie's price mostly reflected the table's appealing aristocratic provenance. Without this, the table was sold on artistic merit alone. Moreover, apparently Christie's and McNally's world-class furniture experts had failed to spot a problem that was readily apparent to the provincial dealers: the base of the table was a later substitution. This greatly reduced its market value. Thus, he argued, Mohune had indeed paid a fair price for the card table.

Unfortunately, the expert's evidence directly contradicted Mohune's sales pitch to Psmith that the table was 'special' and of 'museum quality', and on offer for £50,000. The truth of the matter would be for the court to explore. At the last minute, the October 2013 trial was adjourned to mid-January 2014. A further adjournment was ordered in January 2014, as the defendant's expert witness was unavoidably detained in the USA because of adverse weather conditions. The Circuit Court would be in touch with a new trial date in due course. In mid-May Radcliffe and his expert were asked to come back to Ireland for 19 June 2014. They wearily booked their flights, again.

A surreal trial and sentence

A large number of jurors and the witnesses for both sides converged on the imposing Georgian Court House in Monaghan. They were asked to wait all morning while the prosecution and defence barristers tried to negotiate a complex plea bargain. When this eventually failed, the lengthy process of jury selection began. Finding impartial and unconnected jurors is challenging in a locality where everyone knows everyone else and there is a long history of witness intimidation. Over 120 potential jurors were called before twelve people were found to serve in the trial. When the jury was finally sworn in, the accused stood up and pleaded guilty to the charge of possessing an item of stolen furniture.

The judge dismissed the jury and the witnesses with the immortal words: 'I am sorry, but someone has shot your fox.'[137] One assumes this was particularly frustrating for those who had travelled hundreds of miles for the chase. Finally, after spending more than four years in a police store room the precious antique could finally be released to its lawful owner. The sentence, however, was bizarre. Having pleaded guilty to possessing the stolen table but having no previous convictions, Mohune walked out of the court without a criminal record. He had played the system well.

The insurer finally recovered the mahogany table from Ireland in September 2014. It offered the table to McNally, who was very pleased to buy it back. He had collected its 2004 value as an insurance premium in 2005, but would repurchase it at its 2014 market value. The aftermath of the 2008 financial crisis had hammered the market for brown antique furniture and Irish collectors had been particularly affected. Thanks to the numerous delays of the criminal justice system, the insurer received only £28,000, minus the 15 per cent ALR recovery fee. It felt like a belated and stale victory.

Let down by the legal system

On one level, the recovery of the table with the hairy hocks is a brilliant adventure story. The villains are worthy of a crime thriller: brazen smugglers, thuggish paramilitaries, devil-may-care thieves and a slippery businessman supplying the moneyed elite with loot from the criminal underworld. The police struggle against the general lawlessness, and the threat of physical violence is pervasive. The subterfuge of Psmith and the drawn-out charm offensive leading to the tea party in the suspect's sitting room provide welcome comedic relief. And in the end, justice sort of prevails. The publishers of crime novels would probably suggest we revise the ending.

The card table case shows how much private engagement may be needed to help the overstretched police fight property crime: gun crime, knife crime, drugs and terrorism automatically take precedence over events that do not 'shout, bang or bleed'. It is in the financial interest of insurers to make law enforcement as effective as possible and keep sending the message to crooks that crime does not pay. The insurance industry has found a committed champion in the ALR to promote that agenda. The investment of time, money and imagination into this retrieval was above and beyond the call of duty. But there is clearly a question of cost-effectiveness. The final recovery fee of £4,200 did not even come close to covering the cost of the many meetings, letters and multiple trips to Ireland. The insurers' subscriptions can of course subsidise some cases like this. With an overall goal of changing the norms of the antiques trade so that it values provenance, it is worthwhile taking on and winning expensive battles, but they need to create wide media coverage or at least excited conversations among dealers. If the Garda had accepted the ALR's offer to be on hand to check Mohune's entire stock this recovery could have become a true deterrent to fences everywhere, but it was not to be.

The story of McNally's card table illustrates beautifully the triumphs and tragedies of public law enforcement. It highlights the ability of police forces to coordinate their actions across county and international borders to collect evidence and apprehend criminals. The police engaged positively with the victims of crime, secured stolen property and worked thoroughly to bring together what eventually resulted in successful court cases. Yet, with regard to the Johnsons, imposing the harshest punishments available did little to change the attitude of the gang members. Their lifestyle makes them largely immune to fines. Long prison sentences – if anything – confirmed their perception that they are outsiders persecuted by the system. Should they compare their sentences with that of Mohune, they would be even angrier.

First, Mohune had managed his affairs such that the police moved very carefully when they came to call. The officers did not conduct a fishing expedition. Although they must have been sorely tempted to look at more of the dealer's antiques, tensions within the local community made it unwise do anything that might have left Mohune feeling victimised. The police demonstrably did their duty in reacting to Radcliffe's witness statement: no more and no less. Second, due process takes an inordinate amount of time, especially if one side is in no rush to achieve a verdict. The four-year delay before the case finally came to court gave

Mohune plenty of time to arrange his affairs in preparation for a verdict against him. Third, the police were not sure of success in court and therefore had a weak negotiating position in the plea bargaining. To impose a prison sentence or a punitive fine, the police needed to prove beyond reasonable doubt that Mohune knowingly bought a stolen table. Mohune's unproven statement that he obtained the table in good faith at a minor fair and his expert witness's testimony explaining the bargain price did not ring true. However, with only one stolen item of furniture under consideration and no concrete evidence of how it had come to be in Mohune's possession, it was at least plausible he had made an innocent mistake. If Mohune Antiques is a fencing operation, relinquishing one disputed item and continuing to trade without a criminal record is not a strong deterrent. If opportunistic dealers buy antiques from crooks and thieves and resell them for up to twenty times the amount, the risk of surrendering an object once in a while can easily be incorporated into the cost of doing business.

The case of the card table thus demonstrates that, despite having the common goal of fighting property crime, incentives do not always align for public and private law enforcement. The ALR invested considerable resources with the aim of warning antiques dealers about turning a blind eye to provenance. The ALR and high net worth insurers had hoped to send a strong signal to the antiques trade that crime does not pay by exposing a fencing operation. Yet the police had a a rather narrower objective: parting Mohune from the stolen table without upsetting community relations and securing a confession to vindicate their decision to prosecute. Their surgical approach generated barely any publicity and did not convey the message to opportunistic dealers that they should revise their modus operandi. If anything, it delivered a pyrrhic victory, leading the ALR to question whether private law enforcement in this sector can be made commercially sustainable. Indeed, Mohune Antiques continues to trade in its conveniently opaque ways. And its reputation is such that we have not disclosed its real name here either. Buyer beware, or at least be aware.

10

Illicit Antiquities: Looters v Archaeologists

On 3 August 1981 the Lebanese Ministry of Tourism received a panicked phone call from a security guard at the Byblos Citadel. The watchmen had been overwhelmed in a surprise attack by rebel forces and had ignominiously retreated from the buildings. The citadel was a veritable treasure trove. Precious antiquities had been sent to Byblos from areas of heavy fighting for safekeeping, among them the finds from the Temple of Eshmun near Sidon in south-western Lebanon. The temple complex had been excavated between 1963 and 1979 by the French archaeologist Maurice Dunand in cooperation with the Lebanese government. The team had discovered around 600 beautiful marble sculptures, statues and reliefs. Many of them were votive offerings brought by pilgrims from all over the ancient world to give thanks for a cure at the famous sanctuary.[138] When fighting threatened to engulf Sidon in 1979, the excavation team hastily packed its finds into crates destined for Byblos and fled.

Unfortunately, the ancient artefacts at Byblos acted like a magnet for revolutionary militias keen to replenish their war chests. A Phalangist brigade spent four days raiding the citadel. The local police looked on helplessly as the rebels removed crate after crate from the storerooms. When Dunand arrived at Byblos a week later, all was calm but the Eshmun treasures were gone. He left angry and dejected: his work of the last two decades was in tatters. The police pleaded with the militia leaders to return the country's priceless cultural patrimony to the citadel. After a few days of intense negotiation, the militants graciously agreed. To the great relief of the security personnel, the Phalangists brought back around sixty sculptures, some pottery and eighty-two apparently untouched boxes of finds. But this was not an act of magnanimity in war or a gesture of repentance. When Dunand returned to Byblos to inspect the boxes in January 1982, he immediately realised the police had been duped. Somebody with an eye for quality had taken their pick of the antiquities. Only the poorest-quality statues had been sent back. The supposedly untouched boxes turned out to be half-empty: they contained a jumble of broken pieces from various excavations around Lebanon.[139] The militants never targeted the citadel again: clearly it no longer contained anything worth stealing.

A 'grey market'

Unfortunately, the looting of the Eshmun treasures in 1981 is just one small episode among thousands of others. The market for antiquities is riddled with objects stolen during civil and international wars, as well as those excavated illegally by hungry locals or greedy treasure hunters. The illicit trade in cultural goods promotes the destruction of humanity's archaeological and historical record. Every hastily dug pit, trench or tunnel destroys and jumbles up the layers of the past. Coin and metal hunters smash thoughtlessly through ancient dwellings, graveyards and vessels. We can learn little or nothing from objects without their archaeological context, or from pillaged and vandalised sites. Collective memory and cultural identity can be damaged irreparably by the theft or forced sale of objects of cultural or religious significance. In areas of political instability and times of economic depression, revenues from looted antiquities can fuel further conflict and terrorism.[140] Artefacts fetching five- and six-figure prices in dealers' showrooms and at exclusive art fairs often cost only a few dollars in the source countries. Crooks exploit farmers and labourers desperate to put food on their family's table, cover a medical bill or raise money to migrate. Armed gangs of looters overcome local and state efforts to protect ancient sites. Criminal networks (and occasionally mafias) can make huge profits from smuggling illicit antiquities into collectors' markets.[141] The governments and museums of developing countries thus miss out on the long-term revenue generated from exhibitions, image sales and tourism. Looting cements structural inequalities.

On the other hand, the rich and educated collected antiquities long before countries implemented their own vesting laws and international laws restricted the trade in illicit cultural goods.[142] Some governments granted excavation concessions and export licences long after implementing vesting laws, so that ancient art could be legally excavated, traded and exported. For collectors the mix of licit and illicit objects is confusing. It requires great expertise and in-depth research to distinguish between clean, unverifiable, deliberately vague and false provenances. Some provenances defy classification altogether. UNESCO therefore describes the market for cultural goods as a 'grey market, where clean and dirty goods circulate together'.[143] For example, in summer 2019 controversy erupted over the £4.7 million sale of a sculpture of the young King Tutankhamun at Christie's. The seller claimed it had been in the collection of the Thurn und Taxis family by the 1960s, but offered no documentary evidence for this. Family members phoned by investigative journalists had no recollection of it. Yet, as the Egyptian government could not prove the sculpture was still in Egypt in the 1970s, the sale went ahead.[144]

The focus on provenance in the antiquities market is a relatively new phenomenon. Until the mid-1990s, most collectors, dealers and even museum curators failed to ask detailed questions about the provenance of their objects of desire. Law enforcement was so lax that illegality simply did not feature as a quality criterion. Academic archaeologists were split into those who refused to handle suspect items on principle and those who provided legitimacy to the trade by studying unprovenanced artefacts and assisting with their identification and authentication.[145] In the late 1990s, however, the trade was rocked by a series of scandals involving looted antiquities in museum collections and auction houses.[146] As major museums, their donors and auction houses were named and shamed and forced to restitute looted vessels and sculptures, the wealthy became increasingly wary of collecting antiquities. Relatively few artefacts had an impeccable provenance. The market norm of not disclosing sellers' names at auctions means the identity of former owners is often shrouded in mystery. It is therefore straightforward to create a false provenance for a looted object by claiming it was 'in a private European collection' before 1970. The secretive nature of the market makes it difficult for non-specialists to prove (or disprove) such vague provenance information.[147]

To prevent the antiquities market from collapsing altogether, dealers in ancient art had to shore up the trust of collectors. In response to increased public scrutiny of their trade, they tightened self-regulation through their trade associations. These are private clubs formed for the benefit of their members.

Dealers' associations select their members for their professional integrity. They expect their members to avoid buying from suspicious dealers and observe specific due diligence standards.[148] As compliance cannot be monitored easily by outsiders, the associations vet and vouch for their members' honesty and promise to expel rule breakers. High standards and effective rule enforcement raise the reputation and status of insiders relative to non-members. Membership (and sticking to the club rules) can be costly, but a dealer's willingness to incur these costs is a signal to collectors that they can buy with confidence. Members can therefore charge a premium over unaffiliated dealers. Whenever collectors' preferences change, the club rules can be adjusted to maximise the net benefit of membership.

This chapter illustrates the slow and patchy process of raising provenance standards in the antiquities market over the last three decades. In February 2018 Lebanon's National Museum in Beirut celebrated the repatriation of five Eshmun statues with a special ceremony to thank the many people involved in their recovery. Their stories exemplify the convoluted paths antiquities take in a grey market that is under pressure to tidy up its act. A wide range of individuals, public and private institutions worked together to identify, seize and repatriate Lebanon's stolen cultural heritage. High-profile seizures and repatriations like this serve to educate collectors and remind museums about the risk of exhibiting antiquities with questionable or missing provenance. But changing social norms is a slow process. In nearly forty years since the theft from the Byblos Citadel only twelve of the hundreds of looted objects from Eshmun have been recovered.[149]

The volunteer watchmen

Archaeologists were the first to raise the alarm on the despoliation of cultural heritage to feed an apparently insatiable demand for antiquities. For some scholars protecting a country's heritage has become a vocation, while excavation leaders generally feel responsible for the protection of 'their' sites long after their investigations are completed. Academics are well placed to publicise thefts and looting and are often able to identify stolen objects when they are asked for expert advice by auction houses, museums and collectors. But it tends to take time for high-quality objects to surface in the market: dealers in illicit antiquities are remarkably patient. The Eshmun treasures lay dormant for a whole decade.

In 1991 the Swiss archaeologist Professor Rolf Stucky, who had visited the Eshmun excavation site regularly in the late 1960s, spotted four of the sculptures advertised for sale at an auction in Zurich.[150] He immediately alert-ed the authorities to have them seized and returned to Beirut, but what about the others? Dunand had passed away in 1987, so Professor Stucky retrieved the excavation diaries from Geneva University and published all the available information about the Eshmun treasures. He thought if dealers and collectors could identify the looted items, they would soon be back where they belonged. His lavishly illustrated book on the Eshmun sculptures

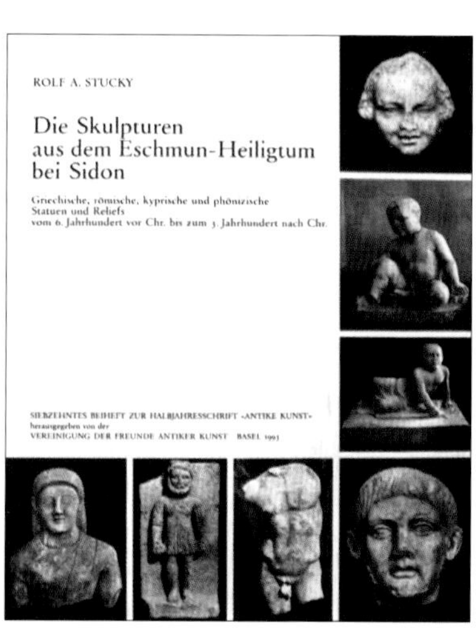

Professor Rolf Stucky's 1993 book on the sculptures from the Temple of Eshmun in Sidon.

was rushed out in record time in 1993 by The Friends of Antique Art in Basel.[151] Professor Stucky personally handed free copies of his book to dealers. He kindly requested they block the sale of the looted Eshmun treasures and urged them to facilitate their return to Lebanon. To his disappointment there was no response. Instead, in 1995 and 1996 Professor Stucky spotted further Eshmun sculptures advertised for auctions and alerted the police.[152] Thereafter, dealers who knew they had the published pieces in their stock adjusted their tactics and avoided the open market.

Shady traders

In private sales, collectors make their own decisions about how many (awkward) questions to ask about an object's provenance. In the American market, readers of Professor Stucky's book (published in German) were few and far between, so the risks of detection were low. One of the five pieces to return to Beirut in 2018 was a beautifully carved bull's head from one of the Eshmun temple's capitals. Despite the glaring gap in its provenance, the antiquities dealer Robin Symes had sold the Bull for US$1.2 million to a couple from Colorado for their dining room in 1996. Lynda and William Beierwaltes were regular customers of Symes: in their social circle, their collection of ancient art marked them out as 'people with intellect and education'.[153]

Like most collectors at the time, the Beierwalteses prized beauty and authenticity but appeared indifferent about provenance. Symes could certainly indulge collectors' passion for rare antiquities. In 2015 the Italian carabinieri found forty-five crates full of precious Roman and Etruscan artefacts bought from tomb raiders in his lock-up at the Geneva Freeport.[154] The Geneva Freeport is mentioned frequently in the context of looted art. Freeports allow their customers to store and trade goods 'in transit' without incurring customs duties or VAT. There is no time limit for storage and usually minimal control of the goods that enter and leave a freeport.[155] Once inside, goods can be traded in complete secrecy between people who have rented spaces within them. Nobody has to check what moves between vaults. The infamous antiquities dealer Giacomo Medici amassed more than 6,000 items looted from what archaeologists reckoned would have been thousands of illegally excavated tombs in his vault. He only took the best of the tomb raiders' haul, according to his maxim 'beauty pays'.[156] He then slowly channelled exquisite objects via a network of blind-eye dealers – such as Symes – to avid collectors of the latest 'must-have' antiquities.

For some US collectors, there was a powerful commercial motive for buying valuable antiquities. Museums often court rich collectors to donate outstanding artefacts to public collections. As a sweetener, 100 per cent of the value of philanthropic donations can be offset against income tax. With a lack of public scrutiny of museum acquisitions, this well-intentioned scheme created a marvellous business opportunity. Crooked dealers would sell exceptionally beautiful objects with flimsy provenances to collectors at a discount price. Broken antique ceramics or sculptures could be sold as fragments and shipped over a period of years to avoid customs or tax officials' attention. Once all the pieces had arrived with the buyer, a skilled restorer could assemble a museum-quality piece. The collector then approached a public institution with a view to making a donation. If interested, the museum curators and directors checked the object for its rarity and authenticity and provided the donor with a valuation. The museum would thus get a free prize object for its display while the gracious benefactor offset their donation against their tax bill. Some museum directors were so keen to swell their collections that they attested valuations that were a multiple of the price paid by the donor. This practice resulted in elaborate fraud schemes whereby dealers, collectors and museums benefited at the expense of taxpayers.[157]

Even if a prestigious museum just takes an object as a loan, the lender is recognised for their generous philanthropy. They save on the insurance, while the artefact's resale value rises: its exhibition in a major museum adds glamour and respectability to its provenance. For the owners of looted antiquities, this was another win-win situation. Sadly, therefore, it was not unusual for looted items to turn up in such august institutions as the New York Metropolitan Museum of Art or the Getty Museum in Los Angeles. However, in the late 1990s investigative journalist Peter Watson started to probe into the commercial practices of Sotheby's in handling suspicious antiquities. Further investigations exposed the complicity of the Met and the Getty Museum.[158] Embarrassed, museums tightened up their procedures around unprovenanced antiquities. This had direct repercussions on the collectors, whose former 'museum-quality' pieces were suddenly tainted, and their suppliers. Antiquities dealers had to take measures to rescue their reputation.

One innovation was for dealers' associations to ask their members to consult the Interpol or ALR database and only sell antiquities with a clean search certificate. However, initially this was mostly a case of 'optical due diligence', that is, appearing to do the right thing. A clean search certificate proves only that the object was not registered as stolen. But neither the ALR nor Interpol had a comprehensive register of looted antiquities. In any case, it would be impossible to create a database to put an end to the illicit trade. First, the pieces must be unique and sufficiently well-photographed to be searchable. Second, one would never capture artefacts that were excavated illicitly and hence never formally documented. At best, one could put together a database of exceptional recorded items stolen from private collectors, museums or official excavations. However, neither source governments nor academics had the money to create it. The ALR therefore stepped into the breach. To improve the quality of its checking service for this new group of customers, the ALR offered to register stolen and looted antiquities for free. In 2000 Professor Stucky was told about the ALR. He immediately sent his Eshmun sculptures book to London and the ALR team registered the lost treasures on behalf of the Lebanese government, the lawful owner of the looted sculptures.

A partially reformed market

When the Beierwalteses entered the antiquities market as prospective sellers in 2004 they found its norms and formal processes transformed. Their earlier cavalier attitude to provenance came back to haunt them. The Head of Antiquities at Christie's provided them with a valuation for the Bull of only 12.5 per cent of its purchase price: US$150,000.[159] Moreover, he pointedly did not offer to include their collection in an auction as it was too hot to touch. Christie's would imperil its reputation by publicly auctioning objects listing the antiquities dealer Robin Symes as their source. Symes had been in and out of court through the early 2000s and during this time over 17,000 (unprovenanced and likely illicit) antiquities owned by him had been found in thirty-three different storage locations.[160] Ever diplomatic, Christie's advised the Beierwalteses that its valuation was conditional on the objects being lawfully exported and that confirmation of this would be sought.[161] The couple probably checked their paperwork at this point and realised they needed a dealer who did not ask unhelpful questions. They approached the Aboutaam brothers of Phoenix Ancient Art who agreed to sell their collection for a commission, but privately rather than at auction. They appraised the Eshmun Bull at a much more satisfactory US$1.5 million and shipped it to their vault in the Geneva Freeport.[162]

The Bull still met the due diligence standards applied by antiquities dealers in the mid-2000s: it had not been registered on the ALR database. Bull sculptures had been used as architectural ornaments on the temple's columns, and the architectural finds were only collated in Professor Stucky's second Eshmun book. This was published in 2005 but did not reach the ALR offices. Thus, in 2008 a clean ALR certificate cleared the way for the Bull's public exhibition in Geneva and Paris.[163] When the hedge fund billionaire Michael Steinhardt requested to see the object, it was shipped back to New York. By 2010, the Beierwalteses were sufficiently disillusioned to agree a sale to Steinhardt at just US700,000 (minus a 20 per cent commission to the Aboutaam brothers). But New York turned out to be a dangerous place for the owners of looted antiquities.

Steinhardt did not add the Bull sculpture to his personal collection. Initially it lingered with Phoenix Ancient Art, which then brokered a loan to the New York Metropolitan Museum. Incredibly, the Met accepted its one-line provenance 'Ex-American private collection, collected in the 1980s–90s', even after being informed the collectors had acquired it from Symes, who by this time had spent seven months in prison for shady dealings in the antiquities market.[164] In 2014 – almost four years after its arrival – a Met curator finally noticed the similarity with the Bull in Professor Stucky's book. The discovery of yet another looted sculpture in the Met would cause public embarrassment, so the Bull was quietly removed from display. But the museum decided against spooking its super-rich donors by calling in the cops over a looted antiquity if the matter could be settled amicably. The Beierwalteses cancelled the sale to Steinhardt and returned his money in full. Yet at this point they considered themselves to be once again the Bull's lawful owners. They instructed their lawyers to request that the Met should not inform the Lebanese authorities. By involving their hard-hitting lawyers, they sent the message that polite, behind-the-scenes private negotiations would not resolve this problem. After a two-and-a-half-year stand-off (with no resolution in sight), the Met finally sent a letter to Beirut.

The 'Pitbull'

When the Lebanese authorities informed the New York district attorney's office of their repatriation claim in December 2016, it did not take the legal team long to verify its legitimacy. The assistant DA – the formidable Colonel Matthew Bogdanos – determined that he was legally required to seize the sculpture. When his office informed the Met of this decision in July 2017, the Bull's head was delivered the very next day. This sudden outburst of eager compliance was not surprising: Colonel Bogdanos has a fearsome reputation in the New York antiquities market. Nicknamed 'Pitbull' by some newspapers for his tenacity,[165] Colonel Bogdanos had at this time already facilitated the return of US$150 million worth of antiquities to their countries of origin. His meticulous and scathing account of the Bull's journey through the shadier parts of the art market also quickly headed off the Beierwalteses' legal case that they were the sculpture's lawful owners. The Lebanese authorities could finally repatriate their long-lost property.

Colonel Bogdanos's colossal court bundle detailing the legal case for the Bull's repatriation is based on subpoenas, search warrants and countless interviews. The investigators went through customs documents, bills of sale, valuations, the ALR's records, shipping bills and proofs of postage, as well as lengthy email correspondences about the object. The painstaking approach of the legal team shed an unforgiving light on the practices and attitudes that allowed the illicit antiquities trade to thrive. Most of the characters involved, whether buyers, sellers, dealers or museum officials, came in for severe criticism. The ALR was on the back foot, too, for providing the 2008 document showing the Bull had not been registered. The DA roundly criticised the trade for accepting this limited bill of

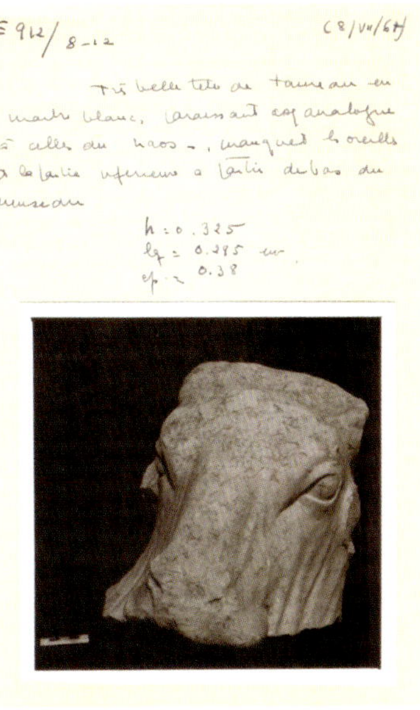

The 1967 excavation inventory catalogue card for the Eshmun Bull from Colonel Matthew Bogdanos's court papers.

clean health to facilitate the exhibition and sale of an object with such a dubious provenance without further enquiry.

A passion for protecting and repatriating the treasures of the ancient world is palpable from Colonel Bogdanos's writing.[166] With his own dedicated antiquities trafficking unit he could turn the New York collectors' market upside down. New York's unusually strict property laws mean that a careless collector could face criminal charges for handling stolen property. Even if they are relatively confident in their legal title, it is often wiser to give up swiftly if an item from their collection attracts the Colonel's attention.[167] Thus, when the Bull was finally repatriated to Lebanon, it did not travel alone. Not one, but three sculptures from Eshmun – their total value estimated at US$5 million – were sent from New York to Beirut. The DA's public announcement of the apparition of two additional marble statues seems deliberately vague and discreet.[168] One torso is reported as having been seized from an unnamed antiques dealer. The other is only described as having been 'recently owned by a private collector'. Apparently one can preserve one's dignity and reputation by settling early and gracefully.

One of the extra statues had in fact been located by the ALR. A London dealer had conducted a search prior to acquiring the sculpture from a private collector in New York in November 2017. As it matched a sculpture from Professor Stucky's book, the ALR warned the dealer and informed the assistant DA of the torso's location, who immediately took steps to have it seized, commending the ALR's valuable role in monitoring the antiquities trade.

Colonel Bogdanos's campaign is largely limited to the antiquities trade in New York, however. In many countries, good faith purchasers obtain legal title (or the right to be compensated) after a statutory period and the bar for what would be considered a good faith purchase can be quite low.[169] Moreover, New York is exceptional in allocating public funding to proactively pursue the trade in looted antiquities. Colonel Bogdanos's legal case for the seizure of the Bull noted that ninety-seven of the ninety-nine antiquities valued by Christie's for the Beierwalteses listed Symes as the only previous owner. In fact, the archaeologist Christos Tsirogiannis painstakingly identified several of these artefacts as coming from Medici's illicit treasure trove of looted antiquities in Geneva in a 1998 edition of *House & Garden* that featured the Beierwalteses' enviable art collection.[170] Thus, the case for repatriation presented by Colonel Bogdanos for the Bull applies to all of these objects. Yet only the Bull was in New York and could be seized. Fascinating as the Bull case is, no-expense-spared, hard-hitting public enforcement like Colonel Bogdanos's iron regime in New York remains the exception rather than the rule.

The art of persuasion

So how does private crime control function when the local law favours the good faith purchaser and there is no fearsome assistant DA to act as a backstop? The case of the fourth Eshmun sculpture to join the repatriation party in Beirut – a further marble torso – shows that it can work surprisingly well, too. This is a classic ALR case. The beautiful Roman torso in question had been chosen by Professor Stucky for the front cover of his Eshmun sculptures book. Yet neither the antiquities dealer in Germany who bought it in 2017 from an Austrian private collection, nor the Austrian collector who had bought it in 1998 in Switzerland had been aware of the professor's campaign on behalf of the Eshmun sculptures. However, there was no question about it: the old and new photographs of the torso were a perfect match.

There was a small problem, though: the sculpture had been registered on the ALR *on behalf of* the Lebanese government, not *by* the Lebanese government. Only the Lebanese authorities could reclaim the statue, either directly from the dealer, or by instructing the ALR to act on its behalf. It

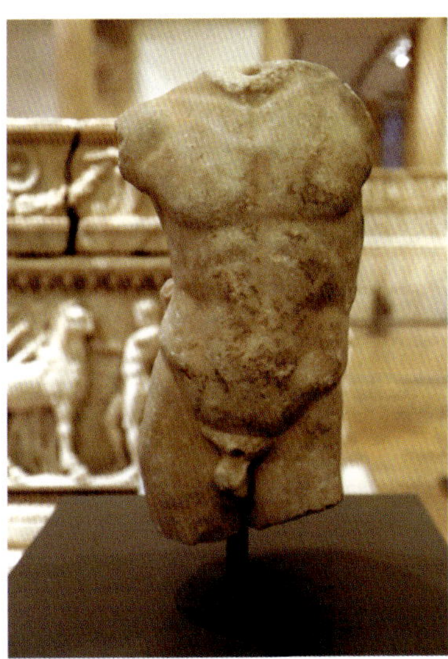

The repatriated marble torso of a nude male in the National Museum of Beirut in 2018.

could also choose to relinquish its claim altogether. The ALR had learnt an important lesson from the drama over the recovery of the Impressionist paintings on behalf of the Museo Nacional de Bellas Artes in Buenos Aires (see Chapter 4). Any work on behalf of governments is undertaken for free; any benefits have to come from positive publicity after a successful recovery.

The repatriation of looted antiquities, however, is not always a political priority. Drawing attention to looting or thefts from national heritage sites, museums or safe storage areas may do far more reputational damage than can be gained from publicity around a repatriation. Moreover, an out-of-the-blue letter from a private company in London offering free help with a restitution may seem a little suspicious. Who is this company working for and why? What is the quid pro quo if the ALR is not charging the source government? Is it better to obtain legal advice before making a decision? A letter from the ALR announcing the good news could sit in a junior official's in tray for some considerable period, before being put into the in tray of a slightly higher-ranking official, slowly making its way up the hierarchy to someone (or a committee) ready, willing and able to make a decision. In the meantime, of course, the object would be in limbo, with the ALR unable to confirm its final status to the (perhaps increasingly exasperated and nervy) client who requested the search.

Fortunately, the Lebanese Ministry of Culture had already worked with the ALR in 2006 to recover a marble head. Still, the ALR did not expect a speedy reply as its previous contacts there had long since moved on. It was therefore surprised to receive a positive answer the very next morning, 12 April 2017: yes please to the 'generous offer' of assistance. The ALR now needed a letter signed by the Minister of Culture to put the recovery process in motion. The office duly despatched all the evidence and a draft letter for the minister to Beirut.

A gentle reminder was sent on 19 April and the reply came back the next day: yes, the letter was with the minister and ready to sign. The German dealer was therefore told of the match on 24 April and given the evidence that the torso was looted. He called the ALR on several occasions over the next days, clearly confused and upset. He had recently bought the sculpture in good faith. The Austrian colleague from whom he had purchased it would surely have had good title after eighteen years? He had a valid export licence from Austria and that had not indicated a problem. Why should he return it to Lebanon? In the notes circulated after one of the more heated phone calls with the dealer on 28 April, the ALR antiquities specialist predicted: 'he is 100 per cent not giving the torso up!'[171].

The ALR maintained that, given the publication of Professor Stucky's book in 1993, the torso could not have been bought in good faith in 1998. The dealer should certainly have conducted the ALR search prior to acquiring an object without location information in 2017. But it was futile to discuss concrete next steps without an official letter from Beirut requesting repatriation. So, another reminder was sent to Beirut on 25 April and another holding email was received on 28 April. The letter had been 'approved' but still needed to be signed.

When the minister's letter finally arrived in London on 8 May, the ALR immediately sent a carefully crafted email to the dealer. First, it set out the law vesting the property rights in the sculpture in the Republic of Lebanon and surmising that under the new German cultural property law of 2016 it would be disadvantageous to fight a repatriation claim in court. Second, the dealer was reminded of his membership in the International Association of Dealers in Ancient Art (IADAA) and its code of conduct. Third, the dealer was reassured that the police had 'not yet' been informed. This was obviously a veiled threat that they might be, even if it was far from clear what the police would do if they were. However, the ALR's central three-line paragraph inviting the dealer to reflect on how his peers would view his conduct was arguably the most powerful part of the missive.

Founded in 1993, the IADAA's main purpose is to maintain public trust in the legitimate market for antiquities that 'does not harm archaeology in any way'.[172] Given increasing public scepticism about private ownership of cultural heritage, the association fully commits itself to preventing art crime. It claims that its members 'understand and tackle issues of provenance that have become prevalent in recent years'.[173] The IADAA requires all members to adhere to 'the highest professional standards as set out in our stringent code of ethics'.[174] Buyers are reassured that IADAA members 'undertake due diligence as a matter of course'.[175] Specifically, members are obliged to search 'every object with a sales value over €5,000' with Interpol and/or the ALR.[176] The IADAA therefore reassures collectors that 'Your dealings with any member of the association can be made with the utmost confidence.'[177]

If the ALR brought the dealer's lapse in due diligence to the IADAA's attention, the professional association 'representing the top international dealers in Classical, Egyptian and Near Eastern ancient art' would have to disown him.[178] As the dealer was a founder member of the IADAA, this would have been particularly awkward for both sides. The day after receiving the ALR's email, the dealer clarified that he had never had any intention of reselling or exporting the torso. In fact, it had been available for collection since 24 April 2017, the day he was informed of the Lebanese claim. All that remained to be done was for the Lebanese embassy in Berlin to come and pick it up. Another marble torso was on its way to the repatriation party in Beirut.

Special powers

The fifth and final statue was seized by customs officials in the port of Tripoli in northern Lebanon. Customs checks are the first line of defence against the international trafficking of antiquities. Arguably, they are also the most powerful. Customs laws allow officials to seize any property that is illegally imported or exported. Customs officers can pre-emptively seize goods or assets where they suspect a link to criminal activity. If the owner of an antiquity seized by customs feels they have been treated unfairly, they must go to court to prove their legal title. Given sufficient resources, customs could stop the trade in illicit antiquities in its tracks.

The series of hugely successful sting operations code-named Pandora is an excellent example of successful transnational law enforcement.[179] In Operation Pandora III in 2018, thousands of police and customs officers from twenty-nine countries joined forces to patrol online markets for antiquities, swoop into auction houses and dealerships, inspect private collections, step up spot checks at borders and visit archaeological sites. Over 18,000 illicit cultural goods were seized and fifty-nine arrests were made in a ten-day period. International coordination greatly boosts the powers of customs in tackling the underground market in looted antiquities. This had first been demonstrated by Operation Pandora I in 2016, when eighteen countries cooperated in a week of enhanced surveillance and checks, seizing around 3,500 objects.[180] Operation Pandora II in 2017 had massively stepped up the pressure with eighty-one countries involved and over 41,000 illicit objects seized.[181] Yet, by the time the Spanish police, Europol and Interpol solicited support for Pandora III, more than half of the countries that had participated so successfully in Pandora II politely declined. Only twenty-nine governments chose to reallocate police and customs resources to a prestigious week-long international collaboration to tackle organised criminals trading in cultural property. So, what is the reality of customs enforcement on a day-to-day basis?

Customs have two problems in enforcing cultural property law. First, random spot checks will catch only a small proportion of illicit antiquities imports, especially when web-based traders use the postal service to send goods directly to customers. To change criminals' perception about the risk of trafficking illicit antiquities, customs officials need accurate and timely information. Customs enforcement therefore regularly work with public institutions and private individuals interested in protecting cultural heritage. Members of the public who become aware of stolen cultural property can provide (anonymous) tip-offs.[182] Ethical collectors, engaged members of the public and professional archaeologists can thus help law enforcement to maximise its effectiveness by doing free detective work for them.

Once an antiquity of dubious origin has been seized, a second potentially even more time-consuming problem arises. How will the recipient react to the official 'notice of seizure' letter? If a small illicit trinket is at stake, then it is probably best to lie low. If the item is matched to one registered on the ALR or with Interpol it is futile to protest. But what about an artefact with a six- or seven-figure retail value that is not registered as looted and could therefore be legitimate? After all, many legitimately owned antiquities have shaky provenance documentation. At this point it turns out the rule that the object can only be reclaimed though the courts is a double-edged sword. Risk-averse recipients of seizure notices will be put off from reclaiming. But if someone calls the customs officers' bluff and starts legal proceedings then officials have a problem: they must prepare a legal case, too.

Law enforcement officials are expert at seizing suspicious cultural artefacts, but are often out of their depth if that assessment is challenged by an irate owner: 'no, this is not a priceless 4,000-year-old pharaonic head, it's a 1920s copy'; 'my daughter made that'; 'this has been in my family for generations, my gran used it as a bird bath'; 'I bought this from a private collector in Geneva in 1968'. Eyes may roll at the mention of Geneva – was it from a 'collection' in the infamous Freeport? – but it is difficult to prove these claims are not true. Who will stand up in court and give expert witness testimony? Who would relish the opportunity to be cross-examined by a ferocious attorney about how exactly they came to the conclusion that a stone relief is genuine and the very one that was last photographed in Palmyra in 1980? A senior expert in the field, preferably a professor at a reputable university, would have credibility when pronouncing an object genuine and looted, but they would also need to collect good evidence to prepare a watertight case.

The market rate for a senior professor's services as an expert witness generally far exceeds the budget devoted to combating illicit antiquities. Therefore, once again law enforcement relies on committed volunteers to take time off work to examine suspicious artefacts, give advice and, if necessary, agree to be drawn into stressful legal proceedings, and all for free. There is a limit to how much *pro bono* work people with full-time jobs can do. Thus, not every seized suspicious artefact will be returned to the source country. For example, the Swiss authorities raided the Geneva Freeport store of Phoenix Ancient Art in October 2017 and seized 11,000 suspicious objects. Yet in August 2018, 5,000 of them were released by a Swiss court. The investigators had been unable to uniquely identify their source countries or establish that they were illicitly exported in the limited time available for their research. Another 6,000 antiquities – including eighteen from the Beierwalteses' collection – remained in the hands of the Swiss authorities for further investigation.[183]

In a legal war of attrition, rich collectors and dealers with million-dollar objects at stake have every chance of prevailing against underfunded police investigators. In jurisdictions that favour bona fide purchasers – such as European civil law countries – collectors have less to fear than in New York. For stretched customs officers, private and public resources such as the ALR and national and international police databases are therefore an invaluable resource when it comes to making a decision to seize an object. The search is free for law enforcement. If there is a match, the cost of pursuing a repatriation and the risk of being challenged is low.

The importance of volunteers in protecting cultural heritage

It is great that the Lebanese government decided to acknowledge and celebrate the people who helped to bring the five Eshmun statues home. This chapter has demonstrated the huge gap that exists between the international law protecting the world's cultural heritage and its formal enforcement. Thankfully, some of that gap is filled by private efforts. Private individuals, NGOs, trade associations and firms like the ALR aid the police and customs by providing information and expertise, by monitoring markets and by taking actions that raise dealers' and auctioneers' cost of trading in suspicious antiquities. Most people expect payment when they collect and pass on information, write detailed reports and publish books. Economic self-interest makes their work sustainable in the long run. Thus, when the IADAA obliges its members to take due diligence seriously, search objects with the ALR and reject antiquities with dubious provenance, it does so to protect the market for licit antiquities. If collectors cannot trust dealers and antiquities collections are widely perceived as tainted, rich people will find something else to collect. Some people may be motivated by status considerations. Academics write books to enhance their reputation, as do investigative journalists who uncover shady deals in major museums or auction houses.

But many people and private organisations who give up time and resources to protect the world's cultural heritage do so almost against their own economic self-interest because they genuinely care. The protestors waving placards outside auction houses feel only the proverbial 'warm glow', as do providers of anonymous tip-offs. Academics helping with police investigations have to be very cautious when talking to their peers about ongoing proceedings, limiting the status gains from doing so. The eagle-eyed curator at the Metropolitan museum who spotted the looted Bull would not have been very popular with the 'donor relations' department. Professor Stucky took time off from his

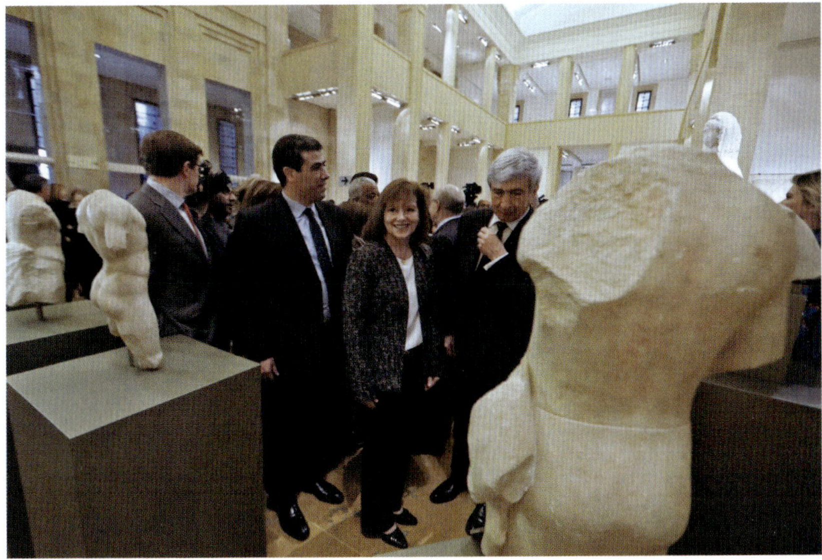

The reception celebrating the repatriation of the five marble statues in the National Museum of Beirut in February 2018.

own research to publish two books on a deceased colleague's excavation. Ancient art lovers donated their money to fund their publication. Christos Tsirogiannis spends his time searching the art world (and glossy interiors magazines) for the looted treasures sold by Giacomo Medici rather than risk crooked dealers gaining access to the Medici archive. The delight and enthusiasm of the ALR staff who facilitated the Eshmun repatriations had little basis in short-run profit considerations either. Other than charging a fee for the dealers' searches, their work was done for free. However, media coverage of discoveries of looted antiquities and successful repatriations raises the profile and credibility of a clean ALR search certificate in the antiquities market. In the long run, increased searches and registrations may make the ALR's work on antiquities commercially sustainable.

Illegal excavations, tomb robbing, theft from museums, smuggling, storing and selling illicit artefacts can be a hugely profitable business. Three cheers to the people who ensure it does not always pay. Numerous volunteers are helping public officials to raise the risks of peddling illicit antiquities. Several hundred sculptures from Eshmun are still missing, but they are definitely not forgotten. Increasing public/private vigilance is changing collectors' attitudes. Significant price discounts for objects of dubious or suspect origin show that people are now taking the caveat emptor warning seriously. Buying provenance-free is no longer a good investment strategy and may backfire spectacularly. We cannot save the world's cultural heritage from destruction without paying for proper law enforcement. At the moment we are spending far too little, but volunteers make that little go a very long way.

11

Some Like It Hot: Fencing Stolen Watches

'Smash-and-grab gang armed with knives target Mayfair jewellers'

It was a brazen attack in broad daylight. In January 2016 four men on motorbikes screeched to a halt outside the Swiss Time Machine jewellers on Avery Row in Mayfair, London. The pillion riders jumped off and forced their way through the front door with a sledgehammer, while the drivers stood guard outside menacingly: shouting and waving hammers and knives at passers-by. Once inside, the robbers smashed open the display cases and swept the contents into plastic bags. Moments later, they jumped back on their motorbikes to make a high-speed getaway with around £1.1 million worth of watches and jewellery. Two of the robbers bungled their escape a few minutes later, when they crashed outside the Chinese embassy in Portland Place. Perhaps they were spooked by the armed diplomatic protection officers outside. They abandoned their crumpled vehicle and ran off, discarding their loot bag when the officers gave chase. The police managed to arrest one of

> *them and also retrieved the bag containing forty-one watches valued at*
> *£650,000. 'It was like something out of a Hollywood movie', commented*
> *an eyewitness.*[184] *Unfortunately, it is all too real. These ruthless raids are*
> *so lucrative that they have become an occupational hazard for jewellers*
> *across the UK.*

A moral conundrum

There is an almost bewildering amount of choice when you are looking to buy a pre-owned luxury watch. If you are browsing online, used watches are offered by dedicated watch dealers, jewellers and general auction websites. You will find hundreds of thousands of watches for sale. One has to narrow the search criteria significantly to end up with a manageable selection. If you prefer to see the watch on your arm before you buy, jewellers and pawnbrokers will be delighted to be of service. One question that invariably comes up is: do you mind if your watch comes without papers and its original box?

In a nutshell: there is a 15–50 per cent discount for luxury watches without boxes and papers, and the more prestigious the watch the higher the discount. There is plenty of advice encouraging buyers to take the plunge. 'You can't wear the box or papers! It's a legitimate way to keep the costs down.'[185] Bloggers list dozens of good reasons for watches to be sold without any documentation. In former times, impulsive buyers often proudly walked out of the jeweller's shop with a shiny new watch on their wrist and never bothered to take the box. Other owners lost or binned the papers later when the warranty ran out. Some watches became detached from their original documents as they were sold on or handed down in families. For some second-hand watch dealers, storing and finding the right box for each purchase may just have been too much of a logistical nightmare to make it worth their while.

Unfortunately, there are also more sinister reasons for undocumented watches to appear on the market. One issue that immediately springs to mind is authenticity: does the discount reflect the risk of inadvertently buying a fake or replica watch? Most counterfeit watches are deliberately bought as fakes: in street markets or from dealers that make no pretence about the objects being genuine, and at prices that fully reflect their low-status origin. No dealer looking for repeat business would pass off these cheap counterfeits as genuine luxury items: it is unlikely fellow traders and serious collectors will be fooled. Should they be taken in initially, bargain watches do not tend to age well. However, there are also so-called 'superfakes' that are extremely well made and hence trickier to spot, as well as 'frankenwatches'. The latter contain a mixture of genuine and fake parts, for example a genuine case with a fake movement inside or a movement culled from a different watch. Here the fraud is more difficult to detect especially as such watches tend to come with credible forged paperwork. Most dealers therefore carefully examine the internal mechanism before acquiring a second-hand timepiece and any damage sustained during the examination is entirely at the seller's risk.

The second issue is theft. Luxury watches make an ideal target for criminals. They are worn openly, light to carry, easily concealed and avidly collected. They are stolen in burglaries, by pickpockets, moped gangs, conmen, prostitutes and dishonest staff. Luxury watches are also a popular purchase for credit card fraudsters. We can alleviate some of the financial risks of these crimes by buying insurance. But criminals inflict far more than monetary losses. Burglaries leave their victims feeling bereft, angry, distrustful, vulnerable and anxious, and can lead to stress-related illnesses. Smash-and-grab raids from jewellery stores in broad daylight put shoppers, staff and passers-by in fear of their lives. Street robbers injure and terrify people, whether intentionally or unintentionally. Knife- and hammer-wielding, acid-throwing moped gangs have become a plague in many inner cities. Innocent people have suffered life-changing injuries or died resisting the theft of a treasured timepiece. This makes buying a watch without documents a moral conundrum: a buoyant secondary market for luxury watches that sidelines their provenance encourages (violent) crime.

Disrupting the market for stolen watches

Much police time is taken up with pursuing the perpetrators of violent and gang crime, while insurance mitigates its financial implications for affected individuals. However, it also makes sense to disrupt the market for stolen watches. Luxury watchmakers produce tens or hundreds of thousands of watches each year, but each one is unique because of its serial number. With a comprehensive database of stolen watches recording the brand, model name and serial number, it would be possible to check whether a watch can be bought and sold in good faith. If we can raise the risk that watches of dubious origins will bring their owners practical, legal or financial headaches, the attitudes of buyers and dealers will change. The greater the discount buyers expect for undocumented watches, the lower the attraction of stealing them in the first place.

Most luxury watch manufacturers have long kept private registers of stolen watches of their brand. Licensed dealers can consult these registers before buying, servicing or repairing watches, and may seize and return stolen watches to their owners (or their insurers). However, watch manufacturers do not allow the secondary market to consult their registers.[186] Until the creation of The Watch Register, independent jewellers and pawnbrokers therefore had no way of checking whether watches offered to them were stolen and this was a deliberate policy. For buyers, stolen watches are not a good investment. Holders of (potentially) stolen watches would avoid sending them to licensed workshops for service and repairs where they might be seized. Using non-specialist repairers and generic spare parts reduces the functionality and resale value of watches. Collectors buying from unlicensed dealers would therefore expect a discount to reflect the probability and cost of inadvertently acquiring a stolen watch. By contrast, licensed dealers with access to the watchmakers' private register could charge a premium for pre-owned watches, because they could certify them as legitimate. Keeping the registers confidential also increased primary sales of expensive collectors' watches through licensed dealerships: many customers were suspicious of non-licensed dealers and speculators selling unused rare watches in the secondary market. The exclusive nature of the registers thus added value to making a licensing agreement with a watch manufacturer: a clear case of private governance for private profit.

When The Watch Register was launched by the ALR as a dedicated service for the watch trade in 2014, there was therefore significant demand among honest jewellers for a reputable database to carry out due diligence checks and facilitate competition with licensed dealers. However, some jewellers and pawnbrokers were happy to ignore the problem of watch thefts. As long as there was no trusted resource to check out watches, it was unlikely they would be caught selling stolen watches. Thieves and fences might offer their loot at a significant discount, but jewellers could sell them at the normal secondary market value. Stolen watches thus offered attractive profit margins. For opportunistic dealers, it requires a broader change in market norms to change their ways. As more theft victims register stolen watches on The Watch Register database, and other dealers, repair workshops and potential customers increasingly check the register before touching pre-owned watches, the probability of being caught rises. A rising risk of having to refund disappointed customers whose watches have been seized and the loss of reputation through local gossip provide incentives for high-street dealers to take greater precautions.

In the online market, however, the barriers to changing practices are higher. Many internet platforms are market makers bringing together buyers and sellers for a commission. The platform does not buy the watch from the seller but merely facilitates the transaction. The buyer's money is often held in escrow for a set period in case difficulties arise. If the buyer spots an undeclared problem with the watch, the transaction is voided. The watch is returned to the consignor and the platform loses only the commission income. Thus, when a super-vigilant theft victim finds their watch advertised for sale online, they do not always get the result they expect when they complain. One theft victim who spotted their stolen watch for sale on the internet confronted the dealer with that information. The company promptly returned it to the person who had consigned it: one Mr M. The former owner was back at square one.

The Watch Register thus set out to reform the business practices underpinning the market for stolen watches. Checking serial numbers is much easier than matching descriptions and photographs of fine art, furniture or other valuables. However, to become effective and self-sustaining as a business it needs many users who pay for its services: both to register stolen watches and to search for them. Could The Watch Register database change the attitude of opportunistic high-street jewellers and online watch dealers and encourage them to adopt due diligence standards for theft comparable to those they already implement for counterfeits? The ALR would need support from law enforcement and the police would need its help in turn.

A shady dealer

In March 2016 an unassuming gentleman approached a watch dealer in the Hatton Garden jewellery emporium. He pulled out a lovely Rolex wristwatch: a vintage GMT-Master 'Tiger Eye' in 18-carat yellow gold. Was the dealer interested in buying it? It was a desirable collectors' piece and certainly of interest, so he decided to have a closer look, including querying its provenance with The Watch Register. Five minutes later he had an answer: the serial number had been matched with a recently stolen watch on the database. The ALR would call the police. Could the dealer please secure the watch in the meantime?

The watch in question had been registered by Swiss Time Machine in Mayfair after the spectacular smash-and-grab raid two months previously. The police were therefore immediately on high alert: this was a very fresh trail that might well lead to the two culprits that had got away. An officer would be sent out directly. The man who had brought in the watch was dismayed when the dealer told him there was a problem. He claimed somebody must have made a mistake. It was definitely his watch. He had bought it legitimately and could prove it. Perhaps it was an insurance fraud? When he grew agitated and demanded his watch back, the dealer made a suggestion to extricate himself from an increasingly awkward situation. Would it be OK if he took his upset customer across the road to talk to the good people from The Watch Register team instead? Everyone agreed and, having delivered both the man and the watch to the ALR office, the relieved dealer returned to his stall at the emporium. He had done his duty.

At the ALR office, the frustrated seller introduced himself as Mr M and explained that he was a watch dealer. He claimed he had bought the watch at an auction, but he did not remember the name of the auction house. Of course, he had all the paperwork at home and the watch had been properly checked by Rolex and against another (nameless) stolen watch database. Clearly this was a case of mistaken identity. Could he please take his watch and go? Thankfully, there was no time for the situation to deteriorate, as two officers from the Metropolitan Police's Flying Squad stepped into the ALR offices to question Mr M.

Mr M was soon on the back foot. It turned out he knew almost nothing about the watch. No, he did not have any paperwork at all. He said he had bought the watch six weeks ago, for £7,500 from a man called 'Chris' at Costa Coffee in Hatton Garden, but there was no receipt. No, he did not have any contact details for Chris either. He recalled that Chris was probably in his fifties, had thinning ginger hair and a Canadian accent. Mr M claimed he was just a small-time trader, mostly peddling watches for spare parts around Hatton Garden. If the watch was stolen it was bad luck: he had certainly bought it for good money and in good faith from Canadian Chris at Costa Coffee.

Predictably, the officers were not convinced by this ropey provenance. They asked Mr M to show them the contents of the plastic bag he had with him. He sulkily upended it on the desk and over two dozen further luxury watches tumbled out. Where were they from? Here and there, a few of them had come from Hong Kong. He had bought them off a man called 'Tony'. He estimated the total value of the watches at around £30,000. It was a surprisingly large and valuable stock for a small-time watch dealer to carry around. So how big was this modest man's business? Despite Mr M's protestations of innocence, the police seized the watches and arrested him. When they later searched his flat, they found a further sixty watches and some fake Rolex certificates. But how many of them were stolen? And should Mr M have known they were 'hot'?

Unravelling a fencing business

Mr M maintained he was an innocent occasional watch dealer. However, the Metropolitan Police already had him on their radar. In July 2015 a young man had been picked up outside a club and whisked off to a nearby hotel. When he woke up, his fleeting acquaintance had disappeared with his Rolex. Soon afterwards, the victim saw his watch for sale on the internet. When he complained to the dealer and tried to reclaim his watch, he was disappointed. Instead of returning the watch to him, it was sent back to the consignor. The theft victim alerted the police who obtained Mr M's details from the internet dealer and phoned him. Mr M claimed he was selling the watch as a favour to 'Chris': a Canadian male whom he had met by a watch repair stall in Bethnal Green. The officer requested he attend Holborn police station with the stolen watch, but Mr M never came and the stolen Rolex vanished.

So, here was the elusive Mr M with an estimated total value of £110,000 watches in his possession, less than a year after first coming to the police's attention in the matter of a stolen watch. He still had no more specific provenance information to give than 'Canadian Chris', 'Tony' and 'as a favour to a mate'. He said he ran a company called 'Chrono Time', but this company was not officially registered and it had never paid a penny in tax. Mr M's large stock of watches suggested it probably should have done. It sounded suspiciously like a business handling stolen goods. The Flying Squad decided to launch an investigation and turned to The Watch Register for help, which was once again offered on a *pro bono* basis.

The next weeks at The Watch Register office were very busy. The staff started by checking the serial numbers of the eighty-seven seized watches against the database. The twenty-one matches they made instantly read like a cross section of the British Crime Survey: a street robbery, a credit card fraud, a theft at a gym, two home burglaries, multiple watches from raids on jewellers … watches stolen in Oxford, Milton Keynes, Twickenham, and most of them within the last few months. But there were also many watches that had not been reported to The Watch Register as stolen. This did not mean Mr M was in the clear, though. Not every watch is insured and not all uninsured theft

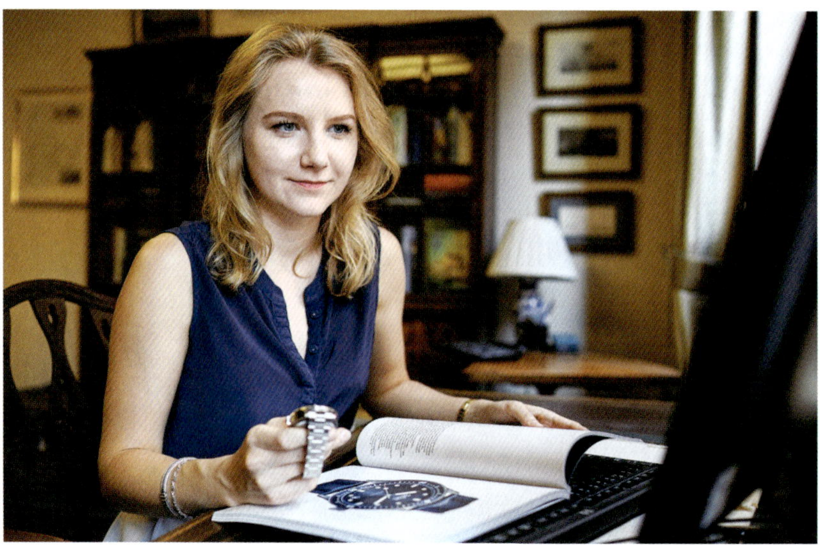

Katya Hills, managing director of The Watch Register, checks a watch against the database.

victims privately register their stolen watches. Not every insurer submits information about stolen watches to the database either. Although insurers of jewellers would most likely know and use the database, not all home insurers may have heard of (or chosen to use) The Watch Register. The secondary market in watches is global and although the initial matches were fairly local the other watches could have been stolen anywhere.

Another issue was the speed at which stolen watches had made their way into Mr M's bag. Insurance claims can take months to process. Thefts from jewellers, however, are quickly reported to the SaferGems scheme, a joint initiative between the British National Association of Jewellers and T.H. March, a specialist insurance broker for jewellery and watches.[187] Again, it takes time to collate information about thefts and email the alerts out to subscribers. The police therefore went directly to SaferGems for the latest data and several further matches were made. In the meantime, the police trawled through their own archive and connected Mr M to four other stolen watches. Another watch was identified by the ALR during a routine check for an auction in west London. When the police enquired with the consignor, the jeweller explained they had bought it from Mr M. The police seized the watch. In April 2016 Mr M was interviewed under caution. This time he claimed he had bought the watch on eBay from someone named 'Lee'. With an ever-growing list of loot there was now a real appetite to prosecute him.

The case against Mr M would be much stronger if the remaining watches in the bag could also be linked to criminal activities. Did the luxury watchmakers have any more information on them on their private databases? The ALR experts started making enquiries, but even with the weight of a British police investigation behind them they often hit a brick wall, especially at the ultra-luxury end of the market. Their watches had been sold to 'very important customers', whose details would naturally be kept confidential. However, if requested to do so by the Geneva police, the makers would contact them to find out if they were stolen. If so, they would inform the Swiss police who in turn would liaise with their British colleagues. In the end, the Swiss police only managed to extract information on the countries to which the watches were originally sold. Thankfully, other watchmakers proved more cooperative, resulting in further matches.

Through this painstaking tracing process fifty out of a total of ninety-four watches seized from Mr M were eventually proven to have been stolen. But the police made another breakthrough. The officer in charge of the investigation went back to two internet watch dealers that had bought from Mr M to find out more about

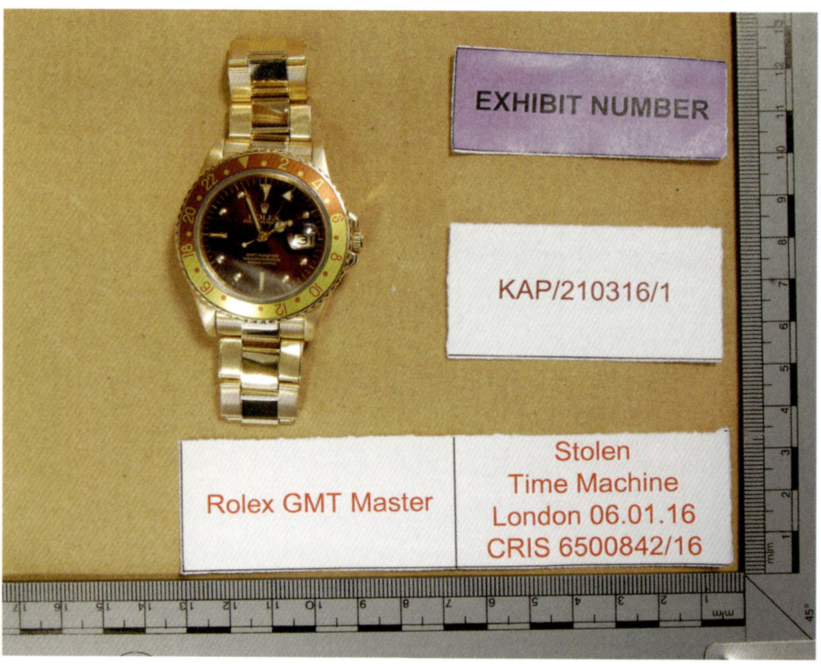

The stolen Rolex GMT-Master 'Tiger Eye' watch valued at £13,500 identified by the ALR in March 2016.

his trading profile. Watchfinder reported it had purchased an astonishing 288 watches from Mr M between 2014 and 2016, with a total value of £691,000. Similarly, BQ Watches had done a roaring trade with Mr M: a total of 247 watches in the previous two years, with a total value of £519,370. Once again, the serial numbers were checked against the ALR database and another fifty-six matches were made.

One watch had a particularly interesting history: it turned up in both the Watchfinder and the BQ Watches list. Mr M had sold the stolen Rolex to BQ Watches in November 2015. BQ Watches sold it on to another jeweller at a watch fair who in turn sold it on to one of its customers. When the buyer identified the watch as stolen and returned it to the jeweller, it was passed up the line back to Mr M. Instead of trying to contact the original owner, Mr M sold the watch again a month later, this time to Watchfinder. Finally, the police had proof that Mr M had sold a watch he knew to be stolen.

The police were now ready to charge Mr M with four offences: possessing criminal property; converting criminal property; possession of articles for use in fraud (the fake Rolex certificates seized in his flat); and cheating the Inland Revenue by failing to pay tax. When the charges were read out to him, Mr M made no reply.

The court case

The police therefore went ahead and prepared their case to be heard at Kingston upon Thames Crown Court in April 2017. The witness statements demonstrated that Mr M could not possibly be the innocent small-time peddler of watches and spare parts for repairs he claimed to be. The stolen watches that had been seized from him were the ALR's largest ever recovery of watches. The total value of the watches that had been identified as stolen was estimated at close to £300,000. Mr M had not provided a credible provenance for a single watch. There were no receipts for any of his purchases and no evidence he had ever undertaken any form of due diligence. Many of the watches had reached him within a few days of the theft, and some of those at his flat still had the jewellers' sales tags and price labels attached to them. As the police case summary points out: 'This clearly shows that [Mr M] is a regular and trusted outlet for criminals to sell stolen watches immediately after offences have been committed.'[188]

Mr M had not registered his business 'Chrono Time' at Companies House either, and there were no business records to document its purchases or sales. Yet his company's turnover based on his trading profile with just two internet dealers (BQ Watches and Watchfinder) was staggering: between September 2014 and June 2016 he had sold watches worth £1.3 million, trading almost on a daily basis. Mr M did not declare any earnings, paid no VAT and even claimed state benefits for a short period. His bank accounts proved he conducted almost all of his transactions in cash.

The evidence produced against Mr M was overwhelming and, realising he had been backed into a corner, he eventually pleaded guilty. The police were delighted with the conviction and the eighteen-months' prison sentence handed down by the court. They also commenced confiscation proceedings to recover any money the fence had gained through his criminal activities. As the officer in charge pointed out, the police usually find it very difficult to secure convictions against jewellery handlers and this success was in no small part due to the credibility of the ALR's record-keeping and its tenacity in compiling the evidence.

Changing business practices

With Mr M in prison (and hopefully subsequently a reformed character) 'Canadian Chris', 'Lee' and 'Tony' must look for alternative outlets for stolen watches. Thanks to Mr M's unhelpful generic descriptions of his trading partners, the police were unable to trace the watches back to the criminal gangs that were responsible for the thefts. Fortunately, the case had much greater repercussions than putting a single criminal behind bars: British watch dealers have become significantly more cautious. Both Watchfinder and BQ Watches are now customers of The Watch Register and routinely check their purchases against it, as do other major online dealerships such as Chronext, Watchmaster and Crown & Caliber. These companies care about their customers' perceptions of them as trustworthy sellers of high-quality watches. The low cost, speed and ease of conducting a due diligence search on a serial number is a tiny fraction of the mark-up in luxury watch sales. And if the seller does not conduct the search, a private buyer can also access the service on a one-off basis. If ever more watch sellers and private buyers adopt this simple precaution, the market for stolen watches will shrink significantly, even if the questionable practice of simply returning the watches to the consignor persists.

Clearly, the detrimental effect on criminal markets would be even greater if all watches matched by The Watch Register were turned over to the police or retained by online dealers until the ownership issue was fully resolved. If a consignor has no paperwork to prove a good faith purchase, that information should be collected and reported to facilitate a rigorous follow-up. With The Watch Register in routine use, suspicious traders could be identified at no cost to the public purse. If all watches at BQ Watches and Watchfinders had been searched from 2014 onwards,

Mr M's name would have come up fifty-six times. Moreover, Mr M was not a registered trader, yet he sold an astonishing volume of luxury watches. There were several things that should have caused suspicion in Mr M's trading profile. Probably there are others like him. With a little more vigilance and cooperation, they can be caught, too.

Making crime pay, or not?

The market for stolen watches is changing as luxury watches have become fashionable collectors' items of rising value. Whereas in former years watch buyers were mostly concerned about authenticity, the issue of provenance is increasingly being recognised. Even the watch bloggers who counsel people to turn a blind eye to missing paperwork usually make clear their advice applies only to buyers who purchase a watch to love and wear forever. Anyone who wants to trade in their watches regularly should be very cautious. But really, everybody should think twice. Street robbery, burglaries, moped gangs and smash-and-grab raids are not just a luxury problem, but a problem for society as a whole. Anyone can become a victim, and those who are lucky to be spared still notice the problem through rising insurance premiums. As citizens we therefore have to decide whether we want to participate in second-hand markets that we know or suspect to be riddled with stolen objects.

For dealers, the calculation is certainly changing. Honest dealers are using The Watch Register database to enhance their reputation by erecting a visible barrier to stolen goods. Running searches and demanding purchase receipts for watches without documentation will straight away put off sellers who know they cut some corners on their watch purchase. However, a reputable high-street dealer politely refusing to buy a stolen watch or an internet trading platform cancelling a sale when a provenance issue is raised is merely an inconvenience for a fence. It takes the kind of public spirit displayed by the watch dealer in Hatton Garden to help the police recover stolen objects and bring crooked traders to justice. The two online dealers questioned by the police could have already noted some irregularities in Mr M's trading profile, but without routine due diligence checks they failed to realise what was happening. Now that they subscribe to The Watch Register such information will be at their fingertips. If watches matched against a reputable stolen watch register were regularly seized pending investigation of their provenance information and the police were alerted to anyone repeatedly attempting to sell undocumented stolen watches fencing would become much trickier and riskier. Even if the police are unable to interview all people with dubious stock, keeping tabs and identifying blatant offenders would raise the probability of law enforcement at relatively low cost.

The Inland Revenue would probably also like to know about online traders with unusually high annual turnovers in markets where buyers and sellers are supposedly private collectors. There is no reason to believe that Mr M's trading was limited to just two online dealers. In fact, he had already told the police he was also trading on eBay. The seven-figure sum uncovered in the investigation could have been the tip of the iceberg. It would be possible to implement reporting requirements if certain monetary thresholds are breached by unregistered online traders. All this can still be circumvented by spreading the business further among various trading platforms. Yet, when selling loot becomes a logistical nightmare and a high-risk occupation, 'Canadian Chris at Costa Coffee', 'Tony' and 'eBay Lee' will find fewer takers for their tainted wares.

Making crime control pay

Matching serial numbers on watches is an obvious extension to the ALR business model, but it brings its own challenges. There is a collective interest in disrupting the market for stolen watches. It would reduce thefts and hence anxiety and stress, losses for insurers and general insecurity on our streets. But these benefits are widely dispersed. Until the foundation of The Watch Register in 2014, nobody managed to organise a broad-based response to the problem. Collective efforts of private crime control often struggle to become commercially viable. When people are asked to make a voluntary contribution to provide a service from which they can benefit regardless of whether or not they paid for it, there is a temptation to freeride on the contributions of others. Private efforts to disrupt the trade in stolen watches were therefore limited and piecemeal, catering mostly to small special interest groups. Watch manufacturers' stolen watch registers are primarily used to confer a competitive advantage to licensed dealers by deliberately excluding the rest of the trade. The SaferGems scheme was set up as a members' club to make it more difficult for gangs to profit from attacks on jewellers' shops. Extending the scheme beyond the club to include thefts from private persons would have cost more than the (paying) members would have gained.

When The Watch Register service was launched, it was immediately accepted by honest unaffiliated jewellers who had been looking for a due diligence product to help them compete with licensed dealers. But this group could not make The Watch Register database commercially sustainable on its own. To build a viable business someone had to make a major investment to establish a comprehensive database of stolen watches that people would pay to search and then change market norms to create broad demand for this service. Fortunately, The Watch Register team did not have to start from scratch: it relied on the ALR's experience, relationships and reputation for tracking down and retrieving stolen artworks. The ALR could also use its existing links to the police and insurers to collate stolen watch data so The Watch Register database quickly became a credible alternative to the private registers of the watch manufacturers. Establishing a stolen watch register would have been a much steeper uphill struggle for anyone else.

A two-way relationship

The story of Mr M illustrates how much law enforcement relies on the cooperation of the private sector. It started off with a vigilant dealer in Hatton Garden spending £2 and sending a brief text message to find out whether he could buy a desirable collectors' watch with a clear conscience. When he discovered there was a problem, he did not take the easy way out by getting rid of his awkward customer and his watch. Instead, he brought them to the ALR offices. It is unlikely that 'entertaining agitated crooks until the police arrive' was part of their job description, but the ALR staff admirably took this unexpected challenge in their stride. The police investigation and their ultimately successful case against Mr M crucially relied on the evidence from The Watch Register database and the free support of the ALR staff. Their testimony helped to secure a well-deserved custodial sentence for Mr M.

While this was another loss-making case for the ALR, the subsequent publicity raised awareness of stolen watches among collectors and dealers. The fact that the Metropolitan Police shone a searchlight into the business practices of online watch sales and exposed the scale of the problem led several dealers to reform their processes regarding undocumented watches. Thus, public/

private cooperation serves both sides. Helping the police can be a sound business investment. Yet it is also clear there is further scope for developing the relationship between private monitoring and public law enforcement: they are complements and not substitutes. Governments could do more to clarify the obligations of dealers to conduct due diligence searches, seize stolen watches and identify suspicious sellers to the police. Anyone buying a watch registered on a reputable searchable stolen watch database should know they could be sued for fencing when they sell it on afterwards. This massively increases the incentive for buyers to become more vigilant. We already have the necessary tools to make stolen watches too 'hot' to buy and sell. The question is whether we compel people to use them.

12

Conclusion: Transforming the Norms of the Art Market

When outsiders look at the Art Loss Register, they do not see the day-to-day business of carefully registering objects on the huge database, painstakingly checking tens of thousands of artworks against it, examining provenance documents and issuing certificates. The media tend to focus on the recovery side of the company, and then only on the most intriguing and controversial cases. Robert Mardirosian's attorney in the Bakwin trial captured this public image combining both admiration and suspicion in the following words: 'Julian Radcliffe, ladies and gentlemen, thinks he is James Bond … an operative outside law enforcement' (see Chapter 3).[189] As we saw in the preceding chapters, art recovery can be an exciting business and an emotional roller coaster. The contrast between the glamour of the world's most exclusive auction showrooms and the sleaze of the economic underworld adds piquancy to the hunt for stolen treasures. However, the many commentators who use the James Bond comparison tap into public concerns about private law enforcement and agents who break the rules to achieve greater objectives. Where exactly does the public interest lie?

On one level, the ALR's stories of derring-do and subterfuge, bluff and counterbluff are excellent entertainment. On another level, they are fascinating examples of how societies create, change and enforce codes of behaviour. When there are gaps in the law or its enforcement, people often develop private solutions. Some of these grassroots solutions are voluntary and collective, others are provided on a commercial basis, and some mix elements of both. Creating new institutions is an evolutionary process. Many private efforts fail outright, some wither after a brief period of blossoming, while others are superseded by more sophisticated competitors. A precious few succeed brilliantly and become household names. For example, the London Stock Exchange has its origins in a private members' club founded at Jonathan's Coffee House by a group of reputable (and financially sound) brokers. In the early eighteenth century the British government passed a raft of legislation to restrict stockbroking. Many types of transactions became illegal, meaning that brokers could walk away from loss-making contracts. However, private members' clubs could make their own rules and enforce them by excluding cheats and rule-dodgers from the group. Defaults thus became rare and the club members' businesses thrived.[190] Similarly, the Lloyd's insurance market was started in a London coffee house, as a private members' society that empowered a committee to provide arbitration in insurance disputes.[191] Private security companies such as G4S, Securitas, Allied Universal and Control Risks respond to companies' and private individuals' desire to defend themselves and their assets against malicious attacks where states provide only partial protection. In the 'Wild West' of the internet, platforms such as eBay and Airbnb are successful because their customers trust them to deal effectively with cheaters. However, the number of companies and initiatives that failed to gain or maintain their clients' and members' trust, and those that were reined in or closed down by legislators, is orders of magnitude larger.

We should consider the ALR's endeavours to establish its services in the art world as a further example of commercial exploration and experimentation in an underregulated market. The stories in this book document a company finding a profitable niche in one part of the art market and seeking to extend that business model to other areas, with varying degrees of success. We observed the company puzzling out its own norms and procedures responding to the varied, ambiguous and sometimes contradictory needs of a very diverse group of stakeholders. The ALR's rule book was written in the middle of a complex and fast-moving game, often against a slippery opposition. Unprecedented events occasionally prompted rough-and-ready or even emotional responses. Some questions simply do not have a clear and satisfactory answer. What norms of behaviour apply against a criminal opposition? Can you bend the truth occasionally and still maintain your customers' trust? Important lessons were learnt with the benefit of hindsight. Defining and redefining the ALR's relationships with its stakeholders, adversaries and law enforcement remains a work in progress.

The ten cases examined here raise a number of important questions. First, is it in the public interest for the ALR to supplement public law enforcement? Second, under what conditions are its services commercially viable? Will the ALR become such an integral part of the art market that people cannot imagine a world without it? Third, many of the private companies that successfully pioneered new approaches to crime control were subsequently aided and guided by laws and regulations to enhance customer protection and raise overall standards in their industry. Can and should governments intervene in the art market, too?

The ALR database and the public interest

The 'public interest' is often invoked to justify policies or actions, but it is an ambiguous concept.[192] It requires people to make a judgement call as to whether a policy or an action provides an overall benefit to society. In democratic societies laws are intended to protect citizens from harm. Public or private initiatives that make crime more difficult or less profitable are therefore likely to benefit society. It is a crime to forge, steal or deal in stolen or counterfeit art. Societies could choose to fund powerful police art squads tasked with creating and maintaining a global, up-to-date database for stolen, forged and looted objects. The police could routinely monitor the art market, catch art thieves and fraudsters, and put them behind bars. However, in a world of harsh budget constraints, this is the exception rather than the rule. There is little electoral support for policies that overtly and disproportionately benefit the rich, and most art collectors are much better off than the median voter. Co-production of crime control between the public and the private sector in the art market therefore makes political and economic sense. Police forces allocate resources to pursue the most egregious cases of art crime. Wealthy art collectors who need additional law enforcement can choose to employ private providers to augment public provision paid for from general taxation. The ALR is just one of many companies that have stepped in to fill the manifold enforcement gaps in the art market.[193]

Monitoring provenance in the market and blocking the sale of stolen objects reduces the profitability of art, furniture and jewellery theft and increases the probability of detection and punishment for thieves and fences. This makes art crime less attractive and our museums, cultural property, private collections, homes and streets safer. As a result of the ALR's – and others' – vigilance, we can risk keeping masterpieces and heritage sites accessible to the public without overblown security expenditure. For the victims of theft there is a hope of one day retrieving their stolen treasures. Insurance premiums

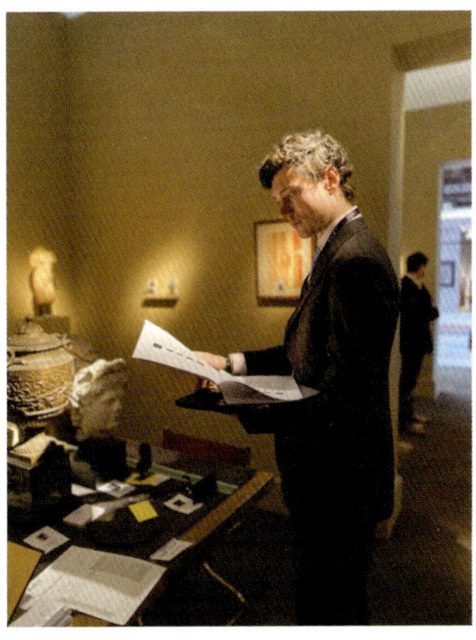

The ALR's Will Korner vetting artworks at BRAFA Art Fair, Brussels, 2020.

for artworks are lower than they would be in the absence of the ALR, enabling more people and institutions to obtain insurance cover. The close monitoring of provenance also makes it more difficult to insert fakes and forgeries into artists' oeuvres. This protects the integrity of the historical record as well as the value of authentic art. Thus, the ALR's stolen art database and The Watch Register are without doubt in the public interest.

The registering of stolen antiquities demonstrates that perceptions about the public interest can change over time. In the past, domestic and international laws to protect cultural heritage were flouted regularly, including by some source country governments that tolerated (and even promoted) the sale of cultural goods to meet short-term income needs. Only a tiny minority of people cared deeply about protecting the world's archaeological heritage. Import and export restrictions were ignored widely, and dealers and collectors routinely turned a blind eye to provenance. In recent years, however, public attitudes towards foreign cultures and religions have become more respectful. As source countries do more to protect their own heritage, public support for restitution campaigns has increased. In addition, policymakers across the world are concerned about the involvement of organised crime, insurgents and terrorist organisations in the looting, smuggling and sale of illicit antiquities. Customs do their best to intercept the flow of looted antiquities between source and market countries, and the police investigate and seize suspicious items brought to their attention. Private monitoring of the antiquities trade in key markets boosts the enhanced public effort to control the illicit trade in antiquities and is therefore also in the public interest.

Art recovery and the public interest

Art recovery is integral to the ALR's business, but it occasionally causes conflict and controversy. People register their losses because it holds out the hope of an eventual recovery. Similarly, insurers use the database to salvage at least some value from the stolen items they acquired by default. However, for traders the recovery side of the ALR's business can be a problem. On the one hand, dealers and auction houses care greatly about their reputation. They want to know about and resolve any issues with an object's provenance before entering into a transaction. Checking the ALR database avoids negative media coverage and involvement in messy and expensive legal disputes at a minimal cost. On the other hand, dealers and auction houses do not want to put off clients from bringing interesting and potentially highly valuable artworks for valuation as they rely on commission income. A confidential warning system would suit them much better than a service that follows up matches by alerting the former owners and – if appropriate – the police. Yet, with a softly-softly approach the ALR's business would never have become commercially viable, because this would not serve the interests of theft victims and insurers.

Thinking more broadly, does art recovery increase social welfare? At first sight, art disputes look like zero-sum games: one party gains at the expense of another. However, commercial resolutions can be in the public interest because they deliver equitable outcomes. Courts of law treat artworks as indivisible. This creates fierce contests between the parties about which law should be applied to decide the winner and how that law should be interpreted. Most people do not think about the public interest merely in terms of legal compliance; it is also about ethics. For example, laws that deprive crime victims of ownership simply because they are 'too late' to make a claim are generally not perceived as fair. The moral case for restitution, or the compensation of the victims of theft and looting, has no set expiry date. It is much more satisfactory when competing claimants explore the multitude of different ways of sharing ownership (including splitting the proceeds from a sale).

The ALR can use its market power to help current and former owners find compromises that are acceptable to both sides. The case of Nazi-era loot is instructive here (see also Chapter 7). Statutes of limitation make it difficult, if not impossible, for most survivors and their heirs to reconnect with their family's former possessions. The problem had been recognised at the 1998 Washington Conference on Holocaust-Era Assets by political representatives from a wide range of countries, who jointly agreed that public museums should seek to find and implement 'just and fair' solutions. However, lawmakers shied away from making this mandatory and exempted the private sector from implementing this guidance altogether. The role of the ALR in this market is two-fold: helping families track their (ancestors') possessions and encouraging the current owners to act ethically rather than insisting on their legal rights. If the holders refuse to engage in an informal resolution process, the ALR cannot force them to. However, many holders can be persuaded that an amicable, swift and low-cost resolution is preferable to a drawn-out legal process or to hiding the artworks from view. By helping the art market to clean legal titles from the noxious legacy of the Nazi era, objects that were previously hidden or circulated in obscure or underground markets can return to the open market or public display. If the artworks are sold at auction, they go to the collectors or museums that value them most highly. Resolving murky legal titles in the private sector is therefore in the public interest.[194]

It is trickier to define the 'public interest' for recoveries involving shadowy figures from the criminal underworld. In general, paying criminals to return stolen objects defeats the objective of reducing the attractiveness of theft. However, the ALR already limits criminals' expected profits. If thieves sell loot in the open market, they risk detection and their buyers expect a discount if there are issues with the provenance. This diminishes the appeal of stealing art in the first place. Yet some thieves only find out how difficult it is to sell stolen art after the theft. When crooks realise their loot is unsaleable, one can make a case to justify a small 'reward for information' to retrieve stolen masterpieces that would otherwise be destroyed, left to decay in some dank hiding place or used as collateral in underworld transactions. Moreover, entering into a negotiation can reveal information that helps the police catch the criminals. Any judgements must be made on a case-by-case basis and in the knowledge there is likely to be intense public scrutiny. Even well-intentioned deals with minimal payouts can look corrupt and suspicious. Press coverage such as 'The murky world of the art detective' in *The Times*[195] or 'Tracking stolen art, for profit, and blurring a few lines' in the *New York Times*[196] demonstrates the difficulty of explaining commercial transactions with the criminal underworld to sceptical journalists. The ALR has learnt from its own experiences, as well as the misadventures of others, to tread very carefully here. Knowing the entire company's reputation is on the line, the ALR has developed (and continually refines) its own strict guidelines to evaluate the pros and cons of engaging with suspected crooks. As a further precaution, there is a constant dialogue with the relevant authorities. Any payments are cleared with law enforcement beforehand.

Accountability and transparency

By stressing the company's public service ethos, Radcliffe invites people to judge the ALR by a very high standard. The company is accountable to the police, its shareholders, its customers and – importantly – the media. In addition, some collectors have the financial resources to fight the ALR in court. For all these reasons, it would be very damaging for the ALR to abuse its power on behalf of special interests, to channel money to criminals or bully an innocent party into a disadvantageous deal. The case of the Hooke Folio is an interesting illustration (see Chapter 5). The ALR interfered with an auction sale to help the Royal Society barter down the acquisition price of an important manuscript. No crime had been committed by the sellers and arguably they had good title. Was this recovery in the public interest? The ALR judged that the Royal Society's claim had greater social legitimacy than the interest of the owners to maximise their personal profit from selling a windfall gain. The ALR therefore used its market power to facilitate a private sale at a price it considered socially and commercially acceptable. The ALR was also careful not to make a profit from its intervention. The press coverage of the case indicates that this carefully calibrated action attracted broad public support.

The public interest is an ambiguous and mutable concept, but it is well suited for shaping and evaluating the operations of this unusual enterprise. Company policy and procedures evolve through consultation with key stakeholders and under the eye of outside observers who are ready to jump on mistakes and misjudgements. Any possible temptation to engage in operations outside the law is tempered by the anticipation of public scrutiny. This does not mean that errors do not occur. However, accountability ensures that practices that contravene the public interest do not persist. Yet this raises another question: can a public service be provided on a commercial basis in the long run?

Commercial viability

The stories in this book illustrate the ALR fighting crime in every area of the art market with what sometimes comes across as scant regard for economic profitability. Radcliffe is clearly an enthusiast. He seems to be drawn in by the excitement of righting wrongs and bringing criminals to justice. It is not surprising that so many commentators pick up on the James Bond vibe: it appears he is not in this business primarily to make money. Would the ALR be viable without Radcliffe's personal commitment of time and occasional capital injections?

There is certainly a strong commercial core to the business. At the top end of the art market, many customers actively seek out the ALR's services. For buyers who purchase art as an investment, as a showpiece or as a bequest to a museum, it is essential to acquire good title on genuine objects; any disputed item has a much-reduced value. Dealers, fair organisers and auctioneers thus use ALR searches to signal their professional integrity to their customers. The cost of searching the database is low compared to the benefits of obtaining certificates attesting clean titles and the reputational gains from routinely carrying out due diligence checks. Furthermore, former owners are often emotionally attached to unique masterpieces and happy to commit significant resources into retrieving them, creating income from art recovery. Yet, the IFAR stolen art database struggled financially although it served the same highly motivated and wealthy interest group. Radcliffe's key innovation was to bring insurers into the company. Art insurers have a common interest in deterring crime by making art 'too hot to handle' and in mitigating their losses by retrieving stolen objects. There are relatively few insurers that offer art insurance for major collections and exhibitions. In 1990 they provided the start-up funding for a joint initiative for art

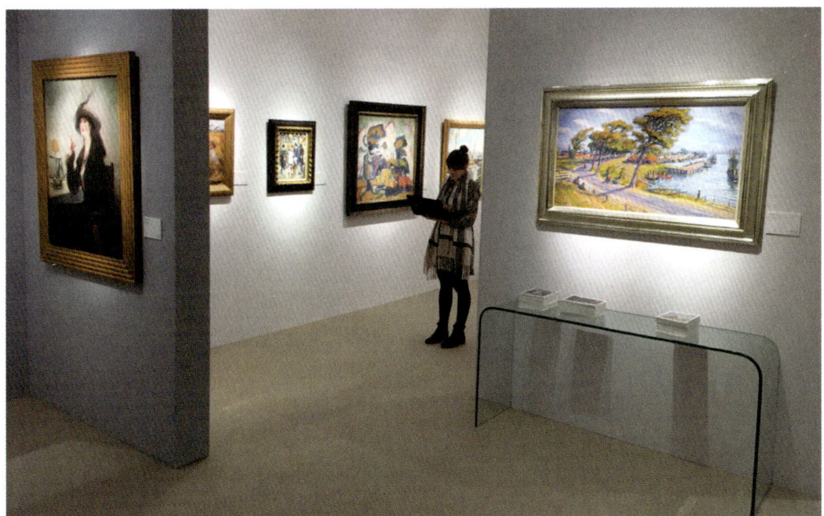

The ALR's Friederike Schwelle vetting paintings at the
PAN Amsterdam Fair, 2019.

crime control, just like banks commit private resources to combat financial fraud. In the early days of the ALR, up to 80 per cent of its annual income came from insurance money.

The further we move away from the glitzy showrooms, auctions and fairs catering to the super-rich, the more reluctant market participants become to pay for the ALR's services. A clean search certificate adds little value to an object worth just a few thousand pounds, while a match causes embarrassment, additional work and perhaps even a financial loss. If domestic law does not require sellers to conduct due diligence checks for a valid transfer of title or only small amounts of money are at stake, it is tempting to rely on the provenance information provided by the vendors. Thefts covered by run-of-the-mill home insurance do not create the large and concentrated losses that cause high net worth and art insurers to band together to tackle the problem at its root. The cost of a recovery can easily dwarf the rewards former owners are prepared to pay to reclaim their possessions. In the case of antiquities, the claimants are mostly governments seeking outright restitution, with no financial reward in sight.

The scope for providing art crime control on a voluntary subscription basis is therefore limited. There is a threshold where the cost of searching the database and the risk of financial loss if a match is made outweigh the benefits from doing so. The search cost does not depend on the value of the object, but on the complexity of identifying a unique match. The cut-off value for searching watches by brand, model and serial number is much lower than that for paintings or sculptures. The fast and cheap watch-checking service is attractive both to dealers and collectors and the business is growing rapidly. Antique furniture is probably the costliest to match, as multiple copies may be in existence and restorers may have obliterated much of the evidence. Antiquities pose a different problem: once identified as looted by a foreign government there is no scope for negotiating compensation for the dealer or current holder, massively increasing the risk of searching the register in the first place.

If short-term profit maximisation is the driving force, companies will opt into significantly less crime control than is in the public interest. Unlike the government, the ALR cannot charge the general public for reducing property crime or the protection of cultural heritage. Yet, we have seen the ALR undertake *pro bono* cases and pursue and prosecute criminals at significant cost. The ALR does not charge the police for assisting with its investigations, Holocaust survivors or their heirs for recording stolen artworks, or governments or archaeologists for registering looted antiquities. Some of these activities may result in further subscriptions, search and recovery income, but the investment may not come to fruition until several years down the line. In the short term, the only way to finance *pro bono* work is by cross-subsidisation with revenues generated from more profitable parts of the business, or from personal resources.

Art recovery is a competitive market, but a stolen art database is a natural monopoly. The art world needs just one database that is as complete and reliable as possible and whose certificates are globally recognised. It would be inefficient for multiple providers to offer an identical service. We know that monopolists can charge their customers more than the cost of providing the service. Indeed, some ALR customers express concern that they are paying over the odds. With short expiry dates for the search certificates, dealers may be asked to search the same object more than once before reselling it. At the top of the market, charging a standard percentage recovery fee can look like bounty hunting. Financially stretched firms in the mid-market can feel bullied into buying services that add negligible value to their business. The ALR's evident commitment to broadening crime control beyond the lucrative top tier of the art market thus causes tensions with some key stakeholders.

However, the ALR is not a classic monopolist making supernormal profits from a captive group of buyers. Although the widely recognised ALR brand name gives the company some market power, the market for clean provenance certificates is contestable. This means that at any time new entrants can take profitable business away from the ALR. Some entrepreneurs already offer premium services to compete at the top of the market or in a lucrative niche. For example, there are firms providing bespoke (and confidential) provenance research. Contemporary artworks whose provenance has been recorded on the blockchain from the outset have no need for an ALR certificate.[197] Foundations protecting the integrity of the oeuvre of particularly fashionable artists could run their own registers of stolen and forged artworks. Some companies have tried to compete at the bottom end of the market, supplying a cursory database search and hence lower reassurance for buyers. With further technological progress in image recognition, it may become possible to automate database searches, reducing response times and costs. Contestable monopolies cannot rest on their laurels or charge excessive fees. If they do, competition quickly arises.

A similar process of contestation can be observed in the area of authentication. In the past, a famous connoisseur may have had the last word on attributing a painting to 'their' artist, effectively making them a monopolist. However, when connoisseurs abused their position to authenticate fakes or arbitrarily blocked the inclusion of certain paintings in a catalogue raisonné, the market looked for alternatives. Art historians entered the market for authentication with a different skill set from connoisseurs. They established their credibility by pointing out glaring mistakes in attribution. Art historians are also in competition with each other: a reputation for accurate attributions is valuable. Forensic scientists then entered the fray with analytical techniques and raised the bar for fakes and forgeries even further. At any one time a particular science laboratory may offer the 'gold standard' test, but there are always others working on developing a better test or supplying standard tests at a lower cost.[198]

The ALR can therefore only charge a premium if it is widely perceived to provide the blue-chip service in the market. The scope for channelling profits from the top of the fine art market towards commercially problematic niches such as stolen furniture and looted antiquities is therefore limited. However, the tightening of industry-wide standards would make it easier to extend commercial crime control services.

Changing the culture of the art market

There have been significant movements in what is considered socially acceptable in the art market in recent decades. The former cavalier attitude to gaps in provenance and reliance on the sellers' reassurance regarding the validity of their title has been largely replaced by a 'new normal': carrying out due diligence title searches and resolving claims before a sale can proceed, at least for valuable artworks. There are four drivers of norm change in the art market, although these are often interwoven. The first is a change in tastes and attitudes among art collectors. Artworks are status goods and public opinion on what conveys status can alter. A good example is objects made from carved ivory and rhino horn. These previously popular collectors' items are now widely perceived to be tainted. Dealers and auction houses must therefore develop credible procedures to exclude poached ivory from sales to save the market for antique ivory carvings. Second, law enforcement can step up, raising the risks of dealing in illicit objects. A prime illustration is the New York district attorney's campaign to return looted antiquities to their source countries, making buyers and dealers much more cautious about provenance (see Chapter 10). Third, over time, the way existing laws are interpreted can shift. For instance, the standards of due diligence for good faith purchases have been tightened considerably, as lawyers and judges respond to changing public attitudes and the increasing availability of provenance-checking services. Finally, new laws and regulations can force the adoption of higher standards.

Looking at the recovery stories in this book, we can see that the ALR is contributing to norm change through three of these pathways. First, the ALR uses media coverage of its cases to change collectors' attitudes to owning stolen, looted and smuggled artworks. By constantly posing the question 'It may be yours, but do you really own it?', the ALR has raised collectors' expectations and demands for improved pre-sale scrutiny. In its resolutions, the ALR invites market participants to consider 'clear title' not purely from a narrow, legal point of view but to take a more ethical approach. Radcliffe and his team engage in moral suasion, nudging dealers and sellers to take 'moral taint' into account when faced with former owners' claims. The ALR employs the concept of 'just and fair' solutions not only for Nazi-looted art but also for other contexts where historical injustices could be righted on a (quasi-) voluntary basis. Subsequent PR praising the generosity and rectitude of owners who restitute artworks or compensate former owners reinforces the new social norm. In case of non-cooperation, the threat of exposure is always implicit and sometimes made explicitly: naming and shaming is a powerful tool for encouraging compliance.

Second, the ALR is putting significant resources into strengthening law enforcement by providing free assistance to police and customs investigations. By making the police more effective at tackling art crime and publicising the successes of this public/private partnership, the ALR encourages more dealers and auction houses to subscribe to its services and take appropriate action when informed of a title problem. Having demonstrably good relations with law enforcement also makes veiled threats highly effective in encouraging cooperative informal resolutions.

Third, the ALR is shaping case law through its lawsuits and expert witness testimony. The increasing prominence of lost art databases in the art market means that not availing oneself of a reputable search service has almost become an indication of bad faith.[199] The ALR's testimony on behalf of Mallett's against its suppliers in Dublin in the case of Lord Roden's bureau helped the firm recover the purchase price (see Chapter 8). However, it also sent a message that while the failure of Mallett's to consult the ALR database was still (just about) acceptable in 2000, it would have been considered negligent by 2005. Similarly, there has been a shift in what is expected of crime victims wishing to reclaim their former property. A demonstrable lack of vigilance makes it difficult to succeed with a restitution claim, so victims of theft or looting who fail to register their claims face an uphill battle when trying to assert their property rights.

Growing a business

The ALR's sustained campaign to improve due diligence standards in the art market created a virtuous cycle of rising registrations, increasing search activities and successful recoveries. The consolidation of the ALR's position in the art market is reflected in the diagram below, which shows the number of registrations of art, antiquities and collectibles, and watches over time. Registrations grew steadily at an average rate of around 9,600 new registrations per year from 1990 to 1999 and 13,600 between 2000 and 2009. The years 2010–19 saw an acceleration in the volume of business with more than 100,000 new registrations in both 2010 and 2017, and an average of 47,000 new registrations per year over the decade. Valuable stolen timepieces had been recorded on the ALR database since its inception but accelerated after the founding of The Watch Register.

Data on the annual number of searches was not systematically collected early on, but it seems that it took several years to push the due diligence product into the market and even longer to convince clients to pay for it. The annual number of searches exceeded 100,000 for the first time in 1998, but in its first decade of operation due diligence checks provided only around 10 per cent of the ALR's total income. Without the insurance industry's support, the enterprise would not have been viable in this period. In the second decade of its operation the ALR became successful in generating both recovery income and publicity. Payouts from major cases like the Bakwin Cézanne (see Chapter 2) and the Landsberg Picasso (see Chapter 7) were essential for the survival of the firm. Any surpluses were invested into marketing the ALR's

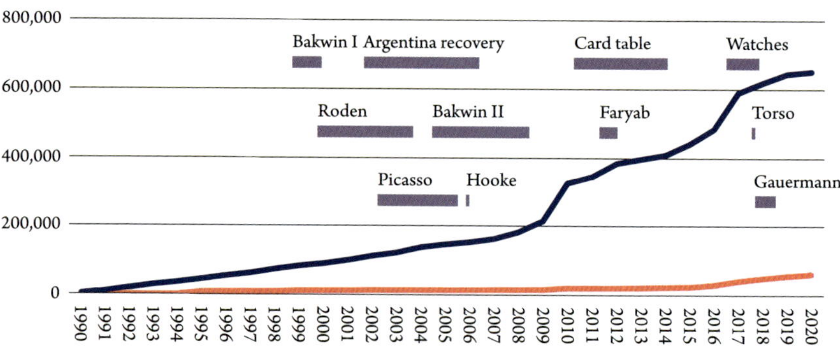

The evolution of registrations on the ALR database over time
(watches in red).

services, high-profile recoveries and expanding the database, including the development of business areas without registration fees, such as antiquities and Nazi-looted artworks. The publicity surrounding recoveries, court cases and cooperation with law enforcement succeeded in encouraging further registrations and searches. In its third decade the ALR's investments came to fruition: increasing search income put the ALR onto a stable financial footing. Between 2013 and 2019 searches fluctuated between 360,000 and 390,000 per year, bringing in between 80 and 90 per cent of its annual income.

The resources spent by the ALR on loss-making recoveries should therefore be seen as investments into changing market practices. Taking on prestigious but costly cases acted as a signal to the market: the ALR demonstrated its commitment to raising standards, leading to further subscriptions and searches down the line. For instance, watch registrations (and searches) took off in 2016/17 when the police investigation into Mr M's fencing operation pierced the complacency of watch dealers. Annual searches on The Watch Register shot up from below 2,000 in 2014 and 2015, to 6,520 in 2016 and 32,490 in 2017 and have grown steadily since.[200] As a successful norm entrepreneur, the ALR has been able to broaden take-up for its services far from its original core business at the top tier of the art market to mid-market fairs, dealers and auction houses.

Again, we can see a parallel in the authentication business. Techniques that originated in response to demand for credible attributions in the top tier of the market percolate down to the mid-market as buyers' expectations of due diligence change (and prices come down). Overall, the art market is surprisingly effective at developing grassroots solutions to the challenges posed by crooks and criminals. There is constant innovation in the methods and processes for producing information. Unfortunately, however, the market does not publicise this information. A large proportion of the private sector's crime control efforts are wasted due to the market's culture of hiding negative information from buyers, competitors and law enforcement. Altering these entrenched norms would require a decisive shift in regulation.

Moving forward: confronting art crime with greater transparency

The art market's focus on protecting the interest of sellers and its 'almost pathological level of discretion' are remarkable.[201] When we buy or sell a car, we have to give our name and address and these are held on a central register. There are comprehensive and reliable vehicle checking services such as HPI in the UK and Autocheck and Carfax in the USA. These allow dealers and buyers to check for a wide range of potential problems: whether the car has been stolen, whether it is encumbered with a loan agreement and whether it has been in a serious accident. When we buy shares and property, our names are recorded. People have to go to extraordinary lengths to conceal their identities within shell companies in these markets. If they do so, it immediately raises questions about their motives. Yet, if someone sells a multimillion-pound painting, they can hide behind an innocuous label such as 'property of a lady' or 'from a central European collection'. We have to trust the auction house has satisfied itself (somehow) that the 'lady' does not run a drug-smuggling business and that the central European collection is not owned by a mafia. Auction houses reveal the identities of consignors only with their explicit permission or when forced to do so by a court order.

The norm of providing utterly discreet services was established in a different age: to spare the blushes of the aristocracy when they divested their family heirlooms to cover embarrassing gambling debts or make the roofs over their heads watertight. This social norm perfectly suits those who enter the market with criminal intent. Policymakers have long been aware of this problem. Financial regulations requiring market makers to 'know their customer' for anti-money-laundering purposes also apply to the art market. However, given the difficulty the ALR faced in tracing Robert Mardirosian – hiding behind the consignor Mr P and Erie International Trading Company – it is unclear how this works in practice (see Chapter 3). Moreover, unless the information is collated and routinely made available for external scrutiny it is difficult to spot when someone makes multiple illicit transactions, or is blocked in their attempt to do so. Peddlers of fakes and forgeries, stolen and looted objects often use several outlets to conceal the extent of their illicit business. The fence in Hatton Garden should not have been able to sell hundreds of luxury watches despite being caught repeatedly with stolen goods (see Chapter 11). Sharing information on the identity of sellers would make it considerably riskier for criminals to build a business around selling fakes, forgeries or stolen art, or engaging in money laundering or tax evasion. Transparency would be improved hugely by requiring all sellers' names to be made public after a period of five or ten years.

After every scandal that hits the art world, the question arises of how much longer the culture of secrecy in the art world will remain viable. The scale of successful fraud, forgery and smuggling operations, and how long some remained in business even after several people had become suspicious, is staggering. At the root of the problem is the caveat emptor principle: it is up to art buyers to fully investigate the works they acquire.[202] Auction houses and dealers are legally obliged to ensure that items in their catalogues are 'as described'. However, the law does not require sellers to present buyers with comprehensive information or to reveal problems that would reduce an object's commercial value.[203] It is therefore tempting to present artworks in the most favourable way. If there are multiple expert opinions, one might select the most positive endorsements and the most prestigious provenance. Negative opinions and half-hearted endorsements often have to be inferred from the absence of a report from a key expert.[204] Thus, highlighting an 'all clear' from the Interpol database could well mean that the ALR refuses to issue a certificate.

This makes it extremely difficult for anyone but highly trained specialists to make informed choices. For the seller, there is a risk–reward trade-off in suppressing negative information. But the risk of being caught is relatively low. If a collector falls in love with and buys an artwork, they have little incentive to invest significant resources to research whether they have been duped. Unless the buyer quickly resells the object, lends it to an exhibition or donates it to a museum, the problem may not come to light until all formal and informal warranties have expired. If a problem is spotted, both sides usually prefer to settle the issue confidentially by voiding the sale. As long as the buyer is reimbursed, any 'mistakes' can usually be hushed up. Fences and peddlers of fakes and forgeries therefore often operate for years without being exposed.

One could change the approach of sweeping problems under the carpet by requiring sellers and auction houses to behave with 'utmost good faith' (*uberrima fides*) rather than merely in good faith. Under this system, sales contracts would be invalidated if the dealer or auction house deliberately withheld relevant information from the buyer, or the seller from the auction house. If auction houses changed their business model to publish balanced information to help buyers make informed choices, opportunities for art crime would diminish and the resolution of legacy cases would be speeded up. It would also be in the public interest to collate information about known fakes, forgeries, condition reports and paintings with disputed titles or attributions in a searchable register. Academics and museum curators should be free to point out problems and engage in scholarly debates about attributions without fear of prosecution by disappointed owners. Making this information accessible would stop (crooked) sellers trying their luck time after time with different dealers, auction houses or private sellers until they finally find someone to hoodwink. It is unlikely that improving disclosure standards would cause an overall contraction in the art market. Paintings on the watch list would lose part but not all of their value. Some art lovers may not mind owning a good fake if they like it. A few entrepreneurs would actively seek out problematic art if they think they can rehabilitate an object or clean up its title. For the remaining blue-chip masterpieces, there would be even greater competition among art investors to own them, protecting the incomes of dealers and auction houses.

Enhancing the public/private partnership

The Introduction to this book examined how the private sector can assist the public sector in fighting art crime. The ALR and other private organisations have succeeded in reducing crime in a sector where – especially in times of fiscal austerity – states have limited public law enforcement resources. Unlike the police, companies can charge the main beneficiaries of their services and thus create revenues to fund their activities, rather than relying on general taxation. Private solutions can also transcend international borders more easily than public law enforcement, which is essential in a global market. However, public/private partnerships are two-way relationships. States could do more to help private companies restrict business opportunities for crooks and criminals in the art market. It is a common pattern that the balance shifts from self-regulation to formal regulation when markets grow, risks increase and less sophisticated market participants require protection. Nowadays, nobody questions the need for financial regulation. Almost every country in the world has a telecommunications regulator. Product labelling regulation addresses unfair and deceptive trade practices in an ever-wider range of sectors. Even organic farming, the former bastion of hippie counterculture, will come under the remit of detailed European Union regulation in 2022.[205] Lawmakers are in an ongoing debate about the regulation of content on the internet to reduce online harm.[206]

When governments become serious about fighting art fraud, money laundering and art theft, and about denying organised crime, terrorists and insurgents the income from looting heritage sites, they need to address the culture of secrecy in the art world. All regulatory initiatives face at least some opposition from the affected sector. Mandating higher disclosure standards will drive some business away from highly regulated markets towards lower-quality jurisdictions. Doubtlessly, some collectors will be disappointed when enhanced scrutiny reveals formerly hidden problems. Their dealers or auction houses will have to cope with the repercussions and therefore will be likely to resist any changes in the law. However, art investors and collectors looking for blue-chip works will flock towards the jurisdictions offering the greatest assurance to buyers that their investments are what they purport to be. New York's stringent property law is not a bar to trading art in the city, but the opposite. It is a strong signal that the seller is truly confident about the provenance of their object and buyers are willing to pay a premium for that. Likewise, jurisdictions that lower the cost of acquiring truthful information by raising disclosure standards will attract sellers that have nothing to hide and buyers in search of genuine, morally and legally unencumbered masterpieces.

A silent revolution in property rights

As a final thought, we should revisit the idea of the ALR as an agent of social change. Private property is at the centre of all market transactions. On a day-to-day basis we take property rights for granted. Yet, the political, philosophical and social debate about the justification of private property is long-standing, stemming back at least to the writings of the Ancient Greek philosophers Democritus and Plato. Every generation must settle the question of how private property can be legitimately acquired, exercised and transferred. Over the last two centuries we have seen massive shifts in what people consider to be socially acceptable. Slave labour, looting and genocide have been outlawed. Former colonies have gained their independence. However, the legacies of unjust former institutions and one-sided aggressions remain embodied in private property rights to this day. Many societies now debate whether the spoils of war truly belong to the victor. Should we address historical injustices by redistribution in favour of the victims of crime, systemic injustices and violent conflict?

Art tends to be at the forefront of the public discourse, with various pressure groups questioning the acceptability of keeping looted art and plundered cultural or religious treasures in museums and private collections.[207] For art collectors and investors, the question of what can be legitimately owned has thus become ever more pressing. The ALR offers an elegant solution to this problem. You can buy something in good faith if no one has registered a legally or socially valid restitution claim. If there is such a claim, it should be resolved before the sale, either amicably or in a court of law. It is fascinating that a private business has developed a practical solution to a thorny social and political issue that politicians have little incentive to tackle. In some jurisdictions lawcourts have already responded to the availability of the ALR's services, realigning property rights with changing social values by redefining 'good faith' sales. Over time, the definition of a 'socially legitimate' claim can become ever broader and the ALR's own policy will continue to evolve, in a constant dialogue with stakeholders, market insiders and outside observers. The stories of the ALR recoveries can therefore also be read as tentative steps towards a fairer society.

Notes

1   'Über-warehouses for the ultra-rich', *The Economist*, 23 November 2013, https://www.
    economist.com/briefing/2013/11/23/uber-warehouses-for-the-ultra-rich (accessed
    4 January 2020); Kris Hollington, 'After drugs and guns, art theft is the biggest
    criminal enterprise in the world', *Newsweek*, 22 July 2014, https://www.newsweek.
    com/2014/07/18/after-drugs-and-guns-art-theft-biggest-criminal-enterprise-
    world-260386.html (accessed 4 January 2021).

2   Clare McAndrew. 2020. *The Art Market 2020*, Art Basel and UBS, https://
    d2u3kfwd92fzu7.cloudfront.net/The_Art_Market_2020-1.pdf (accessed 4 January
    2021).

3   William Goetzmann, Luc Renneboog and Christoph Spaenjers. 2011. 'Art and money',
    American Economic Review, 101(3), pp. 222–6.

4   Peter Watson and Cecilia Todeschini. 2006. *The Medici Conspiracy*, New York: BBS
    Public Affairs.

5   Peter Watson. 1997. *Sotheby's: The Inside Story*, London: Bloomsbury.

6   See, for example, Simon Goodman. 2015. *The Orpheus Clock: My Search for My
    Family's Art Treasures Stolen by the Nazis*, London: Scribe.

7   Rick Muir, email communication with Anja Shortland, 4 October 2019.

8   'Sotheby's declares "Frans Hals" work a forgery', BBC, 6 October 2016, https://www.
    bbc.co.uk/news/entertainment-arts-37574411 (accessed 4 January 2021).

9   See https://www.ifar.org/stolen_art_alert.php (accessed 4 January 2021).

10 For example, objects displayed in museums or archaeological sites in conflict zones.

11 Tom Payne, 'Not just incompetent but brain dead, too! Bulmers cider magnate
    slams police in multi-million pound art heist', *Daily Mail*, 18 June 2018, https://www.
    dailymail.co.uk/news/article-5858475/Bulmers-cider-magnate-slams-police-multi-
    million-pound-art-heist.html (accessed 4 January 2021).

12 'Number of suspects charged by police hits new low', BBC News, 23 January 2020,
    https://www.bbc.co.uk/news/uk-51221054 (accessed 4 January 2021); Danny Shaw,
    'Which crimes are least likely to be solved?', BBC News, 17 October 2019, https://
    www.bbc.co.uk/news/uk-49986849 (accessed 4 January 2021).

13 British Home Office Statistical Bulletin 12/19, Crime outcomes in England and Wales: year ending March 2019, https://assets.publishing.service.gov.uk/government/uploads/system/uploads/attachment_data/file/901028/crime-outcomes-1920-hosb1720.pdf (accessed 4 January 2021).

14 'Crime figures: do the police know how much there really is?', BBC News, 8 October 2019, https://www.bbc.co.uk/news/uk-england-46894162 (accessed 4 January 2021); 'Crimes unreported as public lose faith in police', BBC News, 7 February 2020, https://www.bbc.co.uk/news/uk-51408921 (accessed 4 January 2021).

15 Creating obstacles to profiting from art crime is the greater objective of the two. The bulk of payouts from art insurers is for damage to artworks. Money gained from the recovery of stolen objects is relatively small.

16 'Toy story that led to a round-up of villains', *Lloyd's List*, 22 December 2000.

17 'Spanish police recover three Francis Bacon paintings', BBC, 19 July 2017, https://www.bbc.co.uk/news/world-europe-40659726 (accessed 4 January 2021).

18 ALR news release, 10 December 2015, 'The Art Loss Register recovers cherished family heirloom after nearly 15 years', https://www.artloss.com/the-art-loss-register-recovers-cherished-family-heirloom-after-nearly-15-years/ (accessed 12 January 2021).

19 Noah Charney, 'What's the motive behind most art heists?', *The Observer*, 7 September 2018, https://observer.com/2018/07/mafia-heists-provide-clues-to-motive-behind-famous-art-thefts/ (accessed 4 January 2021); Jonathan Jones, 'Gangsters' use of paintings as currency shows a profound belief in art', *The Guardian*, 30 September 2016, https://www.theguardian.com/artanddesign/jonathanjonesblog/2016/sep/30/gangsters-use-of-paintings-as-currency-shows-profound-belief-in-art (accessed 4 January 2021).

20 Severin Carrell, 'The great Leonardo da Vinci heist: solicitor accused of £4m extortion plot', *The Guardian*, 1 March 2010, https://www.theguardian.com/artanddesign/2010/mar/01/leonardo-davinci-masterpiece-extortion-plot (accessed 4 January 2021).

21 'Bulmers art theft trial: Detective calls police "incompetent"', BBC, 26 June 2018, https://www.bbc.co.uk/news/uk-england-somerset-44619236 (accessed 4 January 2021).

22 Martin Bailey. 'Sandy Nairne and his life as an undercover negotiator: the ethics of retrieving Tate's Turners', *The Art Newspaper*, 30 June 2011, https://www.theartnewspaper.com/archive/my-life-as-an-undercover-negotiator (accessed 4 January 2021).

23 Michael Daley, 'Questions and grey answers on the Tate Gallery's recovered Turners, *ArtWatch UK*, 11 July 2011, http://artwatch.org.uk/questions-and-grey-answers-on-the-tate-gallerys-recovered-turners/ (accessed 4 January 2021).

24 Martha Finnemore and Kathryn Sikkink. 1998. 'International norm dynamics and political change', *International Organization at Fifty*, 52(4), pp. 887–917.

25 Carol Vogel, 'A Cézanne leads a $128 million auction of the Whitney Art Collection', *New York Times*, 11 May 1999, https://www.nytimes.com/1999/05/11/arts/a-cezanne-leads-a-128-million-auction-of-the-whitney-art-collection.html (accessed 4 January 2021).

26 As the transaction was to take place in Switzerland between an American citizen and the unknown holder acting through a Swiss intermediary, the deal required consent from both police forces.

27 'Cézanne still life from important collection to be sold at Sotheby's in London on December 7', https://sothebys.gcs-web.com/static-files/a294bb82-72fe-453c-9f52-07ab824ae995 (accessed 4 January 2021).

28 Bryan Hood, 'A Cézanne once owned by Condé Nast's S.I. Newhouse sells for $59.3 million at Christie's', *Robb Report*, 14 May 2019, https://robbreport.com/shelter/auctions/a-cezanne-once-owned-by-conde-nasts-s-i-newhouse-sells-for-59-3-million-at-christies-2850601/ (accessed 4 January 2021).

29 Stephen Kurkjian, 'Lost and found', *Boston Globe*, 17 December 2000, http://graphics.boston.com/globe/magazine/2000/12-17/featurestory1.shtml (accessed 4 January 2021).

30 United States of America v Robert M. Mardirosian No 07-CR-10075-MLW, Government's sentencing memorandum, p. 2.

31 United States District Court, District of Massachusetts: United States v Robert M. Mardirosian. Case 1:07-cr-10075-MLW, Judgment in a criminal case, p. 2.

32 Martha Neil, 'Retired lawyer, 74, a "glorified fence," gets 7 years in Cézanne case', *ABA Journal*, 16 December 2008, https://www.abajournal.com/news/article/retired_lawyer_74_a_glorified_fence_gets_7_years_in_cezanne_case (accessed 5 January 2021).

33 Oliver Bullough. 2018. *Moneyland: Why Thieves & Crooks Now Rule the World & How To Take It Back*, London: Profile Books.

34 The High Court of Justice Queen's Bench Division, 31 January 2006. Case number HQ05X1794 Proceedings (Tape Transcription) pp. 6–7.

35 Email to Michael Bakwin, 30 November 2006.

36 United States of America v Robert M. Mardirosian No 07-CR-10075-MLW, Judge's sentencing memorandum, p. 13.

37 John Guilfoil, 'Art owner wins $3m civil award in theft case', *Boston Globe*, 24 August 2011, http://archive.boston.com/news/local/massachusetts/articles/2011/08/24/art_owner_awarded_3m_in_stockbridge_theft_case/ (accessed 5 January 2021).

38 Civil Action, Michael Bakwin v Robert M. Mardirosian & others. SJC-11393. Barnstable. Dec. 3, 2013 – April 2, 2014 Judgment, https://law.justia.com/cases/massachusetts/supreme-court/2014/sjc-11393.html (accessed 5 January 2021).

39 United States of America v Robert M. Mardirosian No 07-CR-10075-MLW, Judge's sentencing memorandum, p. 2.

40 *Ibid.*

41 '$25 million in art works stolen from a museum in Buenos Aires', *New York Times*, 28 December 1980, https://www.nytimes.com/1980/12/28/archives/25-million-in-art-works-stolen-from-a-museum-in-buenos-aires-museum.html.

42 Simon Worrall, 'Art for arms' sake', *The Independent*, 22 September 2011, https://www.independent.co.uk/news/uk/crime/art-for-arms-sake-412306.html (accessed 5 January 2021).

43 *Ibid.*

44 'Valuable loot, difficult to sell', *La Nación*, 22 September 2002; 'Stolen art may be recovered', *Ámbito Financiero*, 22 September 2002; 'Complex negotiation upon notorious art theft', *Clarín*, 22 September 2002.

45 'Interpol agent recovers stolen works of art', *The Independent*, 21 July 2003.

46 Stolen paintings recovered 23 years after theft', *New Zealand Herald*, 20 July 2003, https://www.nzherald.co.nz/world/stolen-paintings-recovered-23-years-after-theft/ PGK2WVZ6UMWE5VTHC5QYK53AKQ/ (accessed 5 January 2021).

47 Ryan Dube and Santiago Pérez, 'Argentina defaults on sovereign debt amid coronavirus crisis', *Wall Street Journal*, 22 May 2020, https://www.wsj.com/ articles/argentina-moves-closer-to-sovereign-debt-default-amid-coronavirus-crisis-11590160035 (accessed 5 January 2021).

48 Lewis Smith, '£1m scientific "gospel" of Newton's greatest rival', *The Times*, 9 February 2006, https://www.thetimes.co.uk/article/pound1m-scientific-gospel-of-newtons-greatest-rival-65x5n6npcgz (accessed 6 January 2021).

49 Ian Sample, 'Eureka! Lost manuscript found in cupboard', *The Guardian*, 9 February 2006, https://www.theguardian.com/uk/2006/feb/09/science.research (accessed 6 January 2021).

50 Rebecca Morelle, '"Lost" manuscript valued at £1mn', BBC, 9 February 2006, http:// news.bbc.co.uk/1/hi/england/hampshire/4696484.stm (accessed 6 January 2021).

51 Lewis Smith, 'Royal Society wants £1m book back', *The Times*, 23 February 2006, https://www.thetimes.co.uk/article/royal-society-wants-pound1m-book-back-8dwrh5gvmx9 (accessed 6 January 2021).

52 Detailed information on Robert Hooke's library is available from the Hooke's Books online database: https://hookesbooks.yeldanasifoglu.com (accessed 6 January 2021).

53 Email from Bonhams to the Royal Society.

54 See the British Arts Council on 'Private Treaty Sales', https://www.artscouncil.org. uk/tax-incentives/private-treaty-sales#section-1 (accessed 6 January 2021).

55 The British Arts Council's Reviewing Committee can delay or bar the export of cultural property from the UK. See https://www.artscouncil.org.uk/supporting-arts-museums-and-libraries/supporting-collections-and-cultural-property (accessed 6 January 2021).

56 Email from the ALR to the Royal Society and its legal team.

57 Email from the ALR to the Royal Society summarising a conversation with Bonhams.

58 Email from Bonhams to Julian Radcliffe.

59 File copy of a letter from the ALR to the Royal Society, 13 April 2006.

60 Laney Salisbury and Aly Sujo. 2009. *Provenance: How a Con Man and a Forger Rewrote the History of Modern Art*, New York: Penguin Books.

61 Anthony Amore. 2015. *The Art of the Con*, New York: Palgrave Macmillan, chapter 1.

62 *Ibid.*, chapter 7; 'Art gallery owner pleads guilty in forgery found by coincidence', *New York Times*, 14 December 2004, https://www.nytimes.com/2004/12/14/nyregion/ art-gallery-owner-pleads-guilty-in-forgery-found-by-coincidence.html (accessed 6 January 2021).

63 Ben Lewis. 2019. *The Last Leonardo: The Secret Lives of the World's Most Expensive Painting*, London: William Collins.

64　David Jenkins, 'The Inigo Philbrick saga: from Wunderkind to art fraudster', 11 August 2020, https://itsartlaw.org/2020/08/11/the-inigo-philbrick-saga/ (accessed 6 January 2021); Jacob Bernstein, 'The talented Mr. Philbrick', *New York Times*, 13 March 2020, https://www.nytimes.com/2020/03/13/style/inigo-philbrick.html (accessed 6 January 2021).

65　Letter from the restorer to Frank Faryab.

66　The Tate has a number of 'Late Unfinished Sea Pieces' from the Turner Bequest in its collection, whose authenticity is in doubt. They are of unusual formats and appear to be very close imitations of Turner's late period style. The curators believe them to be the work of Turner's studio assistant, Francis Sherrell. Several of these works were left in the studio at Turner's death and passed into the hands of the Pound family. See, for example, the Tate's entry on the painting *Stormy Sea with Dolphins*, https://www.tate.org.uk/art/artworks/turner-stormy-sea-with-dolphins-n04664 (accessed 6 January 2021).

67　Email from the gallery owner to Frank Faryab.

68　James Hamilton cited in Rob Preece, 'Art dealer spends £2million proving obscure oil painting he bought "on a hunch" is lost Turner masterpiece', *Mail Online*, 29 April 2012, https://www.dailymail.co.uk/news/article-2136865/Art-dealer-Frank-Faryab-spends-2million-proving-painting-lost-JMW-Turner-masterpiece.html (accessed 6 January 2021).

69　James Hamilton is primarily a writer and the discovery of a 'lost Turner' would provide excellent publicity. Dealers and academics guard their reputations more closely: there is a high cost to being contradicted or proved wrong by their peers.

70　England and Wales Court of Appeal (Criminal Division) Decisions. Frank Faryab R v [1999] EWCA Crim 446 (22 February 1999).

71　See *Whalers* (*c.* 1845) in the Metropolitan Museum's online catalogue, https://www.metmuseum.org/art/collection/search/437854 (accessed 6 January 2021).

72　Natural Resources Wales, The Hafod Estate near Aberytstwyth, https://naturalresources.wales/days-out/places-to-visit/mid-wales/hafod-estate/?lang=en (accessed 6 January 2021).

73　Lisburne, Earl of (I, 1776), *Cacroft's Peerage*, http://www.cracroftspeerage.co.uk/lisburne1776.htm (accessed 6 January 2021).

74　Internal ALR email.

75　Internal ALR email.

76　See, for example, https://www.tate.org.uk/art/artworks/turner-stormy-sea-with-dolphins-n04664 (accessed 6 January 2021).

77　Ted Hynds and Richard Brooke, 'Grubby seascape is a lost Turner', *Sunday Times*, 29 April 2012, https://www.thetimes.co.uk/article/grubby-seascape-is-a-lost-turner-n0859csk32x (accessed 6 January 2021).

78　Rob Preece, 'Art dealer spends £2million proving obscure oil painting he bought "on a hunch" is lost Turner masterpiece', *Mail Online*, 29 April 2012, https://www.dailymail.co.uk/news/article-2136865/Art-dealer-Frank-Faryab-spends-2million-proving-painting-lost-JMW-Turner-masterpiece.html (accessed 6 January 2021).

79　Bendor Grosvenor, 'You spent how much?', *Art History News* blog, 30 April 2012, https://www.arthistorynews.com/articles/1287_You_spent_how_much (accessed 6 January 2021).

80 Email from the ALR to Sotheby's.

81 See, for example, Vincent Noce, 'Sotheby's wins case over alleged forged Frans Hals', *The Art Newspaper*, 11 December 2019, https://www.theartnewspaper.com/news/sotheby-s-frans-hals (accessed 6 January 2021). Following the discovery of the forgery, Sotheby's refunded the sale price to the buyer but it took more than three years and an acrimonious court case to get a repayment from the consignor.

82 Letter from Sotheby's to Frank Faryab.

83 *Ibid.*

84 Letter from fingerprint analyst to Frank Faryab.

85 'Former historic buildings owner in court for unpaid fines, *Wilts and Gloucestershire Standard*, 4 March 2014, https://www.wiltsglosstandard.co.uk/news/11051188.former-historic-buildings-owner-in-court-for-unpaid-fines/ (accessed 6 January 2021).

86 *Woman in Gold*, 2015, directed by Simon Curtis, produced by David M. Thompson.

87 US Department of State, Office of the Special Envoy for Holocaust Issues, Washington Conference Principles on Nazi-Confiscated art, https://www.state.gov/washington-conference-principles-on-nazi-confiscated-art/ (accessed 8 January 2021).

88 For example, the Dutch Restitutions Committee, https://www.restitutiecommissie.nl/en (accessed 8 January 2021), and the UK's Spoliation Advisory Panel, https://www.gov.uk/government/groups/spoliation-advisory-panel (accessed 8 January 2021).

89 Catherine Hickley, 'Washington principles: the restitution of Nazi-looted art is still a work in progress, 20 years on', https://www.theartnewspaper.com/news/restitution-of-nazi-looted-art-a-work-in-progress (accessed 8 January 2021).

90 Catherine Hickley, 'Berlin museums appeal to US Supreme Court in dispute over €200m Guelph Treasure', *The Art Newspaper*, 24 June 2019, https://www.theartnewspaper.com/news/berlin-museums-appeal-to-us-supreme-court-in-dispute-over-guelph-treasure (accessed 8 January 2021).

91 David Cassirer, et al. v Thyssen-Bornemisza Collection Foundation CV 05-3459-JFW (Ex), 30 April 2019, p. 34.

92 The website of the International Foundation for Art Research provides an overview of court cases on restitution, https://www.ifar.org/case_law.php?ID=1 (accessed 8 January 2021).

93 Simon Goodman. 2015. *The Orpheus Clock: My Search for My Family's Art Treasures Stolen by the Nazis*, London: Scribe.

94 Author interview with lawyer specialising in art dispute resolution, 27 July 2018.

95 Norman Rosenthal, 'The time has come for a statute of limitations', *The Art Newspaper*, 1 December 2008, https://www.theartnewspaper.com/archive/the-time-has-come-for-a-statute-of-limitations (accessed 8 January 2021).

96 Robin Cembalest, 'Inconvenient truths', *ARTnews*, 1 March 2009, http://www.artnews.com/2009/03/01/inconvenient-truths/ (accessed 8 January 2021).

97 See, for example, Nils Prately, 'Christie's hid Nazi past of painting', *The Guardian*, 24 October 2003, https://www.theguardian.com/uk/2003/oct/24/germany.arttheft (accessed 8 January 2021); Naomi Rea, 'Christie's sold this Swiss dealer a painting likely looted by the Nazis. Now he wants his money back', *Artnet News*, 31 May 2018, https://news.artnet.com/art-world/christies-nazi-restitution-1295141 (accessed 8 January 2021).

98 *Le Répertoire des biens spoliés en France durant la guerre 1939–1945*, available at https://www.lootedart.com/MFEU4B37276 (accessed 8 January 2021).

99 See, for example, the Guggenheim Museum's Thannhauser Collection, https://www.guggenheim.org/artwork/special_collection/thannhauser-collection (accessed 8 January 2021).

100 GA Silva-Casa Gesellschaftsarchiv Silva-Casa Stiftung, 1966–2010, available at http://katalog.burgerbib.ch/detail.aspx?ID=123541 (accessed 8 January 2021).

101 'The collection of James and Marilynn Alsdorf', *Christie's*, 19 August 2020, https://www.christies.com/features/The-Collection-of-James-and-Marilynn-Alsdorf-10107-3.aspx (accessed 8 January 2021).

102 In Memoriam: Marilynn B. Alsdorf, https://mcachicago.org/About/Who-We-Are/In-Memoriam/Marilyn-B-Alsdorf (accessed 8 January 2021).

103 'The collection of James and Marilynn Alsdorf', *Christie's*, 19 August 2020, https://www.christies.com/features/The-Collection-of-James-and-Marilynn-Alsdorf-10107-3.aspx (accessed 8 January 2021); Graydon Megan, 'Marilynn Alsdorf, arts patron and collector who gave generously to the Art Institute, dies at 94', *Chicago Tribune*, 24 August 2019, https://www.chicagotribune.com/news/obituaries/ct-marilynn-alsdorf-obituary-20190823-gbldpeibxzemljztaqfyl3obgm-story.html (accessed 8 January 2021).

104 'Renou et Colle. Paris, 165 rue du Fbg St Honore. Firm of art dealers who handled looted art, notably from the Paul Rosenberg Collection. Contact of Gurlitt and Skira. Schenker documents indicate sales to German buyers', see https://www.lootedart.com/MVI3RM469661 (accessed 8 January 2021).

105 Oscar Schürer. 1927. *Junge Kunst: Pablo Picasso*, Berlin and Leipzig: Klinkhardt & Bierman.

106 The Wiedergutmachungsämter and Entschädigungsamt in Berlin. The archive has since been digitised and is publicly accessible, but in 2002 power of attorney was required to retrieve any information: http://www.wga-datenbank.de/starten.php?s=1 (accessed 8 January 2021).

107 The German office tasked with restitution of losses in the Nazi period founded in 1949: http://www.wga-datenbank.de/die-wiedergutmachungsaemter-von-berlin.php?s=2&sub=2 (accessed 8 January 2021).

108 Kara Platoni, 'The ten million dollar woman', *East Bay Express*, 4 August 2004, https://www.eastbayexpress.com/oakland/the-ten-million-dollar-woman/Content?oid=1074828 (accessed 8 January 2021).

109 Donald S. Burris and E. Randol Schoenberg. 2005. 'Reflections on litigating Holocaust stolen art cases', *Vanderbilt Journal of Transnational Law*, 38(4), pp. 1041–50; Anne-Marie O'Connor. 2015. *The Lady in Gold: The Extraordinary Tale of Gustav Klimt's Masterpiece, Portrait of Adele Bloch-Bauer*, New York: Knopf Publishing Group.

110 Tina Spee, 'Judge dumps Nazi-looted painting case', *Daily Journal*, 17 June 2003, http://www.bslaw.net/news/030617.html (accessed 8 January 2021).

111 Donald S. Burris and E. Randol Schoenberg. 2005. 'Reflections on litigating Holocaust stolen art cases', *Vanderbilt Journal of Transnational Law*, 38(4), pp. 1041–50.

112 James Wyllie. 2006. *Goering and Goering: Hitler's Henchman and his Anti-Nazi Brother*, Stroud: The History Press, p. 79.

113 The Federal Monuments Authority Austria: https://bda.gv.at/english/ (accessed 8 January 2021).

114 Thomas Trenkler, 'Kinsky nimmt Gauermann aus der Auktion', *Der Standard*, 20 February 2009, https://www.derstandard.at/story/1234507637041/ns-raubkunst-kinsky-nimmt-gauermann-aus-der-auktion (accessed 8 January 2021).

115 *Ibid.*

116 Paul Williams, '"Tango One's down" – recalling the life and crimes and brutal death of Martin Cahill', *The Independent*, 16 August 2019, https://www.independent.ie/life/paul-williams-tango-ones-down-recalling-the-life-and-crimes-and-brutal-death-of-martin-cahill-38410325.html (accessed 7 January 2021).

117 An Garda Síochána – commonly referred to as the Garda or Gardaí – is the national police service of the Republic of Ireland.

118 In 1994 Martin Cahill was assassinated by the Provisional IRA in retribution for assisting members of the Ulster Volunteer Force. See Liam Collins, 'The General's "spectacular" heist that led to his bloody downfall', *The Independent*, 24 April 2016, https://www.independent.ie/opinion/analysis/the-generals-spectacular-heist-that-led-to-his-bloody-downfall-34654234.html (accessed 7 January 2021).

119 'Grosvenor House: furniture to the fore', *The Art Newspaper*, 116, July–August 2001.

120 Sotheby's senior furniture expert's evidence in the high court case of Mallet and Son (Antiques) v the supplier of the bureau.

121 *Ibid.*

122 *Ibid.*

123 Sotheby's second furniture expert's witness statement in the high court case of Mallet and Son (Antiques) v the supplier of the bureau.

124 The argument would be based on the Roman law doctrine of *specificatio*. If someone creates an object using stolen material obtained in good faith, the creator becomes the lawful owner of the object unless the stolen material can be recovered without destroying the object. The creator only has to compensate the former owner for the cost of the material.

125 Tom Peterkin, 'Antique that caused deadly vendetta ends up in war veterans' home', *The Telegraph*, 27 June 2005, https://www.telegraph.co.uk/news/uknews/1492862/Antique-that-caused-deadly-vendetta-ends-up-in-war-veterans-home.html (accessed 7 January 2021).

126 Email from the ALR to the Roden Trust.

127 Judgment of Mr Justice Quirke on 12 May 2005 in the case of Mallet and Son (Antiques) v the supplier of the bureau, p. 13.

128 *Summer with the Johnsons*, 2005, BBC documentary.

129 Judge Christopher Critchlow reported in 'Jailed for 50 years: the "stately home gypsy gang" that carried out Britain's biggest burglary in £80million spree', *Daily Mail*, 6 August 2008, https://www.dailymail.co.uk/news/article-1042133/Jailed-50-years-The-stately-home-gypsy-gang-carried-Britains-biggest-burglary-80million-crime-spree.html (accessed 8 January 2021).

130 'Johnson gang leader faces longer sentence', *Antiques Trade Gazette*, 10 May 2010, https://www.antiquestradegazette.com/news/2010/johnson-gang-leader-faces-longer-sentence/ (accessed 8 January 2021).

131 *Ibid.*

132 Name changed.

133 See, for example, 'Border policing: law and disorder in the land of omerta', *The Irish Times*, 15 November 2019, https://www.irishtimes.com/news/crime-and-law/border-policing-law-and-disorder-in-the-land-of-omerta-1.4084259 (accessed 8 January 2021); *Cross Border Organised Crime: Threat Assessment* by the Police Service of Northern Ireland and An Garda Síochána, available at https://www.octf.gov.uk/Publications (accessed 8 January 2021).

134 An Garda Síochána – commonly referred to as the Garda or Gardaí – is the national police service of the Republic of Ireland.

135 ALR file note.

136 Email from the ALR to the Superintendent of Carrickmacross District.

137 ALR file note.

138 The large, ancient complex dedicated to Eshmun – a god of healing – was in use from the seventh century BC to AD 800.

139 Matthew Bogdanos. 2017. Application for a warrant to search the premises of the Metropolitan Museum of Art, New York, p. 10. Main text available at http://www.artcrimeresearch.org/wp-content/uploads/2017/10/Bogdanos-Bulls-Head-Case-Application-for-Turnover-Order.pdf; appendices available at http://www.artcrimeresearch.org/wp-content/uploads/2017/10/Bogdanos-Bulls-Head-Case-Exhibits-31-67-147-287.pdf (accessed 8 January 2021).

140 Jake Plenderleith, 'How the art market helps fund terrorism', *Insight*, 28 October 2019, https://www.int-comp.org/insight/2019/october/how-the-art-market-helps-fund-terrorism/ (accessed 8 January 2021); Steven Lee Myers and Nicholas Kulish, '"Broken system" allows ISIS to profit from looted antiquities', *New York Times*, 9 January 2016, https://www.nytimes.com/2016/01/10/world/europe/iraq-syria-antiquities-islamic-state.html (accessed 8 January 2021); Benoit Faucon, Georgi Kantchev and Alistair MacDonald, 'The men who trade ISIS loot', *Wall Street Journal*, 6 August 2017, https://www.wsj.com/articles/the-men-who-trade-isis-loot-1502017200 (accessed 8 January 2021); Heather Pringle, 'ISIS cashing in on looted antiquities to fuel Iraq insurgency', *National Geographic*, 17 June 2014, https://www.nationalgeographic.com/news/2014/6/140626-isis-insurgents-syria-iraq-looting-antiquities-archaeology/ (accessed 8 January 2021).

141 Jessica Dietzler. 2013. 'On "organized crime" in the illicit antiquities trade: moving beyond the definitional debate', *Trends in Organised Crime*, 16, pp. 329–42.

142 The 1954 Hague Convention for the Protection of Cultural Property in the event of Armed Conflict; the 1970 UNESCO Convention on the Means of Prohibiting and Preventing the Illicit Import, Export and Transfer of Ownership of Cultural Property; the 1995 UNIDROIT Convention on Stolen or Illegally Exported Objects.

143 Samuel Hardy, 'Curbing the spoils of war', *The UNESCO Courier*, October–December 2017, https://en.unesco.org/courier/october-december-2017/curbing-spoils-war (accessed 11 January 2021).

144 Julia Rodrigues Casella Hommes, 'To deal or not to deal: provenance and morality in recent sale at Christie's', Institute of Art & Law blog, 26 July 2019, https://ial.uk.com/to-deal-or-not-to-deal-provenance-and-morality-in-recent-sale-at-christies/ (accessed 8 January 2021).

145 Neil Brodie. 2011. 'Congenial bedfellows? The academy and the antiquities trade', *Journal of Contemporary Criminal Justice*, 27(4), pp. 408–37.

146 Peter Watson and Cecilia Todeschini. 2006. *The Medici Conspiracy*, New York: BBS Public Affairs; Jason Felch and Ralph Frammolino. 2011, *Chasing Aphrodite*, New York: Houghton Mifflin Harcourt.

147 Credible provenance information adds considerable value to an antiquity, so locating documentary evidence that objects were on the market before the 1970 UNESCO Convention has become a business. One can hire researchers to study major collections and auction catalogues and look for old photographs showing an object in a former owner's house published in books or magazines featuring the homes of the rich and famous such as *Country Life*.

148 For example, obliging members to search the ALR register for all objects above a certain value to reassure buyers that nobody is actively looking for the objects on sale is one way of raising the reputation of the members of a trade association.

149 'Another looted conflict antiquity from the Temple of Eshmun in Sidon, Lebanon seized. This time at Royal Athena Galleries in New York', *Association for Research into Crimes against Art* blog, 24 June 2020, https://art-crime.blogspot.com/2020/06/another-looted-conflict-antiquity-from.html (accessed 8 January 2021).

150 Susanne Brunner, 'Rolf Stucky und die Skulpturen aus dem Eshmun-Heiligtum', *SRF Interview*, 6 February 2018, https://www.srf.ch/sendungen/tagesgespraech/rolf-stucky-und-die-skulpturen-aus-dem-eschmun-heiligtum (accessed 8 January 2021).

151 Rolf Stucky. 1993. *Die Skulpturen aus dem Eschmun-Heiligtum bei Sidon*, Basel: Vereinigung Der Freunde Antiker Kunst 1993, https://www.antikekunst.org (accessed 8 January 2021).

152 Matthew Bogdanos. 2017. Application for a warrant to search the premises of the Metropolitan Museum of Art, New York, pp. 134–5.

153 *House & Garden*, June 1998, p. 133.

154 Nick Squires, 'Disgraced British art dealer's priceless treasure trove discovered hidden in Geneva', *The Telegraph*, 1 February 2016, https://www.telegraph.co.uk/news/worldnews/europe/switzerland/12134541/Disgraced-British-art-dealers-priceless-treasure-trove-discovered-hidden-in-Geneva.html (accessed 8 January 2021).

155 Owners wishing to bring antiquities into the Geneva Freeport have to submit them for approval, but this has only been the case since 2016!

156 Peter Watson and Cecilia Todeschini. 2006. *The Medici Conspiracy*, New York: BBS Public Affairs; Jason Felch and Ralph Frammolino. 2011. *Chasing Aphrodite*, New York: Houghton Mifflin Harcourt.

157 Jason Felch and Ralph Frammolino. 2011. *Chasing Aphrodite*, New York: Houghton Mifflin Harcourt.

158 Peter Watson and Cecilia Todeschini. 2006. *The Medici Conspiracy*, New York: BBS Public Affairs; Jason Felch and Ralph Frammolino. 2011. *Chasing Aphrodite*, New York: Houghton Mifflin Harcourt.

159 Matthew Bogdanos. 2017. Application for a warrant to search the premises of the Metropolitan Museum of Art, New York, p. 245.

160 Peter Watson and Cecilia Todeschini. 2006. *The Medici Conspiracy*, New York: BBS Public Affairs, pp. 254–8.

161 Matthew Bogdanos. 2017. Application for a warrant to search the premises of the Metropolitan Museum of Art, New York, p. 246.

162 Phoenix Ancient Art has since been investigated in several countries for trafficking in illicit antiquities: Benoit Faucon and Georgi Kantchev, 'Prominent art family entangled in ISIS antiquities-looting investigations', *Wall Street Journal*, 31 March 2017, https://www.wsj.com/articles/prominent-art-family-entangled-in-investigations-of-looted-antiquities-1496246740 (accessed 8 January 2021); 'Swiss prosecutor returns "Mesopotamian" terracotta animal made by dealer's 11-year-old daughter – along with 5,000 seized antiquities', *The Art Newspaper*, 31 August 2018, https://www.theartnewspaper.com/news/swiss-prosecutor-returns-mesopotamian-terracotta-animal-made-by-dealer-s-11-year-old-daughter-along-with-5-000-other-seized-antiquities (accessed 8 January 2021).

163 Matthew Bogdanos. 2017. Application for a warrant to search the premises of the Metropolitan Museum of Art, New York, p. 203.

164 *Ibid.*, p. 140.

165 Bob Crilly, '"Pit bull" lawyer and former marine hunts down world's stolen treasures', *The National*, 25 November 2017, https://www.thenational.ae/world/the-americas/pit-bull-lawyer-and-former-marine-hunts-down-world-s-stolen-treasures-1.678704 (accessed 8 January 2021).

166 See, for example, Matthew Bogdanos. 2005. *Thieves of Baghdad*, New York: Bloomsbury.

167 Laura Gilbert, 'Tough new scrutiny by district attorney rattles New York antiquities trade', *The Art Newspaper*, 9 March 2018, https://www.theartnewspaper.com/news/tough-new-scrutiny-rattles-collectors-and-dealers (accessed 8 January 2021).

168 Vera Dobnik, 'Manhattan prosecutor returns 3 ancient sculptures to Lebanon', *AP News*, 15 December 2017, https://apnews.com/article/faf31fb1853a440592a57d610d63fbff (accessed 8 January 2021).

169 Bruno Boesch and Sterpi Massimo (eds) 2016. *The Art Collecting Handbook*, London: Thomson Reuters.

170 Christos Tsirogiannis. 2015. 'Mapping the supply: usual suspects and identified antiquities in "reputable" auction houses in 2013', *Cuadernos de Prehistoria y Arqueología*, 25 (2015), pp. 107–44.

171 ALR file note.

172 'Chairman's address', https://iadaa.org (accessed 8 January 2021).

173 *Ibid.*

174 *Ibid.*

175 *Ibid.*

176 *Ibid.* See also 'Annex 1: Code of Ethics and Practice', https://iadaa.org/about-us/ (accessed 8 January 2021).

177 'Chairman's address', https://iadaa.org (accessed 8 January 2021).

178 *Ibid.*

179 'Over 18 000 items seized and 59 arrests made in operation targeting cultural goods', 29 July 2019, press release, https://www.europol.europa.eu/newsroom/news/ over-18-000-items-seized-and-59-arrests-made-in-operation-targeting-cultural-goods (accessed 8 January 2021).

180 '3561 artefacts seized in Operation Pandora', 23 January 2017, press release, https:// www.europol.europa.eu/newsroom/news/3561-artefacts-seized-in-operation-pandora (accessed 8 January 2021).

181 'Over 41 000 artefacts seized in global operation targeting the illicit trafficking of cultural goods', 21 February 2018, press release, https://www.europol.europa.eu/ newsroom/news/over-41-000-artefacts-seized-in-global-operation-targeting-illicit-trafficking-of-cultural-goods (accessed 8 January 2021).

182 See, for example, US Immigration and Customs enforcement Cultural Property, Art and Antiquities Investigations, https://www.ice.gov/features/cpaa (accessed 14 January 2021). Examples of tip forms are available at https://www.ice.gov/webform/ ice-tip-form (accessed 14 January 2021) and https://www.gov.uk/report-immigration-crime (accessed 14 January 2021).

183 'Swiss prosecutor returns "Mesopotamian" terracotta animal made by dealer's 11-year-old daughter – along with 5,000 seized antiquities', *The Art Newspaper*, 31 August 2018, https://www.theartnewspaper.com/news/ swiss-prosecutor-returns-mesopotamian-terracotta-animal-made-by-dealer-s-11-year-old-daughter-along-with-5-000-other-seized-antiquities (accessed 8 January 2021).

184 'Smash-and-grab gang armed with knives and hammers target Mayfair jewellers', *Evening Standard*, 6 January 2016, https://www.standard.co.uk/news/smashandgrab-gang-target-mayfair-jewellers-a3149766.html (accessed 10 January 2021).

185 'The FAQs: Should I buy a luxury watch without the box and papers', *KeepTheTime* blog, entry from 'wishywatchy' on the Rolex Forums, 10 July 2012, https://www. keepthetime.com/blog/should-i-buy-a-watch-without-the-box-and-papers/ (accessed 10 January 2021).

186 Rolex had allowed the secondary market to access its lost and stolen register for many years but stopped doing so in the years prior to the launch of The Watch Register database.

187 In 2018 the ALR entered into a formal partnership with SaferGems to consolidate its watch data within The Watch Register database.

188 Draft of police case summary sent to the ALR.

189 Transcript of United States of America v Robert M. Mardirosian No 07-CR-10075-MLW, Monday 18 August 2008, p. 63.

190 Edward Stringham. 2015. *Private Governance: Creating Order in Economic and Social Life*, New York: Oxford University Press, pp. 64–78.

191 *Ibid.*, p. 48.

192 Jane Johnston, 'Whose interests? Why defining the "public interest" is such a challenge', *The Conversation*, 21 September 2017, https://theconversation.com/whose-interests-why-defining-the-public-interest-is-such-a-challenge-84278 (accessed 12 January 2021).

193 For example, private security services to protect collections, art detectives and recovery services, art authentication and provenance research. Please see Further Reading.

194 When restituting paintings previously displayed in public museums to former owners, public access is often reduced afterwards. However, the ALR does not search museum collections but detects privately held looted artworks.

195 Alexi Mostrous, 'The murky world of the art detective', *The Times*, 9 August 2014, https://www.thetimes.co.uk/article/the-murky-world-of-the-art-detective-cggslfjtvxz (accessed 12 January 2021).

196 Martin Cleaver, 'Tracking stolen art, for profit, and blurring a few lines', *New York Times*, 23 September 2013, https://www.nytimes.com/2013/09/21/arts/design/tracking-stolen-art-for-profit-and-blurring-a-few-lines.html (accessed 12 January 2021).

197 Melanie Gerlis, 'Can blockchain clean up the art market?', *Financial Times*, 25 May 2018, https://www.ft.com/content/feedf512-5eae-11e8-ab47-8fd33f423c09 (accessed 12 January 2021).

198 Anja Shortland and Andrew Shortland. 2020. 'Governance under the shadow of the law: trading high value fine art', *Public Choice*, 184, pp. 157–74.

199 See, for example, the case of Nicole De Preval v Adrian Alan Limited (1997) Queens Bench Division (Justice Arden). The original owner was able to reclaim their stolen property, as the dealer in possession of the artefacts had failed to check their provenance and therefore could not prove he had bought them in good faith. See also Nina M. Neuhaus and Sophie Balay. 2014. 'Databases on lost and stolen art: is consulting a database an inherent requirement of good faith?', *Art, Antiquity & Law*, 19(2), https://ial.uk.com/product/databases-on-lost-and-stolen-art-is-consulting-a-database-an-inherent-requirement-of-good-faith-(nina-m-neuhaus-and-sophie-balay)/ (accessed 12 January 2021).

200 Internal ALR data.

201 M.H. Miller, 'The big fake: behind the scenes of Knoedler Gallery's downfall', *ARTnews*, 25 April 2016, https://www.artnews.com/art-news/artists/the-big-fake-behind-the-scenes-of-knoedler-gallerys-downfall-6179/ (accessed 12 January 2021).

202 The alternative is the caveat venditor principle, whereby it is the seller's responsibility to deliver goods fit for purpose and provide the buyer with the necessary information to make an informed choice.

203 By contrast, many governments have increased the protection of investors since the 2008 financial crisis, by requiring the seller to disclose clear, timely and standardised information about the assets and declare any conflicts of interest.

204 Some academic experts refuse to give negative opinions because they cannot afford to be drawn into a court case about product disparagement with a high-powered collector.

205 Organics at a Glance, https://ec.europa.eu/info/food-farming-fisheries/farming/
    organic-farming/organics-glance_en (accessed 12 January 2021).
206 Adam Satariano, 'Britain to create regulator for internet content', *New York Times*, 12
    February 2020, https://www.nytimes.com/2020/02/12/technology/britain-internet-
    regulator.html (accessed 12 January 2021).
207 Tiffany Jenkins. 2016. *Keeping their Marbles: How the Treasures of the Past Ended Up in
    Museums … and Why They Should Stay There*, Oxford: Oxford University Press.

Further Reading

The art market, art crime in its manifold incarnations, art law and institution-building are large and vibrant areas of academic research. Art crime and its cultural context provides a rich seam for investigative journalists, historians and novelists. Dealers, forgers, private detectives and law enforcement officials have penned fascinating memoirs of their personal experiences in the market and their adventures in the economic underworld. Creating a complete bibliography of this vast field would be a book project in itself. Below is a small selection of books that have caught my attention in recent years. They are either comprehensive overviews of their field, offer interesting additional perspectives, or provide further background to the material covered in this book.

Art crime and the art market

Georgina Adam. 2017. *Dark Side of the Boom: The Excesses of the Art Market in the 21st Century*, London: Lund Humphries
Simon Houpt. 2006. *Museum of the Missing: A History of Art Theft*, New York: Sterling Publishing

Riah Pryor. 2016. *Crime and the Art Market*, London:
    Lund Humphries
Robert Spiel. 2000. *Art Theft and Forgery Investigation:
    The Complete Field Manual*, Springfield, Illinois:
    Charles C. Thomas
Arthur Tompkins (ed.) 2016. *Art Crime and its Prevention:
    A Handbook for Collectors and Art Professionals*, London:
    Lund Humphries
Arthur Tompkins (ed.) 2020. *Provenance Research Today:
    Principles, Practice, Problems*, London: Lund Humphries
Jonathan Webb. 2009. *Stolen: The Gallery of Missing Masterpieces*,
    Toronto: Madison Press Books

Art theft and recovery

Anthony Amore and Tom Mashberg. 2012. *Stealing Rembrandts:
    The Untold Stories of Notorious Art Heists*, New York:
    Palgrave MacMillan
Michael Blanding. 2014. *The Map Thief*, New York:
    Penguin Books
Myles J. Connor Jr with Jenny Siler. 2010. *The Art Of the Heist:
    Confessions of a Master Thief*, New York: Harper Perennial
Thomas McShane with Dary Matera. 2006. *Stolen Masterpiece
    Tracker: The Dangerous Life of the FBI's #1 Art Sleuth*, Fort
    Lee, New Jersey: Barricade Books
Philip Mould. 2011. Sleuth: The Amazing Quest for Lost Art
    Treasures, London: HarperCollins
Sandy Nairne. 2011. Art Theft and the Case of the Stolen
    Turners, London: Reaktion Books

Robert K. Wittman with John Shiffman. 2011. *Priceless: How I Went Undercover to Rescue the World's Stolen Treasures*, New York: Broadway Books / Crown Publishing Group

Authenticity

Megan Aldrich and Jos Hackforth-Jones (eds) 2012. *Art and Authenticity*. Farnham, Surrey: Lund Humphries

Anthony Amore. 2015. *The Art of the Con: The Most Notorious Fakes, Frauds and Forgeries in the Art World*, New York: Palgrave MacMillan

Noah Charney. 2015. *The Art of Forgery: The Minds, Motives and Methods of Master Forgers*, London: Phaidon

Paul Craddock. 2009. *Scientific Investigation of Copies, Fakes and Forgeries*, Oxford: Butterworth-Heinemann (Elsevier)

Jean-Jacques Fiechter. 2009. *Egyptian Fakes: Masterpieces That Duped the Art World and the Experts Who Uncovered Them*, Paris: Flammarion

Eric Hebborn. 1997. *The Art Forger's Handbook*, New York: Overlook Press

Mark Jones (ed.) 1990. *Fake? the Art of Deception*, Berkeley: University of California Press

Kenneth Lapatin. 2002. *Mysteries of the Snake Goddess: Art, Desire, and the Forging of History*, Boston, Massachusetts: Da Capo Press (US Perseus Book Group)

Jehane Ragai. 2018. *The Scientist and the Forger: Probing a Turbulent Art World* (2nd edition), London: World Scientific Publishing

Laney Salisbury and Aly Sujo. 2009. *Provenance: How a Con Man and a Forger Rewrote the History of Art*, New York: Penguin Books

Ronald D. Spencer (ed.) 2004. *The Expert versus the Object: Judging Fakes and False Attributions in the Visual Arts,* New York: Oxford University Press

Frank Wynne. 2006. *I Was Vermeer: The Legend of the Forger Who Swindled the Nazis,* London: Bloomsbury Publishing

Legal scholarship

Brian Harvey and Franklin Meisel. 2006. *Auctions Law and Practice* (3rd edition), Oxford: Oxford University Press

Saskia Hufnagel and Duncan Chappell (eds) 2019. *The Palgrave Handbook on Art Crime,* London: Palgrave Macmillan UK

James A.R. Nafziger and Robert Kirkwood Paterson (eds) 2014. *Handbook on the Law of Cultural Heritage and International Trade,* Cheltenham, Gloucestershire: Edward Elgar

Norman Palmer (ed.) 1998. *The Recovery of Stolen Art: A Collection of Essays,* The Hague: Kluwer Law International

Christa Roodt. 2015. *Private International Law, Art and Cultural Heritage,* Cheltenham, Gloucestershire: Edward Elgar

Janet Ulph and Ian Smith. 2012. *The Illicit Trade in Art and Antiquities: International Recovery and Criminal and Civil Liability,* Oxford: Hart Publishing

Martin Wilson. 2019. *Art Law and the Business of Art,* Cheltenham, Gloucestershire: Edward Elgar

Looted antiquities

Matthew Bogdanos. 2005. *Thieves of Baghdad,* New York: Bloomsbury

Jason Felch and Ralph Frammolino. 2011. *Chasing Aphrodite*, New York: Houghton Mifflin Harcourt

Dan Hicks. 2020. *The Brutish Museums: The Benin Bronzes, Colonial Violence and Cultural Restitution*, London: Pluto Press

Tiffany Jenkins. 2016. *Keeping their Marbles: How the Treasures of the Past Ended Up in Museums … and Why They Should Stay There*, Oxford: Oxford University Press

Simon Mackenzie. 2005. *Going, Going, Gone: Regulating the Market in Illicit Antiquities*, Leicester: Institute of Art and Law

Simon Mackenzie, Neil Brodie, Donna Yates and Christos Tsirogiannis. 2019. *Trafficking Culture: New Directions in Researching the Global Market in Illicit Antiquities*, London: Routledge

Peter Watson. 1997. *Sotheby's: The Inside Story*, London: Bloomsbury

Peter Watson and Cecilia Todeschini. 2006. *The Medici Conspiracy*, New York: BBS Public Affairs

Nazi-era losses and restitution

Konstantin Akinsha and Grigori Kozlov. 1995. *Stolen Treasure: The Hunt for the World's Lost Masterpieces*, London: Weidenfeld & Nicolson

Simon Goodman. 2015. *The Orpheus Clock: The Search for My Family's Art Treasures Stolen by the Nazis*, London: Scribe Publications

Bruce L. Hay. 2017. *Nazi-looted Art and the Law*, Cham, Switzerland: Springer International Publishing

Lynn H. Nicholas. 1994. *The Rape of Europa: The Fate of Europe's Treasures in the Third Reich and the Second World War*, New York: Alfred A. Knopf

Nicholas O'Donnell. 2017. *A Tragic Fate: Law and Ethics in the Battle Over Nazi-Looted Art*, Chicago, Illinois: American Bar Association

Norman Palmer. 2000. *Museums and the Holocaust*, Leicester: Institute of Art and Law

Private governance and self-regulation

Peter T. Leeson. 2009. *The Invisible Hook: The Hidden Economics of Pirates*, Princeton, New Jersey: Princeton University Press

Barak D. Richman. 2017. *Stateless Commerce: The Diamond Network and the Persistence of Relational Exchange*, Cambridge, Massachusetts: Harvard University Press

Anja Shortland. 2019. *Kidnap: Inside the Ransom Business*, Oxford: Oxford University Press

David Skarbek. 2014. *The Social Order of the Underworld: How Prison Gangs Govern the American Penal System*, New York: Oxford University Press

Edward Stringham. 2015. *Private Governance: Creating Order in Economic and Social Life*, New York: Oxford University Press

Acknowledgements

I am utterly intrigued by un- and under-regulated markets. The potential for profitable trade in the absence of law enforcement unleashes boundless human creativity, both legal and criminal. The international art market offers perfect conditions to observe private enterprises finding ingenious solutions for a wide variety of crimes, and criminals innovating just as cleverly to circumvent them. It is a very dynamic setting, tailor-made for studying institution-building. I am deeply grateful to the artists, auctioneers, dealers, insurers, lawyers and researchers who welcomed me into their world, shared their in-depth knowledge and discussed the manifold challenges of this fascinating market with me.

This book focuses on a business that deters art theft by increasing the risk of detection and reducing its profitability. The research reflects many hours of conversation, observation and occasionally interrogation of current and former staff members at the Art Loss Register, and especially its founder Julian Radcliffe. A big thank you to all of you: for opening the treasure trove of your archive to me, for your enthusiasm for sharing your work and for being patient with a curious academic's endless questions. It has been absolutely fascinating to watch you build this business defining, enforcing and resolving contested property rights, while navigating between the conflicting demands of your very diverse stakeholders.

I am deeply grateful to my academic peers across the world who have encouraged, guided and challenged me along the way. King's College London granted me a sabbatical to write this book and my amazing colleagues in the Department of Political Economy gave me the headspace and every assistance to do so. I greatly benefited from a long visit to the effervescent Mercatus Center at George Mason University in Virginia. Thank you, Paul Aligica, Peter Boettke, Rosolino Candela, Giorgio Castiglia, Chris Coyne, Bobbi Herzberg, Peter Leeson and Virgil Storr, for being the perfect hosts – as were David Skarbek in Providence and Ed Stringham in New York. Thank you also to my friends at the Society for Institutional & Organizational Economics, especially Lisa Bernstein and Gillian Hadfield, for your encouragement and for being my inspiration. I remain ever grateful to my mentors Ben Bowling and Federico Varese for their advice and support.

I have greatly enjoyed the company of my students in my art-world research. A special thank you to Florian Bartsch, Daphne Friedrich, Florian Hartjen, Christian Payer, Ewa Puzniak, Sami Winton and Cristina Zheng Ji. The book has been thoroughly revised in response to a multitude of perceptive comments and questions by Daniel Klerman and Paco Tomás-Valiente Jordá. Sarah Lavington and E. Randol Schoenberg kindly provided additional insights on the restitution of Nazi-looted art. Thank you so much for your time, your attention to detail and for sharing your expertise. I also want to thank my editor Linda Schofield for expunging my linguistic infelicities and improving the clarity of the text.

This book was written during a global pandemic, and much of it during lockdown. I am deeply indebted to my children Henry and Ellie, who decided very quickly that I was completely unsuitable as a home-educator and got on with their schoolwork by themselves. My wonderful friends, especially Camilla Darling, Keith Panting, Caroline Pooley and Chris Williams, supported me from a careful social distance. I could not have finished this project without you. As always, my husband Andrew held everything together – only grumbling occasionally about my treasure trove of fifty or so large boxes of very exciting (if slightly dusty) ALR documents. You are a rock, and you will get your drawing room and study back soon. Promise. I am almost finished.

I was a very inquisitive child, forever questioning everything and everyone around. My parents set only one ground rule: 'No "why" questions before breakfast.' But fortified by several cups of super-strong coffee, they were always ready to explain the world. There is no greater gift they could have given to me. This book is dedicated to them.

Index

N

O